"Wrenching, painful, and finally triumphant."
—Arthur Salm, *The San Diego Union Tribune*

"This book comes at a time when it is greatly needed, both as part of our collective history and as an example of using the difficult past toward a hopeful and creative future. Robert Meeropol tells his story in language that is direct, unflinching, meticulous, and elequent."
—Adrienne Rich

"Robert Meeropol knows firsthand about the effects of world politics on the lives of children. He has not only lived through a maelstrom and survived to tell the tale, but has dedicated his life and his work to helping children who have lost their parents through imprisonment and persecution. In this touching memoir, Meeropol's honest and gripping story has never been more relevant than in the present erosion of civil liberties and mistrust of dissent."
—Marge Piercy

"A powerful tale of Meeropol's lifelong struggle to overcome the fear brought on by our government's legal murder of his parents and to transform it—as he does—into a force to build a better world for children."
—Michael Moore

"*An Execution in the Family* offers both a wrenching personal account of capital punishment, and a sharp analysis of its failure as an instrument of 'justice.' Intelligent, intimate, scrupulous in its honesty, Meeropol's work transcends victimization. Here is a clear-eyed witness to history; here is a true voice of conscience at a time of crisis."
—Martín Espada, author of *Alabanza: New and Selected Poems*

"Although the Rosenbergs were no ordinary capital defendants, Robert Meeropol's efforts to honor their legacy reveals the inescapable flaws in the system that failed them. *An Execution in the Family* offers a well-timed reminder that state-sanctioned injustice is best answered by constructive action."
—Steven W. Hawkins, executive director, National Coalition to Abolish the Death Penalty

"Fortunately for us all, Robby Meeropol reveals a soul-wrenching journey of personal courage and political discovery. *An Execution in the Family* is both timely and revealing. It is also a disturbing reminder of how, in the name of national security, our preciously guarded constitutional guarantees can be easily trampled. It's a deeply moving account, with painfully personal insights, into one of the most controversial cases in American history—and one we must never forget."
—Danny Glover

"In the final analysis, Meeropol's sense of responsiblity for humanity—and toward the pursuit of justice for all—has triumphed over the pain."
—Silja Talvi, *AlterNet*

Also by Robert Meeropol

We Are Your Sons: The Legacy of Ethel and Julius Rosenberg
(with Michael Meeropol)

An
Execution
in the Family

One Son's Journey

ROBERT MEEROPOL

ST. MARTIN'S GRIFFIN ♠ NEW YORK

www.stmartins.com

Design by The Book Design Group

Library of Congress Cataloging-in-Publication Data

Meeropol, Robert.
    An execution in the family : one son's journey / Robert Meeropol.—1st ed.
        p. cm.
    Includes index.
    ISBN 0-312-30636-9 (hc)
    ISBN 0-312-30637-7 (pbk)
    EAN 978-0312-30637-3
    1. Meeropol, Robert. 2. Social reformers—United States—Biography. 3. Political activists—United States—Biography. 4. Social action—United States. 5. Social problems—United States. I. Title.

HV28.M365A3 2003
364.66'092—dc21
[B]

                                                          2003043117

First St. Martin's Griffin Edition: June 2004

P1

For Elli, life partner in everything

CONTENTS

ACKNOWLEDGMENTS

———◆·▸◀·◆———

AS I SUSPECT IS THE CASE WITH ALMOST ALL BOOKS, THIS ONE IS NOT
mine alone. My wife, Elli, helped me more than anyone else and to a
large degree this manuscript is a product of our partnership. She provided encouragement from start to finish, major editorial input, and
was my principal sounding board throughout the process. My
brother, Michael, also discussed the contents of the manuscript with
me at great length, provided very thorough and useful critiques of
each chapter, and saved me from making numerous errors. My
daughters, Jenn and Rachel, read and responded to the manuscript.
Jenn gave me editorial advice, and Rachel, now a lawyer, did legal
research I used in Chapter nine. I am grateful to my friends Martín
Espada, Bill Newman, and Ann I. Weber for their substantive and
helpful editorial suggestions. I also thank Jonathan Kozol, Adrienne
Rich, and Howard Zinn for their critiques of my initial essays and
encouragement with this project.

I wish to express my appreciation to agents Frances Goldin and
Sydelle Kramer for their useful consultation and generosity with their

time. I am particularly grateful to Senior Editor Diane Higgins, whose faith in this project is why St. Martin's Press has published this book. She and Assistant Editor Nichole Argyres provided a great deal of very valuable content, editorial pointers, and enthusiastic support.

The Rosenberg Fund Board of Directors, led by Board Chair Bob Winston, granted me the sabbatical to get started, and their ongoing support of my writing helped me to finish. Discussions with dozens of other people over the past decade have contributed to my understanding of many of the topics covered. Since I can't create an exhaustive list without slighting some, I will only single out Kathlyn Conway and David Rosner, Nancy Meyer and Marc Weiss, Bruce and Jane Miller, Lou Shaw and Arlene Tyner.

While many have helped me to minimize errors in this book, those errors that remain are mine alone.

Finally, I wish to thank the Rosenberg Fund for Children, a community of more than ten thousand people. Without their support my life would have followed a different course and this memoir probably would never have been written.

PREFACE

I DIDN'T PLAN TO WRITE A MEMOIR. IN 1999 AT THE END OF OUR two-week summer vacation, my wife, Elli, and I were spinning our typical fantasies, scheming to get away for a substantial chunk of time the following summer. But this time Elli came up with a plan that enabled us to take a two-month "mini-sabbatical" in August and September of 2000. When I described this plan to my friend Martín Espada, he urged me to use the time to convert various talks he'd heard me give into a book of essays. Elli encouraged me to do the same. I was skeptical about publishing anything, but writing seemed like a worthwhile project to undertake while on sabbatical.

After the sabbatical I made a halfhearted effort to find a publisher. I considered giving up in the spring of 2001, but Elli pushed me to present what I'd written to literary agent Frances Goldin. Frances and her colleague Sydelle Kramer urged me to transform and expand what I'd written into a political memoir. They felt the upcoming fiftieth anniversary of my parents' execution would be an ideal time for me to reflect on the evolution of my views on my parents' case, capital punishment, and how the course of my life led me to create the Rosenberg Fund for Children.

I agonized over writing such a revealing document, but ultimately decided to take the chance. Sydelle presented my proposal to Diane Higgins, a senior editor at St. Martin's Press, and this book resulted.

This book is very different from *We Are Your Sons*, the book I wrote with my brother, Michael Meeropol, in 1974. *An Execution in the Family* is really my first book, since my individual portion of *We Are Your Sons* was just eighty pages long (pages 259 to 338). Almost thirty years have passed since that book was published. In those years I've learned vital new information about my parents' case, developed a more nuanced perspective, and perhaps even gained a little wisdom.

A few pages scattered throughout this book contain revised versions of what I've published since 1985 about my life and my understanding of my parents' case. Reviewing the same period twice, once at age twenty-six and again at the age of fifty-five, reveals the vagaries of memory. I've done my best to cover honestly and thoroughly those aspects of my life on which I've chosen to focus. There are instances when my current memory of personal events varies from the recorded account of those same events in *We Are Your Sons*. In those instances I've determined to stick with my current recollections rather than revert to a memory I no longer have or distract the reader with footnotes that detail what I view as unimportant discrepancies.

Some readers and reviewers may treat this memoir as another book about the facts of the Rosenberg case. Some may use the reviews they write as a platform to present their position on my parents' case. I have written about my parents' case here to explain the evolution of my own views rather than to prove my position. I hope readers will understand this distinction. While this book is a product of my parents' case, it is not primarily about it.

CHAPTER 1

Losing at Monopoly

———◆◆◆◆◆———

I WAS SIX YEARS, ONE MONTH, AND ONE DAY OLD ON MONDAY, JUNE 15, 1953—four days before my parents' execution. That hot June my ten-year-old brother, Michael, and I were living with friends of my parents, Ben and Sonia Bach, in Toms River, New Jersey. I was a thin, dark-haired, olive-skinned child of average height. My face tapered from a high forehead to a somewhat pointed chin. I'm told my most striking feature was brown eyes that were so deep set they often appeared ringed like a raccoon's. I was finishing my kindergarten year at Toms River Elementary School. That summer I played a lot of ball with my brother and several older neighborhood kids in the Bachs' front yard. I was fairly well coordinated: quick with my hands but not particularly nimble on my feet. Better at athletics than most but always not as good as some. It helped having a big brother who looked out for me.

I played a lot of Monopoly while I lived in New Jersey. By the time I was five I loved to play endless games with my brother and any other competitors I could find. Even though my opponents were almost always older, I held my own. I quickly learned that, with the exception of the Utilities, it was smartest to buy every property you landed on to maximize your chances of getting a "monopoly." This rapidly used up your meager initial allotment of fifteen hundred dollars. There was even a slim chance you'd quickly go bankrupt and be out of the game if you followed this strategy. It was much more likely that you'd prevent others from getting a monopoly, secure one of your own, and eventually win. Of course, if the dice weren't with you there was nothing you could do. Since my brother played similarly, winning our games had more to do with luck than skill. But my peers had favorite properties and would decline to purchase ones they disdained. They often appeared to be winning because they had more money than I did early in the game. But with more properties I usually acquired the first monopoly and ultimately drove my opponents out of the game. This was quite a life lesson for the child of Communists.

My attitude toward Monopoly reflected my survival strategy. I usually had a plan. Adults found me quiet and withdrawn, although I was very quick to climb into the lap of any adult woman I felt the slightest bit comfortable with. I sought shelter whenever I could. Fuss and commotion usually meant that bad things were happening, and I kept quiet to insulate myself from the tumult and to avoid creating more uproar. I was quietly observing, and my observations inevitably led to strategy. I endured my parents' absence, bided my time, and planned cautiously while cradling hope of winning even when the odds appeared long.

Although at six I was too young to comprehend the world beyond the Bachs' house, my neighborhood, and school, I knew that there was something dangerous "out there," lurking near enough to strike again, that was somehow involved in taking my parents away. A dark cloud of generalized anxiety hovered at the edge of my consciousness—a sense that something about my family was terribly wrong and that my circumstances might get even worse. Most of the time, when I ignored or forgot about the upheavals of my life, I felt reasonably safe with the Bachs, and not too bad. But "we" (whoever that was) were under attack from whatever was out there, and I wanted to keep a low profile, beneath the notice of any enemies.

I felt particularly vulnerable whenever I left the Bachs' home or protection. I was anxious taking the school bus to kindergarten. I remember another small, dark bus rider who, unlike me, had a nervous tic and stuttered. Some of the other kids teased him. Once his mother, a Holocaust survivor with a strong Yiddish accent, got on the bus and screamed at the driver that the teasing made her son more nervous. I observed that her yelling did not help. My mortification for this other boy confirmed my resolve to suppress any habits or outbursts that might attract notice. While I felt I could easily become that tormented boy, I made no effort to befriend him lest I draw attention to myself.

I often put myself in others' shoes. This sense of understanding what others felt led me to sympathize with those who were picked on. However, I was not courageous; I didn't stand up for the victims. While I never physically bullied anyone, there were times when I joined the group in ridiculing social outcasts. I was reluctant to inflict petty cruelty because it left me feeling so remorseful. But I delighted in inventing clever and derogatory nicknames that stuck to my intended target like stepped-on, freshly discarded chewing gum. I still do.

I noticed that being nice and making others laugh without being loud and obnoxious provided social acceptance and safety. I found that if you were friendly to others they were more likely to be friendly to you, but I was wary of the few who might be hostile anyway. This careful approach to new situations made it hard to make new friends. I usually managed to become part of a group but avoided being the ringleader. Willy Loman, the protagonist of Arthur Miller's *Death of a Salesman*, denigrated those who were "liked, but not well liked." I was content to be liked, because being well liked might attract too much interest.

Michael was much more outgoing, talkative, and assertive. With our parents gone, I became his charge, a responsibility he took very seriously. I was content to follow his lead and stay in the background whenever possible. He was used to getting his way, and prone to fits of temper when he was thwarted. Although I do not recall this, I am told that before my parents' arrests he constantly engaged my mother in a battle of wills. After our parents' arrests, adults were even more willing to cater to his whims. His behavior was a focus for adult attention, and I was content to let him have it.

Michael was the one constant presence in an unfathomable kaleidoscope of cameo appearances in my life. Our four-year age difference diminished our sibling rivalry. Instead, we were allies—the two of us against the world. We always slept in the same room. Although the Bachs were also our protectors, Michael was the only person I felt 100 percent safe with. He was a great comfort to me. We woke up early in the morning and held long whispered conversations during which he'd pour out his precocious ten-year-old's wisdom while we played Monopoly. He explained to me why the Dodgers were going to win the pennant in 1953. He told me that although it would be much better if we could live with our parents, at least this was not the shelter we'd spent six months in. He also gave me history lessons, proudly reciting all the presidents from Washington to Eisenhower.

I remember being content, but not happy, as long as I was left to do what other kids did—go to school and play afterward. But there was something out there that would not leave me alone, and that kindergarten year was punctuated with visits to my parents in Sing Sing prison. Then I could not keep beneath "their" notice (whoever "they" were). I remember entering the prison courtyard through a big iron gate and bounding after my brother, who had trouble containing his energy after a long car ride. But I'd quickly return to hide behind my parents' attorney, Manny Bloch, when I saw photographers snapping pictures as we entered and exited.

I have surprisingly sharp memories of much of what I did and even of some of the world-shaking events that swirled about me during the week of June 15. On Monday, when the Supreme Court adjourned for the summer, my parents, who had been convicted more than two years earlier, were scheduled to die on Thursday, June 18, their fourteenth wedding anniversary. On Tuesday a special petition was presented to Justice William Douglas as he left for vacation. On Wednesday, Douglas stayed the execution and went on vacation. On Thursday the Supreme Court was called into special session. On Friday morning Douglas's stay was overturned by a 6–3 vote. My parents were executed that evening, Friday, June 19, one minute before sundown, so as not to violate the Jewish Sabbath. But that is not how I remember the week of Monday, June 15.

Although I couldn't read the newspapers, I saw reports of these last-minute maneuvers on TV and heard about them on radio. I remember thinking that prior to the fifteenth, the judges (whatever *they* were) asked Manny to give them ten reasons why my parents should not be killed—and he did. So my parents were not killed. But that Thursday they asked Manny for an eleventh reason. When he could not provide it, my parents were killed.

I think I confused repeated radio references to "eleventh-hour appeals" with giving an eleventh reason. Michael tells me that we were whisked away to a friend's house in the next town on Friday to avoid the photographers and reporters who had finally discovered us at the Bachs'. I don't remember leaving the Bachs', but I do recall playing ball with my friend Mark that evening, while my brother played with Mark's older brother, Steve. We'd been watching a ball game on TV around suppertime when news flashed across the screen that plans for the executions were going forward. I could not read the words and do not recall Michael's reaction, but he remembers moaning, "That's it, good-bye, good-bye."

Michael's reaction and the urgency behind the adults' decision to send us outside gave me the sense that something especially bad was happening. We came back inside only when it got too dark to see the ball. I remember that Michael was distraught because he'd missed some vital news about the case, and that the adults tried to console him. I doubt I fully comprehended that my parents had just been killed, but I feigned complete ignorance to avoid the commotion, and went to bed. Adults persuaded Michael not to tell me about it that evening or the next day. Although it might not have been on the evening of Friday, June 19, sometime soon I knew that my parents had been killed. Michael says he told me a week later that "Mommy and Daddy are never coming home; they're dead," but I still did not act as if I understood.

I'm not sure I knew what death was. My friend Mark had a tree he had planted in the spring that he told me was almost dead. In fact it showed no signs of life, just a few bare branches stark against the endless light sky of early summer evenings. He packed chicken manure around it as medicine, but it seemed beyond cure. In my mind, that bare dead sapling was mixed up with my parents' death, a bleak and bitter sense of loss in the summer sun.

I pretended not to understand what was going on so adults would not fuss over me. While in some ways I did not understand, by the end of the summer I knew the essential facts: "They" had killed my parents, and I would never see my parents again. That summer of 1953 began with what I now see as the climax of my personal horror story. But the onset of this nightmare was hidden in the mist of my earliest memories. I am told that the nightmare started three years earlier with FBI agents knocking on our Lower East Side apartment door on July 17, 1950. We had finished dinner, and I was already asleep. Several agents entered and later left with my father. I have no memories of this event, but I have heard my brother describe it many times. Michael was listening to an episode of *The Lone Ranger* on the radio, but an FBI agent turned it off. Michael was not cowed and turned it back on. Michael's first battle with the FBI continued until he heard my mother shout, "I want a lawyer!" He recalled becoming worried, and that then our father was gone.

• • •

I have very few memories of my parents, and I will never know such basic attributes as how they interacted in social settings or even the sound of their voices. What is known about my parents is that until 1950, they were a left-wing working-class Jewish couple with two children living on New York City's Lower East Side. They were people with their share of familial problems, personal limitations, and future aspirations.

Julius Rosenberg was born in New York City in 1918. He graduated Seward Park High School on Manhattan's Lower East Side and also received religious training at Downtown Talmud Torah and Hebrew High School. At sixteen he still took religion seriously, but by the time he was eighteen he had become a Marxist. In February 1939 he graduated from the City College of New York (CCNY) with a degree in electrical engineering and married Ethel Greenglass shortly afterward. He held a job with the Army Signal Corps until 1945, when he was fired after an investigation revealed that he had falsely sworn that he was not a member of the Communist Party in order to obtain the job. Next he worked for Emerson Radio until he was laid off. Ultimately he started a machine shop, hiring his brother-in-law, David Greenglass. In 1950, at the time of my father's arrest, the business was failing.

Ethel Greenglass was born on the Lower East Side in 1916 and also attended Seward Park. A star student, graduating before her sixteenth birthday, she was picked to sing the national anthem at high school assemblies because of her extraordinary voice. A close high school friend recently told me that she and Ethel were both so poor that they stuffed old newspapers into the holes in their shoes to keep their feet from freezing during the long walk to school on winter mornings. Acting and singing were her passions. She was a member of the Clark Street Players, an amateur theater group, and worked as a secretary after graduation. She had become an active union organizer by 1935 and left the Clark Street Players to join the more politically oriented Lavanburg Players.

Julius, two years younger, met Ethel when she sang at a union-organizing meeting in 1936. They became a couple almost immediately but did not marry until after Julius graduated college in 1939. Michael was born on March 10, 1943, and I was born on May 14, 1947.

After my father's arrest, Michael, my mother, and I continued to live in our eleventh-floor three-room apartment, in a high-rise development called Knickerbocker Village. The only thing I remember about that apartment was that it was small. (An apartment that appears small to a three-year-old must have been tiny.) We lived with our mother for only a few more weeks. One morning in August she left us with a neighbor because she had been subpoenaed to testify before the grand jury that was investigating what the newspapers were calling the "Atomic Bomb Conspiracy." At the conclusion of her testimony that day, she too was arrested. Except for a dozen or so brief prison visits, neither my brother nor I ever saw either of our parents again.

When our mother did not return that evening, the neighbor wasn't sure what to do with us. Our maternal grandmother, Tessie Greenglass, lived only a few blocks away, so the sitter took us there. Though this seemed like the most reasonable thing to do, it didn't work out very well. David and Ruth Greenglass, my mother's younger brother and his wife, who also had two young children, were caught up in the "Atomic Bomb Conspiracy" as well. In fact, David had been arrested before my father. David and Ruth were urged to cooperate, to say what the FBI and Justice Department wanted them to say, and to name the others who were involved with them. The government threatened David with execution if they did not. The Greenglasses made a deal with the government that spared David's life and kept Ruth out of prison, becoming the prosecution's chief witnesses. Tessie Greenglass backed her son's decision to cooperate with the FBI and collaborated with the government to force her daughter, Ethel, to back David's version of events.

From shortly after their arrests until the hour of my parents' death, they were offered a similar deal. They were pressured to confess that they had helped to engineer the Soviet Union's theft of vital atomic secrets, and to name all others they had worked with to accomplish this feat. They were told that they faced the death penalty and were reminded to think about the impact their execution would have on their children. From the beginning, my brother and I were used as pawns to extort my parents' cooperation. But, unlike the Greenglasses, they refused. There is little doubt that the only reason they were killed was because they resisted.

Tessie wanted nothing to do with us from the moment the babysitter deposited us at her apartment. Tessie complained that my brother and I were driving her crazy and running wild. She said she couldn't handle us and threatened to place us in a shelter. When my imprisoned mother was unable to ease Tessie's burden, our grandmother carried out her threat.

The government was determined to use all the weapons at its disposal, including exploiting family divisions in order to get my parents to confess. At the time of the arrests my father's business was failing, and he and David were angry at each other. My mother did not get along with her mother, Tessie, who favored David. Decades later, through our Freedom of Information Act (FOIA) lawsuit, my brother and I forced the release of secret government documents that detailed Tessie's cooperation. In early 1953, at the government's urging, Tessie visited my mother in prison. My mother reported in a letter to my father that at this visit, Tessie asked her to back David's story even if it was a lie. Tessie pointed out that Ruth had not been arrested and was home with her children. Tessie told her daughter that if she cooperated, she would be released to be with *her* children.

I knew none of this at the time. Tessie did not tell us the real reason why we had to leave her apartment. Her excuse is the source of one of my first clear memories. She said that the apartment was a cold-water flat, without hot water, and that the toilet water froze in the winter. She explained that this made the apartment an unsanitary place to raise children in winter, and so we would have to leave. I remember walking into the bathroom and peering into the toilet bowl, blackened where the enamel had been eaten away. I found the idea of ice in the toilet intriguing. It was barely November, and of course there was no ice.

There were relatives on both sides of the family, but no one would take us into their homes. This was the McCarthy period, and the family was terrified of being associated with Communists accused of atomic espionage. My father's older sister was very close to him and wanted to take us in despite having three children of her own. But her husband, who owned a small store in Queens, said she could not. He told her that it would ruin his business if word leaked that the Rosenberg children were living in his home. This was probably an accurate assessment.

I doubt I minded leaving Grandma Tessie's all that much. She was a sour and nasty woman who was mean to me. Her sister, who I knew only as Aunt Chutcha, also spent a lot of time in the house. I didn't like her either. After Tessie dumped us in the shelter, I dubbed the hated dessert of stewed pears we were often fed there "the Chutcha thing."

We were placed in a shelter in the Bronx. I didn't understand why we were there, but I knew something was profoundly wrong. I was glad to be out of Tessie's apartment, but I remember being very unhappy in the shelter. I recall it as loveless. There were lots of other kids, but I don't remember playing with or talking to any of them. I also remember thinking that my parents were in prison and that the shelter was my prison.

My father wrote to my brother, who had evidently complained about my crying, that I cried because I was too young to understand what was going on. I have no memory of crying, but I do not doubt

Michael's report. One routine from that place sticks in my mind. We were supposed to pray at our bedside before going to sleep each night. I resisted this, but Michael told me I had to or I would go to hell. I knelt by the side of the bed, folded my hands together, and repeated what he told me to say, but upset him by giggling and muttering: "Goddammit." Maybe I was just being silly, or maybe this was the first indication that religion would never make much sense to me.

Fortunately we stayed at the shelter for only a few months. My father's mother, Sophie Rosenberg, had been hospitalized that fall, but had recovered sufficiently by mid-1951 to take us into a new, larger apartment her family rented for her near 180th Street, overlooking the Harlem River. Living with Grandma Sophie was an improvement, but not ideal. Grandma's husband, Harry, died suddenly not long before my birth. My middle name, Harry, is in memory of him. She never got over Harry's death, and now her youngest son faced execution. I lived surrounded by her fear and sorrow.

When fall came my brother went to school every morning, in the third grade in the New York City public school system. But I was still too young for school. I remember playing on the floor by myself with a few small metal toy cars or staring out the window watching the giant earthmovers build what would become the roadbed of the southernmost extension of the New York State Thruway on the other side of the Harlem River.

Although I was lonely, at least I was insulated from "them" while staying at home with my Bubbie Sophie.* Michael was not. William Reuben's series of articles concluding that my parents had not received a fair trial began appearing in the *National Guardian* in August. Michael proudly told his school friends from the neighborhood about them and said that his parents were not guilty. This led to several nasty incidents. Michael remembers visiting a friend after school whose mother threw him out of the house when she found out

---

*Also spelled *bubbe*, the Yiddish word is an endearment meaning "grandmother."

who his parents were. Michael heard his friend's mother yell at her son, after the door to their apartment had been slammed behind him, "That's the last of your Communist friend."

It was decided to get us out of New York City to live more anonymously with friends of our parents in rural New Jersey. But it took a while to arrange, and we did not move in with the Bachs until June 1952. Prior to this move my memories were like a few flickering bursts of candlelight in an otherwise dark haze, but now the candle's flame burned steadily, throwing a small but growing circle of vision around me. I'd lived in Manhattan for my entire life, and the green lawns, scrub forests, and fenced-in chicken pens of New Jersey chicken-farm country were a revelation. The luxury of playing on grass instead of cement enchanted me. I was drawn by the fresh smell of crops growing in fields, touched still-warm chicken eggs, and basked in the openness of the land and sky.

My brother and I had been moved four times in less than two years. I craved the stability this new home promised. Ben and Sonia Bach were nurturing and kind, and had a son, Leo, a year younger than me. Now I had someone to play with when Michael went to school. We lived in semisecrecy. Although our names weren't changed, no one in Toms River seemed to notice who we were, and the press stayed away.

In late 1951, while we were still at Grandma's, we had begun visiting our parents in prison but I only remember the visits that took place after we moved to New Jersey. We must have visited over a dozen times in the next twenty months, but my memory doesn't distinguish one visit from another. I recall more about the process of visiting, the car trip up the Jersey Turnpike, craning my neck—in that pre-booster-seat era—to see out the side window. Sometimes we were driven to Grandma Sophie's and stayed overnight in her apartment before continuing along the Henry Hudson and Saw Mill River parkways to Ossining, where Sing Sing is located.

The prison was built like a fortress, surrounded by high gray walls.

I was always anxious to get inside, away from any reporters and photographers. We'd walk down blank, dun-colored, windowless corridors through a pervasive grimness into a brighter, airier room, where
we visited with our parents. My mother looked shorter than I remembered her, and I sat on my father's lap, but I don't know how we spent
those precious hours. I felt comforted, rather than traumatized, by
the visits. My parents wrote in their letters that they wanted things to
be as normal as possible, and I wanted the same. I was easy to fool,
and if there were unhappy moments during those visits I have
repressed all memory of them.

In September 1952 I started kindergarten at Toms River Elementary School. Although this period was punctuated with prison visits,
all else remained fairly quiet until the week of my parents' execution.
I suppose, like other children, I was the center of my universe. While
many children have this sense of self-importance reinforced by their
families, my family had been wrenched apart. I was shuffled about so
much and even overheard snippets of conversations about relatives
not wanting Michael and me. Other than from Grandma Sophie, I
never got a sense of belonging from my extended family. But with the
exception of the time in the shelter, I'd never felt abandoned. In fact I
was often surrounded by friendly, but unrelated, adults, like the Bachs
and Dave and Emily Alman, who had never met my parents but knew
of them from Knickerbocker Village. Dave and Emily started the
public campaign to save my parents' lives and paid special attention to
Michael and me. I could see that my situation was different from my
friends and my many cousins who lived with their parents. Looking
back, my sense of self and belonging at this critical formative time
was more intimately connected to a political community of support
than to family.

It seemed to me that I was somehow seen as important by those
same outside forces ("they"). Photographers didn't take pictures of
other kids when they went places. We also had a secret of great con-
sequence. The photographers and the secrecy gave me a sense that I

was particularly important, but I didn't understand why. While I derived little benefit from it at the time, I believe that this sense of not being ordinary has driven me to attempt unusual projects as an adult.

The Bachs, the Almans, and other supporters of my parents worked hard to shield my brother and me from public notice. In his fictionalization of my parents' case, *The Book of Daniel*, E.L. Doctorow depicts the movement that worked to save my parents as insensitive to the needs of the accused couple's children. This insensitivity is powerfully dramatized in a scene from *Daniel*, Paramount Pictures' 1983 film version of the book. The two small children of the couple who have been condemned to death for stealing the secret of the atomic bomb are brought to a huge clemency rally. The throng is so tightly packed that the children can't walk through the crowd to the front. So they are lifted up and passed from person to person over the heads of the crowd and deposited onstage while thousands chant, "The children, the children!" The children, of course, are traumatized.

Nothing like the scene depicted in the movie *Daniel* ever happened to us. The people who sheltered us did everything in their power to protect us. They would ultimately become my heroes and role models for how I wanted to live my life. I don't remember being brought to demonstrations, except for the one we went to in Washington, D.C., the last week of my parents' lives. Again, the process of getting there stands out more than the actual event. We went to New York or Philadelphia and got on a bus with many others going to Washington. I peered out the window as we drove south on Route 1, apparently racing a passenger train I believed was filled with people going to the same place; it was exciting to observe and imagine everyone rushing to a common destination. But once we got off the bus and became part of the commotion, it wasn't fun anymore. Then I was a small person amid crowds of milling adult legs. I observed the process of getting to the demonstration so closely because I wanted so much to understand what was happening. I could see how we got there with my own eyes, but no one told me why we were doing this or what was happening once we got there, and incomprehension left me anxious.

The September after the executions I entered first grade in Toms River Elementary School as if there had been no major change in my life. I think I knew by the time I started school that I would never see my parents again, but I refused to acknowledge it. I stopped asking my brother when the next prison visit would take place. I knew there would be no more visits. And yet he reports I'd still occasionally say, "when Mommy and Daddy come home." I must have repressed thoughts of my parents' deaths so fiercely that there were still times when I believed they would come home. Perhaps at the age of six I still believed that you could magically make something happen if you really, really, really wanted to. I can't remember a specific time when I admitted to myself that I would never see my parents again.

That December we were pulled out of school. We spent several days just after Christmas at Grandma Sophie's apartment in New York City. At the time no one told us why we were removed from school. I learned the reason only later.

Over the summer following the executions, some of the citizens of Toms River expressed their concern to the New Jersey Board of Education that their children were attending school with the children of the Rosenbergs. In response the board determined that only children of New Jersey residents could attend New Jersey public schools. Since my parents were New York State residents, Michael and I had the dubious honor of being banished from the New Jersey public school system at the age of ten and six! The board did not want it to appear that we had been singled out. They combed their records, found several other students whose parents were not New Jersey residents, and expelled them as well. Assuming they're all alive, somewhere in this country are a half dozen or so people in their fifties and sixties who were ejected from school because of us. I have this possibly perverse desire to meet some of these people who have this experience in common. I have mentioned this in dozens of public presentations, but so far no one has stepped forward to claim this bond.

Although our grandmother's apartment was familiar territory, the situation was temporary. My grandmother's health was not good. She still grieved for her husband, and her youngest child's execution earlier in the year remained a raw wound. My grandmother was a mournful and disturbing presence. I can still hear her repeated malediction that my father's murderers "should burn!" She couldn't keep up with two active boys who, in the words of a therapist we began seeing around this time, were showing increasing "signs of disturbance." Michael raged, and I withdrew.

At my parents' request, their lawyer, Manny Bloch, had become our legal guardian after the execution. Anne and Abel Meeropol had offered to take care of us when we had been placed in the shelter in 1950, but my parents did not want us to live with people they did not know. In late 1953 the Meeropols repeated their request to Manny through a mutual friend. Manny met them and quickly agreed that the Meeropols would adopt us.

We did not arrive at Grandma's until late Christmas Eve. Earlier that day Ben Bach drove Michael and me from New Jersey through dense traffic to Brooklyn. We were shepherded up the front steps of the largest house I had ever entered. I walked into a big room where lots of other kids sat around a giant Christmas tree with a pile of presents underneath it. I was told the presents were all for my brother and me. I wondered why none of the other kids was getting any. The disparity seemed very unfair. Anyway, why did I need so many? My toy collection at my grandma's house still consisted of four little metal cars and two tiny cowboy figures. I could have used a few more, but not dozens!

This wealth of presents was the first indication of my new life. We were at the home of W. E. B. Du Bois in Brooklyn Heights, and at this party on Christmas Eve 1953, we were introduced to Abel and Anne Meeropol.

The trip back to Grandma's was without traffic jams, but it still took an hour for the Meeropols to drive us home in their big black 1948 Pontiac. During the drive they asked us if we wanted to live with them. I remember passively saying okay. We'd been shipped around so much by that point that, as always, I just tried to ride the current and not make waves. We moved into the Meeropols' apartment on Riverside Drive and 149th Street at the turn of the New Year. I felt at home with them instantly. Anne was warm and loving, and Abel was funny. Manny visited and reported to Gloria Agrin, the young attorney who had assisted him in our parents' defense, that the transformation in us was almost miraculous. A month later, on January 30, 1954, Manny had a massive heart attack and died.

Manny did not have time before his death to complete the legal transfer of our guardianship to the Meeropols. The Jewish Board of Guardians and the Society for Prevention of Cruelty to Children, both dominated by conservatives, found out about this and started legal action to have us taken from our new home. They filed a petition in Children's Court correctly claiming that the Meeropols were not our legal guardians, and falsely charging that we were being abused. They claimed that this abuse was not physical but political. The legal papers stated that we were forced to attend rallies where we heard grisly descriptions of executions, and that we were being taught to hate our country. These accusations weren't true; we did not attend any rallies after our parents' execution, but a judge ordered that we be removed from the Meeropols' and brought to his court for a hearing.

This time the knock on the door came after we were both asleep. The New York City Police demanded that the Meeropols turn us over immediately. At first Abel and Anne would not open the door, and a loud argument ensued through it. Abel had great physical courage. He was an unarmed man facing several armed officers, but ultimately they backed down. Frantic calls to lawyers and tense negotiations led to an agreement that allowed us to stay at home overnight. The next day the Meeropols brought us before the judge, who ruled that we should be institutionalized; we were carted off to the Pleasantville Cottage School, an orphanage, immediately. Fortunately a quick legal maneuver before a second judge had us out of there in a few days.

Once again "they" were trying to do bad things to us. I still didn't know who "they" were, but I knew there was a "bad judge" and a "good judge," and that the good judge was going to give us another chance to live with the Meeropols. Although I had lived with them for only a month, I had already determined that staying with them meant that "we" would win and "they" would lose. But this was not the end of our odyssey. The good judge granted temporary custody to Grandma and ruled that we had to stay with her until a final decision was made about whom we would live with.

Fortunately Grandma did not live too far from the Meeropols, and amid the bewildering changes, it helped that we continued to attend the same public school. A tall, thin, balding supporter picked us up some mornings and drove us to school. On other mornings a short woman rode to school with us on the bus. These simple acts of kindness were not without risk, although I did not know it at the time. FBI agents often took pictures of those engaged in Rosenberg-related support work. They could easily have snapped a picture of our driver's license plate to find the car's owner. FBI agents might then visit the owner's employer and tell him that a Communist who was helping the Rosenbergs' children worked for him. These kind people could have been harassed or fired, as happened to hundreds, even thousands, of other left-wingers during that period.

After school Michael and I would walk to the Meeropols' house. We'd stay through dinner, and they'd drive us back to Grandma's. I do not know how much of this was done with the judge's approval and how much was done surreptitiously. But I kept my mouth shut for fear of saying the wrong thing to the wrong person. Wariness had become my norm. Grandma cooperated, although grudgingly. She lamented the possibility of our names being changed and our going to live permanently with the Meeropols. She would say in her accented English, "You should go mit your *blut*." But my blood, or *blut*, as she called it, would not take the risk of adopting and raising me. I believe that my adoptive parents provided an upbringing that was much more in tune with my biological parents' values than any of my relatives could have. The fact that Ethel and Julius chose their lawyer, rather than one of their siblings, to be our legal guardian, provides a vital clue that my parents preferred that we be raised by members of the left-wing political community rather than by relatives. My biological parents would have approved of our adoption by Abel and Anne Meeropol.

But our adoption had been placed on hold. Michael's and my semi-nomadic routine persisted until school ended in June. I did not fear the monster under the bed. Instead, the home, as Michael and I came to call the orphanage, was an all-too-real bogeyman. We had to be careful; we were being tested, and I feared what might happen if we failed. These tests were not imaginary. Evelyn Williams, a court-appointed social worker, came to interview us several times. She wrote decades later in her memoirs, *Inadmissible Evidence*, that the initial (or "bad") judge called her into his chambers and threatened that she would be fired if she did not support his position that it was in our best interests to be institutionalized. She wrote: "I made a choice: to base my decision concerning my future recommendations for the children solely on my own investigative findings and the hell with the job."*

The court also appointed Dean Kenneth B. Johnson of the New York School of Social Work to look after our interests. We went with the Meeropols several times to visit him in his spacious and elegant office. These visits were cordial, and Dean Johnson struck me as a kindly old man, but I don't remember what he looked like; I hardly

*Evelyn Williams, *Inadmissible Evidence* (Westport, Conn.: Lawrence Hill, 1993), p. 33.

ever looked at him! I was quiet and kept wandering to the window, playing my little-boy-who-could-not-sit-still card so I'd be freed from his scrutiny to play on the grass courtyard outside. I suspect I seemed like a surprisingly normal seven-year-old to Dean Johnson.

The Meeropols respected Johnson. I must have heard them call him well meaning a million times, and, with him as an ally, they ultimately won legal custody of us. I learned afterward that he was dying of cancer and undertook looking after our needs as a final noble mission. But how was I to know that he was a powerful advocate who would ensure that I would not be carted off at any moment? All I could do was to be even more quiet, observant, and careful, and hope that would not happen.

We were also sent to see Dr. Frederick Wertham, a distinguished therapist known for his work with traumatized juvenile World War II victims. Michael was open about his fears, and his occasionally explosive behavior still focused adult attention upon him. I noted adults' apparent relief that I seemed so unaffected by the events of the last several years. Dr. Wertham commented that I did not really appear to understand what had happened to my parents, and that I was suffering from no significant psychological disturbance. I smiled inwardly as I eavesdropped on these stupid adults, who never realized that I understood all but their most technical terms and that my hearing was better than theirs. I found satisfaction in fooling them because it gave me a sense of control.

My sham good cheer, feigned ignorance, and denial of psychological problems seemed to serve me well, but they prevented me from getting the intense adult intervention I needed to address my frozen emotions. It never occurred to the adults in charge that sending me away from my new "parents," the adults I was most likely to open up to, for a "wonderful summer experience" might not be such a good idea. I'm not sure who paid for and decided that we were to go to sleep-away camp in the summer of 1954. Abel and Anne were strong advocates of summer camp, and might have thought it would be good for us to spend time with our peers. Perhaps they saw how I loved the country (as Manhattan's denizens referred to any unpaved area not occupied by packed multistory buildings). They knew I thrived on outdoor activity. Perhaps the ongoing custody battle also had something to do with the decision, but leaving the Meeropols was the last thing I needed. I was told that we were going to camp only for the summer, and we would return to Grandma and the Meeropols in the fall. But the fall was inscrutably distant for a seven-year-old, and I had already learned that the future was uncertain.

Michael was in a bunk with eleven-year-olds and I lived in a bunk with a dozen seven-year-olds: no biological parents, no grandma, no foster parents, no adoptive parents, and no Michael. Since our parents' arrest, Michael and I had shared a bedroom except for our time at the shelter. At other times I usually had at least one of "us" as a buffer between "them" and me. By this point I classified all outsiders as "them," until people I knew were on our side showed me this was not the case. I'd been in "their" clutches twice before, and it was happening again.

I was miserable, and I wasn't the only one. Michael complained so bitterly that we were granted a special time together every day for his sake. But that was just one more thing that separated me from my bunkmates. They had parents. They were going into third grade, while I was going into second. They could write two-sentence postcards to their parents, I had to have a counselor help me write mine. I had to be coaxed to join any group activity. I wouldn't learn to swim. Watching was safer than doing, and all I remember doing was watching. I had bided my time, hoping to win in the end, but whenever my circumstances seemed to be improving they changed again and became even worse. When I finally landed on a few properties, there seemed to be a new rule for just Michael and me that prevented either of us from buying them. I feared I was going to lose the game.

CHAPTER 2

New Name, New Life

———◆◆◆◆———

I DIDN'T KNOW AS I WATCHED THE OTHER KIDS PLAY THAT SAD SUM-
mer that my life was about to get better. Not only did we return to the
Meeropols when summer camp finally ended, we even slept in our
bedroom there. The "good" judge followed Dean Johnson's recom-
mendation and granted the Meeropols custody. I can't recall anyone
explaining to me what this meant, but my amorphous sense of foreboding faded rapidly. Within weeks we moved from 149th Street to a
bigger apartment in a white ten-story building at the corner of 161st
Street and Broadway. Rather than have separate bedrooms, Michael
and I chose to share one and use the other for a "playroom." Now we
had space for all the toys we'd received at the Christmas party nine
months earlier. The bathroom between these two rooms was also primarily for our use. I accepted as the natural order that Abel and Anne
slept on a pull-out couch in the living room and used the tiny bathroom in what had once been the maid's quarters.

We had enough room to set up a large Lionel electric train set
given to us by Anne and Abel's friends the Posners. The set had

belonged to their son, Richard, and I learned years later that he found this gift problematic. He seemed sullen when he came to visit and saw it set up in our playroom. His parents tried to cajole Richard and boasted of his prowess at chess. Michael also played chess, and I was learning. A match between Michael and Richard was arranged. The visit was hastily terminated after Michael won.

In 1981 President Reagan appointed Richard, then a leading conservative legal scholar at the University of Chicago Law School, a federal Appeals Court judge. Since then he has been elevated to become the chief judge of the U.S. Seventh Circuit Court of Appeals. Many conservatives consider him one of our leading public intellectuals. Michael and I have kidded that we hope his defeating Richard at chess played no part in Richard's turn to the Right. I like to imagine that there is an alternative universe in which the Left in *that* United States is as powerful as the Right is in ours. In that mirror-image America, Michael would have been forced to give his train set to Richard, but Michael would ultimately have become one of our nation's most powerful judges.

Though the Meeropols' new apartment was only a mile from the old one, the location meant yet another new neighborhood and school. This change in the fall of 1954 was different: We were already using the last name Meeropol, although our names were not officially changed until 1957. To my new group of street buddies and classmates I was Robby Meeropol, who lived with his parents, Abel and Anne Meeropol. I had no special living or transportation arrangements, and my picture never appeared in the newspapers.

You might think that our names were changed to protect the children of Julius and Ethel Rosenberg from harassment. But Rosenberg is a common name in New York City. The Manhattan phone book has entire columns of "Rosenbergs" but no "Meeropols." Michael and I have even joked that if we ever wish to resume an anonymous existence we'll change our name back to Rosenberg.

Abel and Anne discussed this matter with child psychologists and were told that a name change would serve us well for two reasons. First, as long as our adoptive parents had one last name and we had another, our classmates were bound to ask about the discrepancy. Answering would repeatedly force us to address and relive our parents' deaths or make up a cover lie. Neither of these alternatives was deemed healthy. Second, after all the turmoil we had been through, creating a normal family life would help us to heal more rapidly. Having the same last name as my parents was part of such normalcy. I don't recall anyone asking me what I thought about the name change.

Michael says he welcomed it, but I had a minor aesthetic quibble. As a seven-year-old I liked name alliteration. I thought it a little unfair that I lost my alliterative "Robert Rosenberg," while my brother, the older one, who usually got the better deal, gained the alliterative "Michael Meeropol." I also wished I could have a more common last name. Meeropol simply sounded a little weird. People constantly goofed it up. I've been called everything from Winipool to Marigold. Sometimes telemarketers butcher the name so badly it sounds like "Miracle." With a name like "Robert Miracle" I could have been an evangelist.

There were other changes as well. Many of the people who had been central during the three previous years disappeared from my life. Manny Bloch died, and Emily and Dave Alman, the Bachs, their son, Leo, and everyone else I knew in New Jersey vanished. I only visited Emily and Dave once every few years. The next time I saw Ben, Sonia, and Leo was in 1959 or 1960, and I do not recall seeing them since. Instead of living with Grandma, Michael and I visited her once a month. We might see a Rosenberg aunt or uncle at Grandma's, but mostly we saw Rosenberg family only at Passover seders. I shed the judges, special guardians, social workers, and psychologists like old skin. At the age of seven, I found it simple to live in the suddenly more pleasant present.

But I never erased my biological parents from my consciousness—Michael and I still had occasional whispered conversations in our room after bedtime about "Mommy and Daddy." By that time we also called Abel and Anne "Mommy and Daddy," but when we said those words in an intimate urgent whisper we both knew whom we were talking about.

Other events also revived unsettling memories. The National Committee to Secure Justice in the Rosenberg Case had been transformed into the Committee to Secure Justice for Morton Sobell. Morton had been convicted along with my parents and was serving a thirty-year prison sentence. The Sobell Committee, as we called it, sold secondhand items to raise money for his lawyers out of a storefront on Broadway about fifteen blocks north of our apartment house. Periodically Anne would gather items and donate them to the store.

Sometimes I accompanied Anne when she walked to the store. I often pressed Anne or Abel to take me on walks in the neighborhoods beyond our immediate area. One or the other was usually willing to indulge me, but I always wanted more. Having the Sobell Committee as a destination enabled Anne both to please me and accomplish an errand. While walking, we noted architectural details, pointed out birds, and exclaimed over the trees', bushes', and flowers' responses to the change of seasons. February's forsythia buds, tightly coiled and black tipped from frost, swelled in March and unfurled into gaudy yellow in April, only to be replaced by neon green leaflets in May.

But when we arrived at the Sobell Committee's store, I did not go in. I found most stores boring, and lingered outside. One day I was happily people-watching outside the store, when a short gray-haired woman with a tear-streaked face came running out and hugged me. Anne came out and quickly shooed her away. I was frozen. I was already so far removed from being a Rosenberg son that I'm not sure I immediately registered why the woman had hugged me. I reverted to denial mode, and within seconds was acting like nothing happened.

Many of my most difficult moments during the late 1950s and early 1960s came not from "them," but from well-meaning supporters of my parents. I'm sure the woman who hugged me in front of the Sobell Committee storefront meant only the best, and would vigorously have denied that she was thoughtlessly using me as an emotional outlet for her own sorrow. I shied away from any emotional outburst, but I particularly hated public displays that might alert others that I was not like everyone else. It also made me queasy to think that people I didn't know knew my secret. I didn't talk with Anne or even Michael about my intense desire to avoid such incidents. But Anne made only solo trips to the Sobell Committee store after that. There were other incidents, but they were infrequent. I learned to treat them as emotional mosquito bites that stopped itching if I ignored them.

Later, years in the future, I had to learn how to deal with being a magnet for people's anguish over my parents' execution. At age eight, however, I had a firm family foundation from which to engage the world. Although I have few clear memories of my biological parents, they are precious. Some people say that much of the important transmission of parental values occurs in the first three years of a child's life. While in my case my biological parents may have sowed the seeds of my values before they were taken from me, I have no way of knowing that consciously. I lived with my biological parents for only three years, but lived full-time in my adoptive parents' household from the age of six to eighteen, until I went away to college.

I refer to and think of both my adoptive and biological parents as "my parents." I've been told that those who do not know me well sometimes have difficulty figuring out which set of parents I am talking about. It may be different for my brother, who spent almost equal time in the Rosenberg and Meeropol homes, but I only spent three years in the Rosenberg home.

I started calling Abel and Anne Meeropol "Mommy" and "Daddy" only a month after meeting them. They rescued me from that vague but constant sense that things were bad and often got worse. They were childless and raised me as their own. I felt they saw me, more than Michael, as theirs. Michael was already half grown when he came to live with them. I am as much, if not more, their child as I am the child of Ethel and Julius Rosenberg. I became Abel and Anne's child so quickly because, after three and a half years of being shuttled from place to place, I required a close parental bond. It also helped that Anne worked part-time while I was growing up, and that Abel worked at home as a songwriter. They were always there for me. I came to take their constant presence for granted.

Before his death, Manny Bloch saw us only once in the Meeropol household, but after that visit he remarked to Emily Alman how quickly we had taken to our new parents. Emily, in an interview for a 1997 video documentary titled *Michael and Robert*, recalled what effective parents the Meeropols were. Emily also stated how pleased the Rosenbergs would have been with the cultural richness and progressive politics of the Meeropol home. Although the Meeropols were more intellectually and culturally oriented than the Rosenbergs, they too had little money. They lived off the modest royalties of Abel's few successful songs,* and could not afford to send us to cultural enrichment classes and summer camps. Manny spent the last six months of his life raising money for a trust fund for our educational and emotional needs from thousands of concerned adults in the United States, Europe, and as far away as Australia. The funds that he raised provided for some living expenses, private school, and ultimately college tuition.

Anne was five foot three, blond, and very pretty. She dressed with unconventional theatrical flamboyance and managed to pull it off— most of the time. She had a knack for motivating young people. Her friends said she had been a very effective elementary schoolteacher in the thirties and forties. In the late fifties and early sixties she ran drama classes and directed productions for teenagers. She was an

---

*Three of Abel Meeropol's songs, "Strange Fruit," "The House I Live In," and "Apples, Peaches, and Cherries" produced a modest but steady stream of royalties.

organizer who knew how to make things happen. She was strong-willed and firm, but very loving. She made my brother and me thrive.

Our household still had conflicts, however. Michael was used to getting his way, but Anne had rules, set limits, and was adamant about them. I observed and noted that Michael's screaming clashes with Anne did little good. During one such battle I pretended to whimper in the corner. Both sides quickly stopped yelling and were remorseful that they were upsetting me. They *were* upsetting me, but since I was unable to display what I felt, I had to fake expressing it. I didn't really lose control of my emotions, but consciously *decided* to whimper.

By the age of eight I recognized a need to maintain emotional control of myself so that I would have more control over my circumstances. I learned to manipulate situations and figure out more devious ways to get what I wanted. But I was not always successful, and this led to occasional battles. Shortly after we started living with them, Anne and Abel initiated "family meetings." We all had titles: Abel was "president"; Anne, "vice president." I remember that Michael was the "sergeant at arms," but Michael tells me that *he* was the "secretary" and *I* was the "sergeant at arms." These meetings went well at first. Although I don't remember this, Michael has told me that as sergeant at arms it was my job to announce the start of the meeting. He reports that I did this with gusto, booming out: "The Meeting of the United Family is about to begin!" But after a few meetings, it dawned on me that they were a sham. I realized that they were designed to make Michael and me feel as if we had a say in things when we really didn't. I had a stubborn streak, an unyielding sense of fairness, and, even at eight, a manipulator's keen awareness of being manipulated. Sometime in 1955 I pointed out that the meetings were unfair unless Michael and I had equal votes. Abel and Anne responded with their mantra for the next decade: "Children are not equal to adults." We could talk, but they would decide. I said that this was the way we always made decisions, so the meetings were worthless. They began to get angry and told me to stop talking. "Now I can't even talk!" I screamed, and stalked off to my room. I ultimately caved in to Anne and Abel's demand and ended up sitting sullenly at a meeting I was now forced to attend. That was the last family meeting, however.

The vague sense from my earliest memories that my family was being treated unfairly no doubt underlies the paramount importance I've always placed on fairness. But I believe that Abel Meeropol played an equal or greater role in shaping my intense sense of evenhandedness. He started working as a high school English teacher in the New York City public school system in the late 1920s. He left teaching in the 1940s and earned a modest income thereafter writing song lyrics. He had tremendous intellectual integrity, and was viscerally outraged by unfairness and injustice. His antilynching anthem "Strange Fruit," which was popularized by Billie Holiday, reflected the ferocity of his antiracist feelings. He once wrote: "I wrote 'Strange Fruit' because I hate lynching . . . , and I hate the people who perpetuate it."

In our household we respected all people, revered those who fought for equality and justice, but hated bigots, oppressors, and exploiters. "Love your enemy" was not part of our moral code.

Abel was dark haired, sported a thin mustache, and was very gentle. He provided an excellent male role model for me. He was funny and could be quite indulgent. I learned quickly how to wheedle almost anything out of him. Anne would return home from an errand to find that I'd received four, instead of my normal allotment of two, Oreos from him. In my mind I can still hear her rueful "Oh, Abel."

Abel and Anne each made important contributions to progressive politics. The two of them often acted as a team. Abel wrote the scripts for secular bar and bat mitzvah programs that celebrated progressive aspects of Jewish cultural history, and Anne directed the thirteen-year-olds who performed them. Later, when I was in high school, Abel wrote and Anne directed pointed political commentaries and satire. I particularly enjoyed watching Anne direct a children's play that Abel wrote, called *Topsy Turvy Town*. Anne organized effective events for a number of organizations. Adopting the orphaned sons of Communists recently executed for "giving the secret of the atomic bomb to the Communist menace" at the height of the McCarthy era was a very brave act. Abel and Anne were not only up to the task; they continued to be politically engaged while they raised us.

Abel and Anne had been active members of New York's Teachers Union Theater Art Group. Abel designed sets and wrote satirical lyrics; Anne acted and sang in the programs. In fact she gave the first public performances of "Strange Fruit" at Teachers Union meetings years before Billie Holiday sang it. Abel quit teaching in 1945 to go to Hollywood after the success of "The House I Live In." They stayed in Hollywood for more than five years. I'm not sure of the circumstances that brought them back to New York City in 1951, but Abel once told me they left Hollywood one step ahead of the blacklist.

They had continuing personal contact and professional relationships with writers and singers. A parade of writers and singers came through our 161st Street apartment. Deep-voiced chain-smoking Cisco Houston looked like he'd just stepped out of a Western movie. Meridel LeSueur, a writer of popular left-wing "young adult" books, visited and gave us a signed copy of her book about teenagers in a mining community, *Zuska of the Burning Hills*. Malvina Reynolds sang her catchy songs in her thin voice on our living-room couch. I couldn't resist making fun of what I considered "mushy" songs. In her schmaltzy "Turn Around," which became quite popular years later, I altered one stanza about a young girl growing up quickly, and "turning around" to discover herself grown:

> *Turn around and you're five*
> *Turn around and you're ten*
> *Oh what the hell*
> *Turn around again!*

Our house was often filled with raucous laughter. Abel was always playing silly word games. I egged him on, was a willing imitator, and was soon inventing my own verbal absurdities. Abel had a repertoire of voices and animal noises he made to entertain friends' children. His bark was so realistic that it was once recorded for a dog-food commercial on radio. Anne would warn Abel about getting me "over-stimulated," but I doubt that either of them was too disturbed by my boisterous shrieking. Abel and Anne were not only dedicated parents, they were also dynamic and productive people whose lives I was privileged to share.

Many people have expressed to me the sadness they feel about my traumatic childhood. I've usually been inclined to emphasize the positive even though experience has taught me that things can go horribly wrong. I don't know if this optimistic tendency is the result of my brain's chemistry, my genetic makeup, the nurturing of so many good and caring people, or a complex combination of all this and more. I do not wish to downplay the fear and anxiety I felt in the years between my parents' arrest and the late 1950s, but this time period had some positive aspects as well. I can't help feeling that I gained as much as I lost during those years.

Being permanently placed with Abel and Anne was a critical personal and political victory. Those who tried to have us taken from the Meeropols were not satisfied with killing our birth parents; they wanted to kill the Rosenbergs' legacy as well. They wanted me to grow up forgetting or rejecting my birth parents. In fact they wanted to prevent my growing up to create something like the Rosenberg Fund for Children. But they failed. Instead I grew up with a positive image of my biological parents, and the most profound and abiding respect for any people who place themselves in harm's way for the good of others. I am convinced that I would not have survived to become a fully functioning adult if we had not won the victory that enabled us to stay with Abel and Anne.

More immediately, I was finally free to be a kid. I spent my days in the neighborhood public school, played at recess with kids from my block, and on the street with those same kids or with my brother until darkness or dinnertime. We were street kids, consciously differentiating ourselves from those with more privileged backgrounds. Because the neighborhood was changing, a euphemism for its becoming more cultural and ethnically diverse, the rent for our large apartment was modest. There was a synagogue directly across the street from my house, but its congregation was shrinking. My best street buddies, Harry, Joey, and Allen, were Jewish or Italian, but the block across Broadway, to the east, was mostly black. I frequently played in front of my house or around the corner to the west, but I never crossed Broadway to play. My school was a mixture of Jews, Italians, Irish, African-Americans, and a small but growing group of Spanish-speaking kids whose parents came from Puerto Rico or the Dominican Republic. I was raised with an overtly antiracist ethic, and ethnic diversity was part of my everyday life, but I was blithely unaware of the contradiction between this and the semisegregated character of my neighborhood.

I learned as much on the streets as I did in school. I spent hundreds of hours hanging out with Catholics and more religious Jews whose parents were not leftists. My group of a half dozen eight- to ten-year-olds would often play for fifteen minutes and then argue for a much longer period of time whether a runner was safe or out. Endless argument, negotiation, and reconciliation served as a rich self-guided social laboratory. Winning was fun, but learning how to do so without alienating those on the other team, who might be your teammates tomorrow, was more important. Coping with losing was even more so. Possibly my most valuable lesson was learning to get along and have a good time with those I didn't always agree with.

The streets also could be pretty tough. It was not unusual for us little kids to have our ball stolen, or to get shoved or even beaten up by older kids. It was particularly unpleasant to be caught alone by bigger kids when there was snow and ice on the streets. Fortunately I had terrific radar: I smelled trouble and avoided it. I could talk my way out of most situations, and when words wouldn't serve me, I kept moving toward home and didn't react. I never endured anything worse than having to scurry home with a lot of dirty snow and ice down my back. Experience had taught me that complaining to adults about such incidents did little good, and I remained reluctant to discuss problems with adults. I channeled my rage at bullies' unfairness into schemes to outwit them, and rationalized each success at avoiding trouble as a victory.

Since the 1930s the Meeropols had been members of the American Communist Party. I believe they left the party in the early 1950s not because of political disagreement but so that they could adopt us. Of course I didn't discuss these adult matters with Abel and Anne when I was a child. Somehow I knew it wasn't safe to talk about the American Communist Party while I was growing up. Ex-party members were more acceptable parents than party members in 1950s America. Raising my brother and me in a manner that was simultaneously true to their ideals and in our best interests was a formidable task. How could they shield us from the particulars of our past without negating its general political and cultural framework? How could we avoid being overly burdened while remaining Rosenberg sons?

I don't know that Anne and Abel thought about these questions in this way, but they were not content to send my brother and me to nonpolitical New York City neighborhood schools, no matter how good they were, and allow us to grow up as street kids. Little by little we were immersed in the New York area's child-oriented left-leaning institutions. In the fall of 1956, with the aid of funds Manny Bloch raised before his death, Michael started ninth grade at Elisabeth Irwin High School, and I started fourth grade at its affiliated elementary school, the Little Red School House.

EI and Little Red, as we quickly came to call these schools, were progressive private schools in Manhattan's Greenwich Village. Some of our teachers were blacklisted members of New York's Teachers Union who had recently lost their jobs in the public school system because they would not sign loyalty oaths. Angela Davis graduated in the class before me. Arthur Miller's son was in my class, and Norman Mailer's daughter was a couple of years behind me.

Entering the fourth grade, or "nines," as grades were designated at Little Red, was a social challenge. The families of my new classmates had a political orientation or artistic interests that were closer to my family's than my former public school classmates had been, but they also came from wealthier homes. Most could walk to school and had been together in the same classroom for three or four years. Breaking into this established group took time, especially because of my continuing caution in new social situations. Fortunately there was one other new boy, Lenny. He did not live in the neighborhood either, and took the subway to school as I did. We quickly became friends.

I was sufficiently aware during my first year at Little Red to know that Stevenson was running against Eisenhower for president that fall of 1956, and that it would be better for our side if Stevenson won. I also knew by then that our side usually lost and so was not surprised when Eisenhower was reelected.

The curriculum at Little Red was designed to teach us about the world. While I knew that my parents had been killed, the circumstances that surrounded their case remained mysterious. I had a vague sense that it had something to do with politics and the world. Why did it happen? Asking directly would open old wounds, so I never asked. But if I learned all about politics, world affairs, and even history I might ferret out the answers. The "nines" focused on Mexico, the "tens" on India, and the "elevens" on China. It was probably no accident that we concentrated on an ally, a neutral country, and a Communist country. I learned that there was a worldwide conflict between the capitalists and the Communists. This was in contrast to my age-mates in most other schools who learned about the battle between democracy and communism.

I pored over maps and globes because I wanted to know more about the world than just its politics. The natural world entranced me. Geography, climate, landforms, and animal and plant life were remarkable. In order to learn all you had to do was observe! I got an old radio and started listening to weather reports. I kept charts of daily high and low temperatures. I converted several two-by-three-foot plywood rectangles from our old electric train setup into backing for the relief maps of the continents I created, using multiple colors of soft clay. Soon miniature continents with snaking blue rivers that emerged from brown molded mountains and crossed green plains were propped against one wall of our playroom.

Politics were daily fare at home, and in general my brother and I agreed with Anne and Abel on the issues. Abel and Anne did not have to force their worldview upon me. In fact, my major political arguments with my parents during this period were generated by their conclusion that I was too young to join my brother and some of his friends, who were picketing the neighborhood Woolworth store with signs that protested: SOUTHERN WOOLWORTHS SEGREGATE! I was furious when they said I still wasn't old enough to attend the first big national civil rights march on Washington in 1957.

We watched the evening news together and Sunday morning news shows like *Meet the Press*. I did not have to be coaxed to watch, and that wasn't only because my other television viewing was tightly rationed.

Watching TV news in our house was not a passive event, particularly for my mother. She'd curse out President Eisenhower, and repeatedly mutter "bastard" at Secretary of State John Foster Dulles. As far as I could tell, my parents always criticized U.S. policy and agreed with the policies of the Soviet Union. They were pleased when the Soviet Union shot down the American U-2 spy plane piloted by Francis Gary Powers because it exposed our government's duplicitous claims that it did not spy on the USSR. I can't remember them criticizing the Soviet invasion of Hungary, or them being distraught when Khrushchev finally exposed Stalin's crimes in 1956. If I voiced any concern about the Soviet Union's righteousness, my father would say: "In the 1930s we thought it was simple. The workers would seize the means of production, and all our problems would be solved. Now we know it's not that simple." He reiterated variations of this left-wing version of "God works in mysterious ways" without explaining further, until Alzheimer's short-circuited his mentation almost twenty-five years later.

My family bought the daily *New York Times*. Although I was interested in current affairs, I was not a good reader and so did not read it. If we got the Communist Party newspaper, the *Daily Worker*, I never saw it. Instead the left-wing but non-Communist *National Guardian* was delivered to our apartment weekly in a plain brown wrapper. The *Guardian* was special to our family. Founded by former *New York Times* reporters Cedric Belfrage, Jim McManus, and Jim Aronson, its publication of William Reuben's multiarticle analysis of my parents' trial in 1951 sparked the public campaign to save their lives.

There was never a question of talking politics with my street friends. I remember trying to find out if I might have a political ally by asking what newspaper their parents read. None of them knew, and I didn't pursue the subject.

My brother and I also attended progressive summer camps. My unhappiness at summer camp in 1954 may explain why the Meeropols did not send me to camp on my own until 1959, after I finished the sixth grade, my final year at Little Red. In the mid-1950s I accompanied my mother to Lincoln Farm, a camp for teenagers, located in New York's Catskill Mountains, where she worked as a drama counselor. There I was a "counselor's brat," free to participate in camp activities or roam the fields if I did not stray too far.

The summers of 1959 and 1960, after my twelfth and thirteenth birthdays, I attended Camp Woodland as a full-fledged camper. At this camp, also located in the Catskills, left-wing views were the norm. It was comforting to be somewhere where I could speak my mind and did not feel alone. None of my bunkmates told me that they thought my parents were heroes. In fact, no one ever mentioned my parents' case, but I blossomed in an atmosphere that was supportive of leading left-wing victims of McCarthyism, like Paul Robeson and Pete Seeger, who performed at Camp Woodland. I had heard my parents described as victims of McCarthyism often enough to feel that these heroes were like my parents and shared their ideas. Once I felt comfortable, I became politically outspoken.

At least some of my bunkmates' parents were Communist Party members. I had a wonderful time with age-mates who shared my worldview. We could develop our own way of responding to world issues, which were in line with, but different from, our parents'. We talked a lot about the burgeoning civil rights movement. One friend wrote a satire about President Eisenhower to the tune of "Sweet Betsy from Pike." I still remember the first stanza:

> *I'll tell you a story about a man named Dwight*
> *Who went to a golf course on a cool summer's night.*
> *It was segregated but he didn't mind*
> *Because he knew he'd be with the ones of his kind.*

Some of my contemporaries who were children of Communists have written popular books about why they turned their backs on their parents' politics. I am not referring to the many "red-diaper babies" who ultimately drifted away from activism or who never became activists in the first place, but rather to those who appear to have gone out of their way to publicly revile their parents' politics and child-rearing practices. Ronald Radosh's recent book, *Commies: A Journey Through the Old Left, the New Left, and the Leftover Left,* is typical of those who have described their progressive school or summer camp experiences as oppressive farces.

That is not the way I felt about my camp experiences. I've never entirely understood why I embraced left-wing culture and politics so wholeheartedly, but I believe this had as much to do with the people I interacted with as it did with the ideas they promoted. School, progressive or otherwise, was just okay. Camp, on the other hand, was the pinnacle of my childhood experience. It is possible that I received special treatment because I was a Rosenberg son, but I do not recall this happening. Many of my camp friends have the same passionate attachment to our summer camp experiences.

I loved that my parents sent me to Commie camp. Like Ike at the golf course, this gave me the chance to be with the "ones of my kind." I viewed the larger society as fostering selfishness, discrimination, and deceit. Summer camp was my liberation because it enabled me to conform, to be like everyone else, without embracing the destructive values of the larger society.

The Meeropols sent me to summer camps that reinforced their politics. But I think these camps were effective in passing on their values because they weren't too heavy-handed. This created an environment in which campers could rebel against orthodoxy without wholesale rejection of those values. This empowered me to engage the political world on my terms.

In the fall of 1959 I started seventh grade at EI. EI's curriculum included typical junior high school subjects, but we also spent class time discussing the civil rights movement. Civil rights activists spoke in schoolwide assemblies. At one assembly my class performed a civil rights play for the school. I played Crispus Attucks, a black man who was the first person shot by British soldiers at the start of the American Revolution. I didn't have any lines, but I got to die dramatically onstage.

We read and studied the *Southern Patriot*, the newspaper published by the Southern Conference Educational Fund (SCEF). I joined with several classmates, including Danny and Jeff, whose minister father had been thrown out of his Brooklyn congregation for being a Communist sympathizer, in publishing the *Northern Patriot* for our classmates.

In addition to becoming more politically outspoken, I started to think about issues of patriotism and civic activism. I noted that the inclusion of the word "patriot" in the title of SCEF's newspaper was one of many efforts the civil rights movement made to prove its loyalty to the United States. I saw pictures on television of southern roadside billboards showing Martin Luther King attending a seminar at Tennessee's Highlander Center. The billboards were captioned: "Martin Luther King at a Communist training school." I believed that communism was the best economic system for the vast majority of humanity, and that working to improve the lives of the world's citizens was the ultimate patriotic act. The sentiment "my country right or wrong" seemed wrongheaded and stupid to me. I agreed with the Soviet Union, not because I supported it as a nation-state, but because I believed it was working for the benefit of all people. I saw no contradiction between supporting the overthrow of the U.S. economic system and being patriotic. I reasoned that American Revolutionary War heroes were our greatest patriots, and they overthrew their government.

Tom Paine was my favorite Revolutionary War hero. His pamphlet *Common Sense* passionately advocated the right of rebellion. I saw him as the common man's hero, an eighteenth-century Che Guevara, who journeyed to France to support French revolutionary forces after the American Revolution was won. I also read his book *The Age of Reason*, and agreed with his arguments against a literal interpretation of the Bible. His cogent dismantling of religious dogma convinced me that the reason religion had never made sense to me was that it didn't make any sense.

Michael and I remained very close. Michael was also attending EI that year, so we even spent our days in the same small school building. But Michael was a senior and would leave for Swarthmore College the next year. Right before he left, he made a big deal of us taking a special final walk together. He told me this walk was important because things would never be the same after he left. I was concerned about the one constant of my entire life leaving, but found his open expression of emotion embarrassing. I liked to talk about politics, sports, or more recently, about girls with him, but by September 1960 I was thirteen years old and preferred, even with Michael, to keep my emotional concerns to myself. Looking back, perhaps I refused to dignify the occasion because I could not confront the true sense of loss I felt. I defused this uncomfortable conversation by making a joke out of Michael's seriousness. Michael was right: We remained close, but for the next five years I was the only child at home while he became a sporadic presence.

Fidel Castro entered Havana triumphantly nineteen months before I entered the eighth grade, without quite as much fanfare, in September 1960. His transformation of Cuban society remained constant front-page news. Our eighth-grade teacher, Murray (Lewis—at Little Red and EI we called our teachers by their first names), encouraged us to read a daily newspaper and clip articles of particular interest. We were supposed to underline the passages we felt were most important and discuss them during the current events period of the school week. Although I still had some difficulty reading, and was embarrassed at how poorly I read aloud, for the entire school year I read, cut out, and underlined every article about Fidel and the Cuban revolution published in the *New York Times*. I taped each clipping into a scrapbook that soon bulged and had pieces of articles protruding from it at all angles. In Fidel I found my contemporary hero.

In the fall of 1960 EI held a mock presidential election, as was typical of high schools throughout the nation. That was the year

Kennedy ran against Nixon. At EI, Kennedy lost. He lost to Norman Thomas, the Socialist Party candidate. As I recall, Thomas received 72 votes, Kennedy 70, and Nixon 2. I think of those 2 votes as the "diversity" votes; Republicans were the minority students at EI.

I was a moderately good student, but was constantly told that I could do much better if I applied myself. I read relatively slowly, had difficulty with spelling, and stumbled painfully when forced to read aloud. I found all arithmetic work very easy but had trouble once they started substituting letters for numbers. This confounded both my parents and teachers because I did so well on all the aptitude tests. I still have a notebook full of spelling and writing exercises that I worked on with my mother after school, but even with her extra tutoring I was told repeatedly that I did not live up to my potential. It did not help that my brother had been a stellar student, a National Merit Scholarship finalist, and was going to Swarthmore.

I think I would have been happier at school if I didn't see myself as a lazy underachiever. Twenty-five years later, observing one of my daughters' struggles with spelling, and having slogged through countless misspellings in my father's four hundred prison letters, I realized that dyslexia ran in the family. Even relatively late in life, recognizing the genetic component of this problem has helped me to deal with it. I still haven't met a word I can't misspell if given half the chance, and will remain forever grateful to the programmer who invented SpelCheck.

My eighth-grade class visited W. E. B. Du Bois at his Brooklyn Heights home in the spring of 1961. If I had a flicker of memory about my previous visit to his house seven years earlier when I first met Anne and Abel Meeropol, I repressed it. This time Du Bois had an enormous impact on me. I sat in awe, literally at his feet, while he described his school experiences in a quiet melodious voice.

I felt as if I had entered an international sanctuary while I sat in his parlor. Its window curtains were red tapestries from China and a Ghanaian flag adorned his wall. His soft voice entranced me first with tales of his childhood and then with stories of his ninety-first birthday while a thunderstorm boomed outside. I was particularly impressed that he didn't talk down to us or give a lecture that overflowed with facts. He seemed brilliant, warm, and full of kindness. I found it incomprehensible that he was virulently hated by so many in our society for his radical antiracism. I was moved to write a short essay about this experience immediately after I returned home from school. I concluded: "The overwhelming power of the setting, and the man, will make a lasting impression on me for the rest of my life."

I did not exaggerate when I wrote I'd remember this visit for the rest of my life. This episode was the climax of my time at Little Red and EI. I'd spent five school years with the same classmates and was at home there. Even with Michael at college, all aspects of my life felt remarkably safe and secure. I was increasingly self-confident, had lots of companions, and even occasionally acted as a leader. I did not suspect that the five years of nurturing in an alternative school and stable home environment were about to end.

CHAPTER 3

Disguised as a Mild-Mannered Liberal

————◆•❉•◆————

I STILL DON'T KNOW THE REASONS ANNE AND ABEL DECIDED TO move from New York City. They explained that the neighborhood was deteriorating, but in retrospect that answer was, at best, incomplete. Since racial diversity did not seem to trouble them, I'm not even sure what they meant by "deteriorating." Leaving my neighborhood friends troubled me less than leaving EI, since my extracurricular social life took up most weekends, and increased homework limited my weekday after school time on the street. But my parents promised that I could stay at EI, even though we were moving to Hastings-on-Hudson.

We moved at the beginning of June 1961. During the final two weeks of the eighth grade my father dropped me off every morning at 242nd Street, the last stop on the subway. He picked me up there at four each afternoon, thus making two forty-minute round trips five days a week. By the end of the first week, my parents told me that this would not work and I would be attending Hastings High School in the fall. I pointed out that I could take the Grand Central Railroad to the Marble Hill Station, where it intersected with the subway at 225th Street, but they declared the two-dollars-a-day round-trip too expensive. I was devastated and angry.

My anger was fueled by the suspicion that they had never intended to let me stay at EI once we moved. They may have had some concerns about how fast kids grew up at EI. My eighth-grade class started having "lights out" parties during which couples made out on every square inch of upholstered or carpeted space. I now had my first girlfriend, Ronnie, and found this agenda delightful. Perhaps they were anxious about my going to school in the middle of Greenwich Village, one of the early incubators of the sexual revolution, and of drugs.

My parents also may have been uncomfortable with the snobbery a private school education often generates. Or they may have felt that I had healed enough to be removed from the cocoon they had created for me. They may even have felt that I had to learn to get along with a broader cross-section of the population if I was going to be a functioning adult in the United States. But I don't know what they thought because we didn't have intergenerational discussions of such matters. I adjusted poorly to my new high school, and until I escaped to college I did not forgive what I viewed as a betrayal. By the time I was old enough to discuss this with my parents as an adult, it no longer seemed important.

A typically self-absorbed fourteen-year-old, I assumed that I was the main reason for the move. It didn't occur to me that my parents were cramped in the old apartment and wanted more space. My parents explained that they paid a bargain price on a very big house at the corner of Broadway and Fraser Place because the previous owner needed cash fast for a business deal. I hated leaving New York City, but this new house was remarkable. Built in 1893, it had served as home and office for a physician. A cobblestone-enclosed porch created a large unheated L-shaped space at least forty feet on a side and ten feet wide. The porch's several, multipane, wood-framed windows (six feet high and eight feet across) could be folded, accordion-style, along their hinged sections during the warmer months. The house sat on a half acre of land that sloped up from Broadway. Visitors climbed several steps at the street, continued up a curved walkway, and mounted more steep stone steps to reach the porch, which they crossed to enter a wide Dutch door. To the left was the doctor's old waiting room, now our downstairs living room. To the right a stone fireplace, almost big enough to walk into, flanked by matching built-in benches. Straight ahead my mother had a desk in what had been the receptionist's space. Also off the entryway, a door opened into an octagonal wood-paneled room that had been the doctor's office and that soon housed our baby grand piano. The second floor had a large kitchen, another dining and living room, my parents' bedroom suite, which included my father's study, and, finally, my bedroom.

My room, which had an extra bed in it for Michael's visits home, was directly above the main entrance and had its own fireplace. When I lay on my stomach at the foot of my bed with my chin resting on my forearms I could gaze across Broadway, over the rooftops of the nearest houses to the sheer stone cliffs of the Palisades beyond the Hudson River several miles away.

Even though we rented out the three-bedroom third floor, our two floors seemed like an extravagant amount of space for three people. After my father's death I came across some of their old income tax returns from the 1950s. I don't see how they could have afforded even a bargain basement price on that house. During that period my father's third biggest source of royalty income came from a song entitled "Apples, Peaches and Cherries." Peggy Lee's recording of it in 1950 had done fairly well, but royalties had dwindled to a trickle after a year or two. Sasha Distel, a French folksinger whose main claim to fame may have been being Brigitte Bardot's boyfriend, caused a minor sensation with a new song "Scoubidou" that soon topped the charts in France. "Scoubidou" was a poorly disguised French translation of "Apples, Peaches and Cherries." Distel, confronted with overwhelming evidence, quickly settled my father's copyright infringement suit, and we received a windfall. My parents told me the money helped pay for our new car, and I bet it covered the down payment on the house as well. To this day my brother and I receive modest royalties from "Scoubidou."

I didn't know how to say good-bye to my friends at EI. I had several mechanisms for deflecting bad news or feelings. I could ignore them or pretend I didn't understand what was going on. When forced to confront something, I usually denied it was all that bad or figured out a way to find its silver lining. But I had no coping strategies for presenting bad news to others.

During the middle of the eighth grade, our teacher, Murray Lewis, who was the most influential teacher I had during my first twelve years of school, made an offhand remark about the difference between people who were really happy and those who just pretended to be. I brooded about his comment that day on the subway ride home. Which was I? I had never ventured beneath my veneer of glib cheeriness. I had a vague sense that I had never addressed my sorrow at losing my parents. I covered it up and thought about other things instead. I can't remember ever crying about their executions as a child. In fact, except when physically hurt, and rarely then, I never cried about anything. I presented myself to my friends at home and at school as if my parents' arrest, imprisonment, and execution had nothing to do with me. I ignored this personal tragedy that was central to me. I couldn't bring myself to tell my left-wing friends at school that I was Ethel and Julius Rosenberg's son, even though I thought some probably knew already. My parents thought I had few problems because I kept them to myself. For the first time I began to wonder if I was just hiding my problems from myself. Looking back, this was my initial glimmer of understanding that while I had developed a persona that was functional in the short term, it might not hold up for the long haul. But I told no one about repressing my feelings because I feared I could not handle whatever I brought to the surface.

In the days after Murray's comment I became increasingly glum. As the days became a week, my parents, teachers, and even a few friends began to ask what was wrong. I just shrugged them off. I felt that the foundation of my psychological edifice was shaky, and if I revealed my crisis to anyone it might all come crashing down. I might have been able to share these feelings with Michael, but he was away at college. Although I don't remember this, Michael's reports in his letters to my biological parents of my constant crying immediately after their arrest revealed my distress. The lesson I had apparently internalized was that expressing my distress did no good. In the spring of 1961, at almost fourteen, I still doubted it would help. There were a couple of kids in my class who were psychological basket cases, and I didn't want to be like them. Some of them saw therapists or had parents who were therapists, but I didn't consider therapy an option. Even though Anne and Abel had taken us to therapists when we first came to live with them, in general they scoffed at what they called psychological mumbo-jumbo. My father made fun of them with a short verse:

> *I've never seen a psychiatrist*
> *Neither a he nor she one*
> *But with the fees they get with ease*
> *I'd rather be than see one.*

About two weeks into this downward spiral, I concluded it was ridiculous to constantly worry about who I really was. I loved my parents, liked my friends, liked my school, and I liked my life. The last two weeks hadn't been fun, so why continue with this stuff? Yes, there were things too frightening to confront, but that was long ago and I'd left them behind. True, I could not bring myself to tell anyone who my biological parents were, but there were special reasons for that. I could be honest and truthful in the present and that was good enough. The squall passed, and the sun came out. I put it in a box and didn't look back.

A few months later when it was time to say good-bye to my friends on the street, I simply said "I'm moving, good-bye" and that was that. I've never seen any of them since. I'd told my school friends that we were moving, but I'd be returning in the ninth grade anyway. When my parents changed their minds about my returning to EI, I told no one. I went to school that last week dreading the moment I'd have to reveal the truth, and feeling bad that I could not bring myself to say a word about it to anybody. Murray Lewis announced on the last day of class that I would not be returning in the fall. My girlfriend and others were dumbfounded that I hadn't told them, and I could only stammer that it was my parents' fault. Then I went home to my new house and tried not to think about it.

I also avoided mulling over what awaited me that fall at Hastings High School. I replaced that dread with anticipation of spending my first summer at Lincoln Farm as a real camper, not just a counselor's brat. Lincoln Farm was a teenage "work camp" set on several hundred acres of hills and valleys at the western edge of New York's Catskill Mountains. More than a hundred campers aged thirteen to sixteen spent the mornings doing farming, construction, or forestry projects, their afternoons playing sports and participating in cultural workshops, and their evenings socializing. I quickly gravitated to a group of left-wing-oriented folk singing kids. During the McCarthy period *Reader's Digest* published the FBI's list of ten ways to spot a Communist. We didn't need a list to spot each other. My closest camp friend, Ellen, was the daughter of Communist Party members.

I worked with farm animals and in the garden most mornings. Some grumbled at weeding, but I found it satisfying to keep the rows neat and clean, and never tired of watching branches sprout, leaves emerge from buds, flowers bloom, and fruit fatten. Working in the garden also enabled me to pick the precise moment to sample perfect raw string beans. Evening campfires or hootenannies capped many near-perfect days, and political discussion, joking with the guys, or flirting with the girls, garnished all these activities. The summer passed by too quickly.

Hastings was an old suburb. For almost a hundred years the commuter railroad had enabled thousands of professionals to pursue careers in New York City, twenty miles to the south, while raising families amid the jumble of thickly wooded hills that overlooked the Hudson River. There were some newer houses on hilltops deeper in the woods, but stately older structures predominated. The Anaconda Copper Company had a big plant along the river, adding a working-class component to the town of ten thousand.

Hastings High was much bigger than EI, but my class had fewer than two hundred students. Although almost all Americans think of themselves as middle class, through my Marxist-oriented lenses almost a quarter of my classmates appeared to come from working-class backgrounds. They dominated the sports teams and were tracked to shop and other technical classes. They were most likely to be Polish or Irish Catholics. They probably weren't all that different from some of my city street friends. I was leery, however, of dealing with working-class kids in school, even though I had coexisted amicably with kids like them on the streets of my old neighborhood. Despite tracking, some working-class kids were in my homeroom and a couple of my classes, at least during freshman and sophomore years. During my first month, I disagreed with something Steve said in English class. The next time the teacher's back was turned Steve got my attention, balled his fists, and pantomimed the question: "Do you want to fight?" I quickly pantomimed back, "No," and remembered to be careful about whom I disagreed with thereafter. The last I heard, Steve was an army master sergeant.

Some of my classmates made overtly racist remarks about Jews and blacks. Bruce commented during a current events and civil rights discussion in history class, that Negroes down south were easier to get along with because they knew their place. Richard, one of the few black kids in my class, shot back angrily, "Exactly what is my place, Bruce?!" Bruce whined in response: "Now you see what I mean." The teacher immediately squelched the discussion. Bruce also made comments about Senator Hubert Humphrey being practically a Communist. I viewed Humphrey as a red-baiting mainstream liberal, and classified Bruce as a racist and a fascist. He and his group of friends were to be avoided.

Although the school had some ethnic and class diversity, my class graduated just a few blacks and Asians. The sons and daughters of Protestant and Jewish professionals dominated the college-bound classes. Hastings High had the typical cliques of jocks, popular cheerleaders, student-government types, along with brains and nerds, but I felt I was in foreign territory. I was shocked to discover that almost none of my classmates had spent any time by themselves in New York City. My classmates refused to believe that I had regularly ridden the subways by myself since I was nine. Soon I was eating lunch regularly with two other boys; the three of us were squarely in the nerd camp. Mostly I lived in my head at school, emerging to have fun on weekends with camp friends in "the City."

I didn't find schoolwork challenging. Since I didn't want to reveal too much of my political perspective or inner thoughts in history and English papers, I dutifully regurgitated the conventional wisdom that was not so subtly set forth in my textbooks. Giving the teachers back what I thought they wanted, instead of really thinking about assignments, made homework even easier. I remember an illustration in a history text that classified people by their politics. The chart showed a parabolic curve with a few fascists and Nazis on the extreme right and an equal number of Communists and anarchists on the extreme left. The descriptive caption read that although Nazis and Communists appeared at opposite ends of the chart, they had more in common with each other than with the majority of us in the middle. I knew "us" didn't refer to me.

I fantasized that I was underground in the enemy camp and that the FBI was looking for me. I was camouflaged as a mild-mannered liberal (to paraphrase the narrator's expression describing Clark Kent in the *Superman* television series). I was not so far off. Decades later, when portions of my FBI files were released in the wake of the FOIA lawsuit my brother and I filed, I learned that the FBI had visited Dr. Phillip Langworthy, the school superintendent in Hastings, and asked him to keep tabs on me. The file indicated that he declined. The story I heard later from others who knew him was that he indignantly threw them out of his office. Perhaps they opened a file on him at that point. I also wonder if they ultimately found someone to do their dirty work. Since I've never asked for my entire FBI file, I don't know if the FBI kept me under surveillance while I was in high school.

Without friends to hang out with after school, I had time to kill at home. I finally began to read. I read a few of the political books shelved in my father's study. My parents had a book series entitled the Little Lenin Library from the International Publishers, the Communist Party's press. I read about the Russian revolution and read the *Communist Manifesto* cover to cover, but couldn't get past the first page of Marx's *Das Kapital* or Lenin's *Imperialism: The Highest Stage of Capitalism*. I read all the books I could find about Fidel Castro and the Cuban revolution. I furthered my political education by attending a Communist Party–sponsored teenage discussion group that was held regularly at the home of my camp friend Ellen, who lived in a neighboring town. I factored what I learned about revolutionary transitions into my fantasies.

My favorite fantasy centered on avenging my parents. In one variation the government was overthrown and the new Communist regime felt it was fitting to appoint me to sit in judgment over all those who had anything to do with my parents' frame-up and execution. I don't recall David and Ruth Greenglass ever being brought before me. Instead I focused my wrath on my parents' trial judge, the prosecutors, and various FBI agents. They would be dragged forward and I would send them off to the firing squad. In another version I got to be on the firing squad. I preferred the former, because even though I craved revenge I couldn't imagine shooting anyone. I supported the idea of fighting the good fight, whether against Nazi Germany or for revolutionary Cuba, but cringed at personal violence. I never got involved in fights and can't remember hitting anyone during my teenage years.

I grew up believing that Ethel and Julius were completely innocent. When I was a child, this belief was based on emotion and trust; Abel and Anne Meeropol and others in my community said that they were not guilty, and I believed them. During high school I knew virtually nothing about the facts of the Rosenberg case. But I considered my parents to have been murder victims and those who engineered their execution as murderers. Far from believing that capital punishment was wrong, I even relished the thought of capital punishment for my parents' murderers.

But I didn't spend that much time fantasizing and when left to my own devices rarely had trouble finding things to do. My fascination with the natural world that first surfaced on the neighborhood walks I took with Anne and Abel and developed at summer camp now focused on the weather. I had kept weather records of the daily temperature range and snowfall amounts every winter since I was eight. I loved snow and cold, and our move only a dozen miles farther up Broadway exposed me to more of both. My window provided an excellent view of the western half of the sky, where most of our weather came from. Thunderheads built over the Palisades, barreled across the Hudson, and battered our relatively exposed location with ferocious wind and rain. Morning sun created ever-changing patterns of light and shadow on the cliff face, and the evening sun illuminated clouds' underbellies with purple and gold. My parents became uncomfortable if I stared out the window too long. "Don't you have something better to do?" my mother would scold.

Our house had a detached two-car garage, and in the spring of

1961 we mounted a basketball backboard on it. I spent hours practicing jump shots, playing imaginary scrimmages or games of "horse." I also liked yardwork, and there was plenty of it in our oversize lot. Pruning bushes, raking leaves, mowing the lawn, and shoveling snow were new and mostly pleasant experiences for a city boy. One morning in November 1960 I went outside and couldn't figure out why the ground was so hard until I realized it had frozen.

I also did household chores. In the fall of 1960 I learned about storm windows. Our apartment in the city had had neither these nor screens. Mosquitoes apparently couldn't survive in the old concrete-covered neighborhood, and one pane of glass was evidently considered sufficient insulation for apartment buildings in winter. Now each fall I struggled to replace fifty-three screen windows with their fifty-three heavy, steel-framed storm counterparts, and each spring I reversed the process. I put my weather knowledge to good use and picked the right time for each change. I was a better candidate for storm-window work than my father, who was now almost sixty. He was in pretty good physical condition and quite a bit stronger than I was, but I was the right option for another reason. My father repeatedly cautioned me not to yank my door key in frustration if the lock stuck, because the key might break off. I never broke my key, but the keys he'd broken in the lock attested to who really needed the warning. Envisioning a trail of shattered windows, I did the work myself.

Abel worked at home, and this gave us time together. When I was bored or procrastinating, I would wander into his study and engage him in conversation. He'd usually be sitting at his ancient black Smith-Corona typewriter amid piles of paper. The study, many times the size of the space he had in the old apartment, quickly became a cluttered mess. Our interactions often followed an opening gambit. I'd hover in the doorway, my eyes surveying the mess. He'd say, "I'm going to clean this up right away." I'd smile knowingly before saying what was on my mind. The mess multiplied as I progressed through high school. We had a second ritual. He'd mutter "shit" every time he'd hit the wrong key. That happened frequently while I was standing unnoticed at his door. I'd feign shock, and he would profusely apologize for his verbal transgression or claim that he'd meant to say "shite." I think he genuinely felt some remorse for saying "shit" in front of his teenage son.

My father was always willing to talk about current affairs. Although he was no longer a member of the American Communist Party, I never heard him voice criticism of it. I remember my brother coming home from college and arguing with him about the American Communist Party's support for the Hitler-Stalin pact in 1939. The party, previously vociferously anti-Nazi, suddenly stopped criticizing Hitler after the pact. This silence about Hitler was both cynical and self-defeating, particularly for Jewish Communists, my brother argued. My father said: "The capitalist countries wanted Germany to attack the Soviet Union; this was necessary for the revolution's survival." Michael countered that he understood why the USSR took this strategic action, but why couldn't the American party still continue to attack Nazism? My father didn't seem to understand that the USSR could do one thing and the American Communist Party another.

In some ways Abel was not politically sophisticated. His politics came more from his heart than his head. The leader of Abel's Communist Party club had put him on report while he was in Hollywood because Abel objected to reading Karl Marx's *Das Kapital* in the theory classes mandated for all party members. He'd spoken up in class: "I know who the workers are, I know who the bosses are, and I know which side I'm on. Why do I need to know more than that?" As far as he was concerned you were either with the oppressed or against them, and once you chose your course you stuck to it.

Politics was not all we talked about. Although I was not a particularly confrontational teenager, I could discuss endlessly a broad range of subjects with either of my parents. If they really got mad, I gave in, at least outwardly.

I took evasive action if I couldn't get what I wanted directly. I would go behind my parents' backs. I developed a taste for reading science fiction. After I'd exhausted the town library's supply of this genre, I started buying science fiction paperbacks at the nearby drugstore. My mother objected to my wasting money on this trash and forbade me to buy any more. I agreed but bought them anyway, stuffing them down the front of my pants to sneak them into the house.

Although I spent more time with my parents than most teenagers did, in some ways we were distant. I remained angry with them for moving, and I believe they knew that, but we never talked about it. More than a generation separated us. They kept up with changing popular culture into the 1950s, but the changes of the 1960s left them baffled. They were unable to see the functional similarity between the forms cultural protest were taking in the 1960s and the rebellious, cutting-edge music and art they had helped to generate as members of the Teachers Union's Theater Arts Committee thirty-five years earlier.

In 1962, when I was fifteen, Abel was fifty-nine and Anne was fifty-two. I could get Abel to listen to what I was saying about the positive political impact of Bob Dylan, but Anne was another story. My parents said that it was important for children to acknowledge when they were wrong, but I noticed my mother never admitted that *she* was wrong, particularly about cultural matters. Once during one of her many attacks on rock and roll music, when she ridiculed the current number-one hit "Running Bear," I laid an ambush: "Ma, you say it's a stupid song; tell me what it's about." She dismissed my question. "Oh, it doesn't matter . . . something about a bear who was running and they couldn't catch him." I pounced: "It's about an Indian named Running Bear who had a tragic love affair. You say the song is stupid, but you don't even know what it's about!" I earned a stiff reprimand for being insulting, which I knew only served to change the subject.

A few years later my mother and I went to Greenwich Village to see a performance of the protest musical *Viet Rock*. I liked it, but she said the music was just noise. Once outside the theater afterward, she complained to Ronnie Gilbert, one of the members of the blacklisted folk group the Weavers, that the blaring music detracted from the political message. I winked at Ronnie behind my mother's back as Ronnie rolled her eyes at my mother's stodginess.

My parents believed in the separation of adult and children's worlds. Certain subjects were taboo. Adults did not discuss sex or curse around children, even teenagers. Adults made decisions, which were not subject to reconsideration. I could argue, but once they set down a rule, it would not change. I grudgingly accepted their dictum that children, and teenagers for that matter, were not equal to adults. But I felt regardless of who you were, you should admit mistakes and change if you were wrong. I wondered if my parents' rigidness grew out of their being so much older. I wondered if they would have been able to see my point of view a little better if they had been ten or fifteen years younger.

Looking back, I see that their parenting inspired me to want children of my own, but their style encouraged me to have them earlier in life. I felt it was important to be young enough to see things from my children's viewpoint—I didn't want to miss out on the things they could teach me. And I swore to alter my opinions and decisions if my children could demonstrate that they were right, and believe I kept this vow. I adhered to a modified version of Abel and Anne's style of setting limits on activities and discussion with my children, but parents and children did not live in separate worlds in Elli's and my household.

My brother was only a flickering presence after he went to college, but what he did had a powerful influence on me. He was the first to tell about a new left-wing organization I ultimately joined, Students for a Democratic Society (SDS). He had traveled to Mexico in the summer of 1961, so I wanted to spend my next summer there. In order to accommodate me without spending any money, my mother organized a tour of teenagers, and she and I went for free. Her financial motivation, in this instance, may have overcome her good sense. I found it mortifying to be on a coed tour with a dozen fifteen- and sixteen-year-olds with my mother as the leader and chief chaperone! The trip did not compare favorably with my wonderful camp experiences. Even worse, it left me without a new set of camp friends to hang out with once I began the tenth grade after the summer of 1962.

I never felt so isolated as I did during the first half of my sophomore year. The Cuban missile crisis occurred that fall. My classmates, those who thought about it at all, uniformly accepted that we had the right to tell Cuba and the Soviet Union what weapons could be deployed on Cuban soil. Everyone was all in a dither about Soviet missiles just ninety miles from our shore, without thinking that Cuba had a lot more than a few missiles just ninety miles from *its* shore. No one mentioned all the nuclear-tipped missiles we had in Turkey pointing at the Soviet Union. The Soviets were always portrayed as the aggressor, even though our country was the one with a worldwide military presence. But I knew better than to say any of this. I did pipe up when some of my classmates predicted that nuclear war was imminent. I dismissed such fears, saying that both sides would bluff, but there would be no shooting. This reflected my tendency to deny potential catastrophes more than it did my political acumen. We now know how close we came to nuclear annihilation.

Although the Cuban predicament passed, my loneliness remained. The low point was not having a New Year's Eve party to attend, and not even having a friend to stay up till midnight with. Perhaps this forced me to become a bit more outgoing during the second half of my sophomore year. I first started having lunch with Alex toward the end of my freshman year, and by spring of our sophomore year we were visiting back and forth after school. We'd shoot baskets at my house and take turns being each other's catcher/umpire for imaginary baseball games we pitched. I think one reason we got along so well is that neither one of us tried to cheat the other by calling a strike a ball.

We were well matched and more interested in playing than winning. His parents were practicing Jews, and he was politically on the Right. But we enjoyed arguing, my "liberal Democratic" counterpoint to his "conservative Republican."

I remember telling myself in June 1963 that my four years of high school were almost half over. Just two more years, then things will get better. I also made sure not to repeat the mistake of the previous summer, and returned to Lincoln Farm for the summer of 1963. Delighted to be ensconced once again in a progressive community and now one of the older campers, I returned to camp exploding with social energy. It helped to be sixteen and, with the aid of a recent growth spurt, to be approaching six feet tall.

I quickly became very close with my bunkmates Michael and Hector. Hector's parents were Argentinean Jews who had immigrated after one of that country's numerous purges of left-wingers. Hector had been in the country since he was nine, lived in New York City's borough of Queens and attended the Bronx High School of Science. Hector looked the part of a science nerd. A few extra pounds hung on his six-foot frame and he kept his asthma inhaler close at hand. He spent much less time than Michael and me playing sports. Michael grew up in a working class home in Brooklyn. I'm not sure how his parents afforded the camp's hefty price tag. Perhaps like my family his parents had a special relationship with the camp's owners. Michael's mother was Irish Catholic and his father Jewish. Michael was a wiry six foot three, with a crop of frizzy white-blond hair that looked a little bit like cartoon pictures of what happened when you stuck your finger in an electric socket.

Although we were all born within a few months of one another, both Michael and Hector were a year ahead of me in school, courtesy of the New York City school system's Special Progress Program, which enabled gifted junior high school students to complete the seventh, eighth, and ninth grades in two years. When we weren't talking about sports or girls, we talked politics. Both came from left-wing backgrounds, but as far as I know neither came from Communist Party families. We agreed with the civil rights movement's call for racial and economic justice. We agreed that the United States should withdraw its troops from Vietnam. We disliked American foreign policy in general, but unlike me, they were equally suspicious of the Soviet Union's policies. They claimed that like the United States, the USSR was motivated by its national interest rather than its love for humanity. Lack of freedom in the USSR, they pointed out, was not just capitalist propaganda. If I attacked the United States for its racism, how could I ignore Soviet anti-Semitism? These questions, plus the Soviet Union's growing rift with China, gave me pause. Maybe the Soviet Union didn't have all the answers, but I was reluctant to abandon the definitive political answers provided by Marxist orthodoxy.

My parents' case never came up in conversation, and it had become easier to ignore. An entire decade had passed, and I lived in the present. I had so much to share with Michael and Hector about our daily activities, who cared about what had happened to any of us during the first six years of our lives?

The climax of the summer actually came a few days after camp ended. On August 23, 1963, Michael, my old EI friend Danny, and I boarded a chartered bus that left from New York City at three A.M. to travel together to a civil rights march on Washington. I was finally old enough to travel on my own with my friends. I celebrated my liberation by bringing thirty-five dollars, a small fortune for me, because it made me feel even more adult. We joined hundreds of thousands who filled the mall between the Capitol and the Lincoln Memorial for the rally that would be remembered for Martin Luther King's "I Have a Dream" speech. I never got close enough to discern more than specks on the distant podium. I believe I heard Dr. King's microphone-mangled speech, but to this day I'm not sure if that was just post hoc wishful thinking. I was most inspired by the numbers and sense of togetherness of all who attended. But what stands out more is that when I returned exhausted to my bus for the long ride home that evening, my thirty-five dollars were gone. I've read at least one account of that march that mentioned what a bonanza it was for pickpockets. I had made my contribution to them.

I entered my junior year at Hastings with Michael, Hector, and other camp friends to party with on weekends. Some camp friends lived in Westchester, and through them I connected with Westchester Students for Peace and Civil Rights. I frequently marched with Arthur and Victor, who lived in Croton-on-Hudson. I would have been nervous about joining protests in Hastings, but marching five miles away in White Plains, the county seat, was another matter.

I still spent most of my weekends in New York City. Within a month or two, Michael, Hector, and I had developed a revolving visiting schedule. The first weekend we met in the city and slept over at Michael's, next we stayed at Hector's, and the third they came to my house. Since other social obligations occasionally intervened, it usually took at least a month to go through this cycle. We had a regular phone schedule as well. In my house any call beyond our local area was considered a luxury. We minimized such calls by taking turns each Thursday, initiating a round robin of conversation. For instance, I'd call Michael, who'd call Hector, who'd then call me. By the end of the third call a Saturday meeting place and a tentative plan had emerged.

The three of us went to folk clubs in Greenwich Village, attended camp parties, and wandered all over the city. I don't know if we were foolhardy to be roaming the streets in the middle of the night, but no one ever bothered us. Mostly we searched for excitement and found very little. None of us had girlfriends. We said we were experts at having a good time while having a bad time. Just playing cards or chess together was fun, even though they were both better players than I was. None of us felt connected to our respective schools. When Kennedy was assassinated that fall, we commiserated with our camp friends, not our classmates.

Kennedy was no hero to Michael, Hector, and me. He'd given the go-ahead to the Bay of Pigs invasion of Cuba. He'd financed counterinsurgency operations all over Latin America to help keep dictatorial elites in power while that continent's masses starved. The Peace Corps was merely window dressing, a transparent and pitifully small buyoff designed to co-opt more basic change. I was amazed by people's reaction to his killing. Kennedy had not been universally loved. The Republicans had been attacking him savagely, and the media had not been particularly supportive. His reelection had not been assured. Suddenly he was dead and everyone loved him. All the magic of "Camelot," which had been a sideshow for the last three years now, became the centerpiece of a major cultural myth. A significant segment of our society was engaged in mass self-deception. After he died people wanted to have liked him. I wondered at their seemingly unlimited capacity to wallow in wishful thinking and fool themselves.

My social life continued to improve in school. I was slowly becoming a part of the college-bound or brainy crowd. At the beginning of the year, I still saw Alex, and we soon formed a triumvirate with another junior named Walter. Walter was one of the mainstays of the high school wrestling team. Though at 180 pounds he won almost all his matches, he was not a typical jock. Walter and I had several passions in common. The son of a high school physics teacher, he believed in science and was an ardent agnostic. While religion never made much sense to me, my attack on it was political. Marxist orthodoxy taught that it was the opiate of the masses, and I agreed. Walter's attack, on the other hand, was based on the scientific method. You learned about the world by observing, experimenting, forming theories, and testing them. To him religious belief was an unverifiable human construct based on ignorance. He was an agnostic, rather than an atheist, because he couldn't disprove God's existence. Walter had articulated another position that explained why religion never made any sense to me. He was also the first person I met who was as fascinated by the weather as I was. We even liked the same kind of weather, snow and cold. I remember my mother shaking her head and marveling when I had hung up after one long weather-related phone conversation with Walter; she had never imagined someone could get so excited about a cold front.

My last two years at Hastings High School were still medicinal, but it went down easier. I had already learned what I could get away with saying and writing without straying beyond the acceptable range of views. During my last two years of high school I became more comfortable voicing unorthodox views. McCarthyism was fading fast by 1963. Walter, Alex, and I organized an informal discussion of religion that a dozen of our honors class friends attended. Most probably thought the discussion was going to be an exchange of religious concepts between Protestants, Catholics, and Jews. They were surprised when Walter and I launched an all-out assault on all religious beliefs. I remember asking if any of my more religious friends found it troubling that if they had been born into a Muslim family they would be just as sure of a different set of religious beliefs. They looked at me as if I had two heads, but this exchange of ideas facilitated more social contact afterward. Despite our disagreements, I became closer with those who had participated in this discussion.

The sixties are often remembered as the time of growing political and cultural radicalism. Television reminds us that Timothy Leary captured young people's imaginations by telling them to "tune in, turn on, and drop out," and hippies traversed the land in funky VW buses. But most of that happened in the late sixties. In 1964 and 1965 only the faintest forerunners of these cultural and political changes began to infiltrate Hastings High School. There were, however, several Hastings High antiwar activists. By 1965 we started wearing peace or antiwar buttons to school.

Discussions in our honors history class became quite lively. Mrs. Lloyd, my favorite high school teacher, put up with quite a bit of political heresy from me. Left-wing historian Philip Foner's two-volume tome on the history of United States relations with Cuba formed the backbone of the first serious research paper I'd ever written. My thesis was simple: The United States had been acting as an imperialist bully toward Cuba since the promulgation of the Monroe Doctrine, and so it was only natural that Fidel Castro was so anti-American. It was hypocritical for the United States to declare our right to intervene in Latin America while self-righteously declaring that continent off-limits to European colonial powers. Mrs. Lloyd gave me a good grade even though she chided me for being too one-sided. I looked forward to her class. Each student was required to complete a career plan. The guidance department wanted us to make a more rigorous attempt to answer that nagging question: "What do you want to be when you grow up." I charted a course for becoming a history professor.

I had a hard time taking this career exercise too seriously because of my previous run-in with the guidance department. Earlier in the year the guidance department had us tested for color blindness. I was shown a series of cards with lots of little circles filled in with two colors. If you could distinguish the colors the little circles of one color formed a number. I saw no number on almost half the cards. The counselor bluntly informed me I was color-blind. I was taken aback to learn I had this disability and asked what I should do. The counselor responded that I shouldn't work in a paint factory.

My brother had spent the previous summer as a counselor at left-wing Camp Thoreau. The summer after my junior year, I joined him as a junior counselor. The summer began on a somber note. Three civil rights workers were missing in Mississippi. We soon learned that they had been murdered and that one of them, Andrew Goodman, had gone to high school with several fellow counselors. Andrew's name was added to a growing list of left-wing martyrs that included my parents. Good people got killed, their murderers went free, and all we could do was tearfully sing "We Shall Overcome." I agreed that we could honor Andrew's memory by sending hundreds more south to replace him, but felt that it also would have been nice to repay his murderers in kind.

That summer was an important social watershed for me and was even more so for my brother. My brother and his best friend, Jerry Markowitz, had worked as counselors at Camp Thoreau during the summer of 1963. Jerry met Adrienne Rosner there, and they were married several years later. Michael spent a lot of time with Jerry and Adrienne over the next year, but he was a third wheel. To correct this imbalance Adrienne introduced Michael to her best friend, Ann, at Camp Thoreau during the summer of 1964, the year that I joined them. Michael and Ann were married two years later. Adrienne's younger brother, David Rosner, also a counselor, became my good friend, and we have been close ever since.

It was a bit of a shock to return to my parents' home as a high school senior after a summer with so much freedom. Although I complained about my lack of independence, Anne and Abel gave me quite a bit of it. My parents now had two cars, even though my mother almost never drove. I had unlimited access to one of them during the week, and they even let me drive it into the city to visit Michael or David on weekends. Hector was now a freshman at Berkeley, so I could only see him during vacations, but Michael and David each lived at home while attending Brooklyn and City colleges, respectively. My best friends were in college, while I still had to put up with high school.

Since I had never gotten into any real trouble or openly defied their limits, my parents trusted me to behave responsibly on my own. I thought I was getting away with murder, but my transgressions were limited to minor speed-limit infractions, eating junk food, and staying out later than I was supposed to. Walter and I explored the remotest corners of Westchester County while sampling its hamburger and ice-cream stands.

During my junior year I began to spend more time with Anita, a classmate who was also involved in Westchester County antiwar activity. Sometime during senior year we began going together. We rarely went on formal dates. We'd have impromptu visits or hang out with groups of friends. Even though she was probably the only person in my class with whom I could be entirely open about my politics, I still never dared to talk with her about my parents' case.

But as college approached I figured that it would only be a matter of time before I crossed paths with people who knew I was a son of the Rosenbergs. I realized that I wouldn't have answers for even the simplest question they might ask about my parents' case. Initially I was more concerned about not looking stupid than consumed with intellectual fervor to find out what really happened. Walter and Miriam Schneir's *Invitation to an Inquest* was published in mid-1965.* Their book was a thoroughly researched effort to prove my parents' innocence. I went with Anne and Abel to meet them. Walter and Miriam gave me an inscribed copy, and I devoured it. I read several other books and portions of the trial transcript as well. My emotional belief in my parents' innocence became an intellectual certainty.

The press usually labeled my parents as atomic spies. According to the media they had been convicted of espionage or treason. The death sentence was warranted because they had stolen the secret of the atomic bomb, which the prosecutors called the greatest secret known to mankind. From the Schneirs' book I learned that they had really been convicted of conspiracy to commit espionage. Our courts had determined that they had joined with others and took at least one act to further a plan to commit espionage. It was hard for me to imagine that you could execute two people who had only been convicted of conspiracy. This fact is so difficult to accept that to this day interviewers doubt my truthfulness when I mention that my parents were convicted only of conspiracy to commit espionage.

*Walter and Miriam Schneir, *Invitation to an Inquest* (New York: Doubleday, 1965; Penguin reprint, 1973; Pantheon reprint, 1983).

The Schneirs also demonstrated that there was no single secret of the atomic bomb. The general theory behind the bomb had been known worldwide prior to World War II. There were lots of technical problems to be solved along the way, but any country that devoted sufficient resources would ultimately succeed in detonating an atomic bomb. The real secret was whether it would work, and that had been given away when we dropped the bomb on Hiroshima. The Schneirs concluded: "Not only were Julius and Ethel Rosenberg—and Morton Sobell—unjustly convicted, they were punished for a crime that never occurred" (p. 403, Penguin, 1973).

I also learned a lot more about the government's three chief prosecution witnesses, my Uncle David and Aunt Ruth, and Harry Gold. David Greenglass had been an army machinist working at Los Alamos, New Mexico, on the atomic bomb project. He had no scientific training; in fact, David's education never progressed beyond high school. He tried to use the GI Bill to go to college, but had flunked all of the courses he took at Brooklyn Polytechnic Institute. How could this man possibly steal advanced scientific secrets? I discovered that Ruth Greenglass had never been charged with a crime, even though she had taken the witness stand and sworn she helped her husband transmit atomic secrets. This was in stark contrast to my mother, who was executed after swearing under oath that she was not involved. I read that David testified that he gave sketches containing a critical atomic secret to Harry Gold, who used the recognition signal "I come from Julius" to identify himself to David when they secretly met in New Mexico.

Gold was a chemist who lived in Philadelphia. Gold swore that he was a spy courier transmitting information to the Soviet Union from a member of the British team working at Los Alamos, the German-born atomic scientist Klaus Fuchs, but that on this one occasion he received information from Greenglass. The Schneirs provided ample proof that Gold was a pathological liar. They even quoted a transcript from another trial at which Gold testified, where Gold admitted that he invented a fantasy life, lied for sixteen years, and he lied so often that "it is a wonder steam didn't come out of my ears at times" (p. 102, Penguin, 1973).

Becoming more knowledgeable about my parents' case did not break down my block against broaching the subject with anyone. Anita and I spent more time together as the last days of high school approached, but we didn't talk about the case. Instead we talked a lot about Vietnam. She painted a doomsday scenario of Johnson constantly increasing our troop strength, now at several hundred thousand, to more than a million. She predicted that Russia and China would enter the war, and that it might become nuclear. I always rejected such pessimistic projections, but a lot of my antiwar friends in Westchester worried that the way things were going we might not live all that much longer. Perhaps this triggered some of my generation's willingness to engage in daredevil experimentation with drugs and lifestyle. We were young but not carefree.

Anita described helping another classmate, Celeste, who was strung out on heroin, slip out of school as she began to have withdrawal symptoms. Celeste was in my homeroom. I never gave her more than a nod, but felt a bond with her because, like me, she seemed so out of place. I learned from Anita that Celeste had gone out with Mick Jagger, and rumor had it that she was the subject of the Rolling Stones song: "Nineteenth Nervous Breakdown."

Anita protected me as well. I believed that my secret was safe, but it hung by a thread. Anita knew who my biological parents were, but I don't know how she found out. Anita told me years afterward that she had to use all her powers of persuasion to keep another classmate who discovered who I was from blurting it out at a class party. I can't imagine how I could have handled that information becoming generally known to my classmates. I doubt I could have functioned in such a fishbowl. The prospect of what might have happened terrifies me to this day. Yet, looking back, I find it amazing that I was never exposed. People love to have and share important secrets about others. I owe an incredible debt to Anita and to all those who kept silent and even ran interference for me.

I learned a decade later that Dr. Langworthy discussed the FBI's visit with my history teacher, Mrs. Lloyd, and that she responded by providing me with additional support. I figured it was just luck that the Rosenberg case never came up in our history class. Now I know that I have Mrs. Lloyd to thank for that. The summer after we graduated Anita went to Europe while I worked at a day camp on Long Island. Anita wrote me that she "knew of my sorrow," and I wrote back that I was glad she knew but that she "shouldn't love me for it." I was much more comfortable being Robert Meeropol than being Ethel and Julius Rosenberg's son.

My childhood was extraordinary but not unique. Like so many others I'd come into contact with a wide range of what humanity had to offer. David and Ruth Greenglass as well as Abel and Anne Meeropol made up my heritage. Powerful people tried to make sure that I never received a positive legacy from my parents' activism and resistance. But Dean Johnson did what he could to protect us before succumbing to cancer, Dr. Langworthy defied the FBI agents, and loyal friends kept my secret. I felt I had survived four years on foreign turf, but was blind to the allies I had in Hastings. My classmates' admonition next to my picture in my high school yearbook, "For happiness mingle with others," was warranted.

I was full of optimism as I headed for Earlham College. I thought I could engage the world on my terms. I was not yet prepared to acknowledge being Julius and Ethel Rosenberg's son, but thought that maybe someday I could handle it. Despite some evidence to the contrary, at eighteen years old I felt that there were more good than bad people in the world. And sometimes the dice rolled your way, and you landed on the right property.

• • •

Looking back on my first eighteen years from a middle-aged perspective, I feel that I was fortunate that the nightmare of 1950–53 was sandwiched between periods of strong parental love from my two sets of parents. My work, the Rosenberg Fund for Children, grew out of the loss of my parents, the spark of their resistance, and the nurturing of their community. Indeed, much of the support the RFC receives comes from those who wish to honor the Rosenbergs' memory. But the connections the RFC makes between culture, family, and activism also bear Anne and Abel Meeropol's imprint. The RFC has produced several large public performances in its ten-year existence. I have been a chief organizer of these productions. One evening, while participating in a rehearsal for an RFC production, I realized I was doing the same kind of work I watched Abel and Anne do when I was a teenager. I'd received valuable on-the-job training from them without even realizing it.

I suppose you could say that the younger son of the Rosenbergs founded the RFC, but the younger son of the Meeropols runs it. The RFC is living proof of how honored I am to be Ethel and Julius Rosenbergs' son. My last name is proof that I feel the same way about Abel and Anne Meeropol.

CHAPTER 4

Mush-Head

———————◆◆◆◆———————

I BASED MY FIRST IMPORTANT ADULT DECISION, CHOOSING A COLLEGE, largely on ignorance. How did someone who felt compelled to keep his radicalism under wraps while living in suburban New York enthusiastically anticipate attending a college in conservative Richmond, Indiana? I had some good reasons for my choice, however. My brother's friend Jerry Markowitz, who had just graduated Earlham with a major in history, reported that the history department was excellent. I knew two other New Yorkers from Old Left families who were students at Earlham, and had heard no complaints from them. I had a romantic vision of walking elm-lined streets and sampling the quiet but friendly small-town lifestyle. Finally, I didn't get into Swarthmore, my first choice.

My first impression of Indiana was not good. I found its endless flat cornfields dull. The ordinary-looking campus buildings widely spaced among stately oak trees were pleasant but uninspired. The adjacent graveyard with its rolling lawns that sloped to Clear Creek was the most scenic part of the setting. It was also the favorite campus make-out spot. The school tried to prevent access to, and conception in, the graveyard by means of a twelve-foot-high chain-link fence, but this was ineffective.

I might have had second thoughts about Earlham if I had known the results of the 1964 presidential election held just ten months before my arrival. Richmond had given Republican conservative Barry Goldwater 60 percent of its votes, even though Lyndon Johnson garnered more than 60 percent nationwide. I didn't know that Earlham's administrators were conservative midwestern Quakers who thought that the Quakers who founded the American Friends Service Committee were dangerously radical. An upperclassman on my dorm hall told me that the townspeople of Richmond were known for their racism and considered "Earlhamites" to be "a bunch of nigger-loving Communists."

I expected Earlham to be a Quaker version of Antioch, the progressive cooperative learning college located seventy miles to the east in Yellow Springs, Ohio. It came as a jolt when Earlham's president Landrum Bolling welcomed incoming freshmen at the end of my first day on campus with the following: "Some of you have the mistaken idea that you've gotten off the bus seventy miles east of here. Earlham is not a Quaker Antioch or a midwestern Swarthmore." My classmates' cheers were chilling.

On the other hand I was astounded when I entered my dorm room for the first time to discover that my roommate had plastered a huge poster of Moscow's Red Square on the wall. Arthur was a pacifist who had just returned from a summer-long Quaker-sponsored "Peace Tour" to the Soviet Union. He was a hulking six foot three, with arms that seemed too long for his body. I figured someone that big and strong probably didn't have his nonviolent ideology challenged often.

I arrived determined not to fade into the social and political background. Earlham had an opinion board on which community members posted notices, statements, and responses. Within a week Arthur and I placed a notice inviting students to attend the first meeting of the Earlham Committee to End the War in Vietnam. The fact that only a couple of dozen students showed up did not dampen our zeal. We proposed a march from campus to the center of town carrying signs urging U.S. withdrawal from Vietnam. The group agreed.

We applied for a parade permit, but the Richmond City Council turned us down. One councillor argued against giving us a permit because granting it might be seen as the council's endorsement of our position. Someone tipped the administration off to our plans. Arthur and I were summoned to a meeting with the college president.

Protests were fine, he told us, but we should remain on campus or risk damaging Earlham's fragile relations with the town. We reported back to the committee, which to my dismay acquiesced by deciding instead to hold a silent vigil in the center of campus. I was outraged by the town's heavy-handed rejection of our basic constitutional rights and by the administration's complicity in squashing dissent. I expressed my indignation by posting a vitriolic blast against the undemocratic nature of Richmond on the opinion board. Within a month of my arrival I had gained campus-wide notoriety as a radical firebrand.

Arthur and I did not give up. As the year progressed, our willingness to argue relentlessly with all comers succeeded in turning some students against the war. Our first convert was Hernán, who lived across the hall. His Eastern European Jewish ancestors had immigrated to Chile at the end of the nineteenth century. Hernán had been born in Chile and moved to the United States when he was twelve. Short, dark, and strong, he wrestled in the 133-pound weight class for Earlham's team.

Arthur received several publications that provided us with war-related information, and my parents paid for a subscription to my current-affairs bible, the *National Guardian*. Arthur and I shared this material with Hernán, and we all compared it with the news in the mainstream press and on television.

The more Hernán read, the more he came to agree with us. The

75

mainstream media portrayed the North Vietnamese as invaders. But the 1954 Geneva accords established one Vietnam, and our information demonstrated that the Vietnamese viewed themselves as one nation. Thus the only foreign power in Vietnam was the United States. North Vietnamese president Ho Chi Minh was a Communist, but he was revered as a national hero for leading a successful war to free Vietnam from French colonialism. The press called the South Vietnamese government democratic, but that government canceled elections in 1956 because, in President Eisenhower's words, Ho Chi Minh would have gotten 80 percent of the vote. We convinced Hernán and gained other converts because we learned the facts and were willing to engage in hours of face-to-face discussion.

Arthur and I did not always agree. We frequently argued about pacifism. I believed in just wars, citing World War II as an example. I demanded to know how we could have nonviolently resisted Hitler. He countered that by defeating Hitler with military might we had set the stage for the nuclear arms race and potential worldwide annihilation. He said that India provided an example of how a population could be mobilized to defeat the military. I responded that although India had thrown off British rule, its lack of revolutionary housecleaning had left it corrupt and impoverished. Arthur and I both wanted the United States to withdraw from Vietnam, but he sought peace while I wanted victory for the Vietnamese.

Although classwork was more challenging than it had been in high school, I remained satisfied with slightly above-average grades. The relatively few hours I spent studying left time for socializing, and I quickly developed close friendships with Arthur, Hernán, and several others. We talked about everything from politics and people to sex and psychology, but I never told a soul that I was Ethel and Julius Rosenberg's son. Starting relationships from scratch far from familiar settings made keeping that part of my identity easier. I rationalized that what had happened during the first six years of my life was not essential to knowing me.

I corresponded with Anita, but finding female companionship on campus was a more immediate concern. This was not easy for freshman men since the upperclassmen were usually more appealing choices for freshman women. One day I plunked my tray down at lunch in Earlham's main dining room at a table already occupied by two attractive girls wearing the East Coast urban uniform of jeans and plaid work shirts. They were sophomores named Dee and Elli. Dee was from Cincinnati, and Elli came from the Washington, D.C., suburbs. Dee was blond with a terrific smile while Elli had very dark, thick long hair that presented a startling contrast to her fair complexion and sparkly blue eyes. We started talking and joking, and they began shredding every napkin on the table and piling the strips onto my tray. They quickly became my preferred dining companions. I would eventually marry Elli, but at first I had my eye on Dee. Unfortunately both women were going out with upperclassmen, so neither relationship got beyond flirting for the time being.

I was absorbed by college life, but off-campus events also engaged me. Antiwar activists announced they would hold a national demonstration in Washington the weekend after Thanksgiving. Our Earlham group chartered a bus to bring students to the march, but we leaders decided to arrive a few days early to attend the founding convention of the National Committee to End the War in Vietnam. Scott, one of our members, had a station wagon. Six of us piled into it, and after one abortive attempt (underinflated tires caused the huge 1959 Chevrolet wagon to fishtail dangerously on the highway), drove the five hundred miles to Arthur's parents' house in D.C.

The organizing meeting was held in a rundown church in northwest D.C. Progressive pacifist-oriented graduates of private Quaker high schools dominated the antiwar movement at Earlham. I was exhilarated that at this gathering my radical positions were more the norm. I absorbed the political debates at lengthy meetings that long weekend, and found Saturday's mass demonstration almost anticlimactic.

Students for a Democratic Society (SDS) had a strong presence. I'd joined SDS as an at-large member during high school. I was proud of my membership card, dutifully kept up my dues, but despaired at being able to find four others at Earlham to form the "minyan" of five required to organize a chapter.

SDS was becoming the predominant left-wing organization of my generation. SDS had grown out of the youth section of the League for Industrial Democracy (LID), a democratic socialist organization that denied membership to Communists. Although SDS broke with the LID when SDS jettisoned this anti-Communist prohibition, SDS did not embrace the Soviet Union. SDS propounded the vaguely socialist politics of "participatory democracy." This meant that people should have direct access to and control over the decision-making processes that affected their lives. I was enchanted by this concept and thought it would resonate well on college campuses. Eighteen-year-olds couldn't vote, but we could be drafted to die in Vietnam's jungles. Why should we follow political leaders blindly when the world they presided over was a cesspool of poverty, racism, and war? I was mature enough to live seven hundred miles from home, but had no say in Earlham's rules, which shackled me. The Earlham administration claimed that they were older and wiser and made these rules for our protection. The administrators acted like our parents, but we observed that many in our parents' generation appeared to lead unhappy and empty lives. The generation before us screwed up their own lives, so why should we let them mess up ours? I doubted that Earlham's rules were for our benefit. I felt, instead, that they were designed to reinforce the administration's power and control. By dissembling about their rules' purpose the administration demonstrated hypocrisy rather than wisdom.

When I returned to New York for winter vacation, the dynamism of the East Coast only served to highlight Indiana's lifelessness. My brother, Michael, and Ann added to the festivities by returning from England to get married. The ceremony took place between Christmas and New Year's in 1965. My biological father's older sister, Ethel, and her husband attended the party afterward. I found it jarring to have Rosenberg relatives in the Hastings house for the reception. While I had visited Aunt Ethel's house once or twice a year throughout high school, I felt I was leaving my current life to visit my past when I did so. It made me anxious to have these reminders of my history intrude upon my new identity. My Rosenberg past was deeply submerged, and I was more comfortable avoiding anything that would bring it to the surface.

I fretted through the winter at Earlham. Attendance at our antiwar committee meetings dwindled. I had little leadership and organizing experience. I urged volunteers to become more active, but my overbearing efforts drove them away. I thought my tightly run meetings were models of efficiency, but other participants evidently found them stifling. I acted as if one female committee member was my secretary, and was perplexed when she stopped attending meetings.

My spirits were low, and academic pursuits failed to raise them. I realized that my uninspired grades needed improvement if I wanted to earn a Ph.D. and become a college professor. But after a semester on campus, I was no longer sure I wanted to spend my life in such a cloistered environment. Politics was my greatest intellectual passion, but I couldn't imagine making a career out of radical activism.

But at eighteen, I could be down one month and up the next. A chance encounter in late March 1966 transformed my February funk into April's exhilaration. My friend Michael came to visit during his spring break, and we spent two days at Antioch. We stayed in Yellow Springs, in a house owned by parents of one of my brother's friends from Swarthmore.

There was another guest as well. This charismatic man, whose name I can't recall, had long dark hair and an arresting stare. I had let my hair grow beyond acceptable midwestern standards and dabbled with facial hair permutations, but I wasn't a hippie. I drew a sharp distinction between my radical activism and the burgeoning countercultural phenomena. This gurulike young man, who was several years older than us, argued that radical politics and hippie culture could be fused. He told us that both hippies and new leftists were in rebellion against America's consumer-oriented society, which was oppressing both the Vietnamese with military might and domestic youth with empty capitalist materialism. If young people united we could end the war and transform the United States into an egalitarian society based on peace and love.

Michael and I discussed this for several days before he returned to New York. I was more skeptical than Michael about this peace and love stuff, but my questioning of college social rules, as well as the captivating concept of participatory democracy, had opened me up to new ways of looking at things. I knew that the American Left had been isolated for decades. If we who were in political rebellion could reach out to the rapidly increasing numbers of those who were in cultural rebellion, we could build the first left-wing mass movement the nation had seen since the 1930s. While I never embraced it fully, I came to feel that there was merit to what some in SDS eventually called the "millions of groovy kids theory" of how we would transform society.

Elli and I became a couple one month before finals of my freshman year. One night another friend and I sprung Elli and her friend from their dorm for an overnight adventure. Earlham had no curfew for its men, but it locked its women up in the dorms at 10:30 every night. My friend and I waited in the bushes to catch the sleeping bags the women tossed out of the dorm's second-floor windows. They darted out a side door of the dorm, and we headed for the woods at the edge of campus. I was having a mild reaction to the typhoid injection I'd received that afternoon in preparation for my summer vacation trip to

Europe. My arm was sore, and I had a slight fever. Settling into a sleeping bag with Elli that night provided an instant cure.

I was falling in love with Elli, but she sensed I was holding something back, and it troubled her. She also found my style of dominating meetings obnoxious. The year ended on a down note. Elli broke up with me shortly before the semester ended. In a letter a couple of weeks after the semester ended, she wrote that she ended our relationship because of its "emotional poverty." I was devastated, but quickly repressed my feelings. In any event she had decided to spend a year in eastern Kentucky doing community organizing and would not be returning to Earlham that fall.

Despite Elli's absence I looked forward to returning to Earlham when the summer ended. The main attraction was the prospect of living on a dorm hall with a group of political troublemakers. Instead of fraternities Earlham had a system that enabled groups of upperclassmen to accumulate points to bid for halls. You gained a point for already residing on a hall and two more for each year of your college career. Since halls averaged twenty residents and incoming freshmen were randomly assigned to each hall, a group of fifteen rising seniors and juniors were almost assured of obtaining the hall of their desire. We didn't think we had much chance at amassing the necessary points because we had only gathered a group of nine and most of us were rising sophomores, but we bid on the semibasement of Barrett Hall. Surprisingly no one else bid on it, and so it was ours.

I still roomed with Arthur, although Hernán was my best friend. Hernán was not a U.S. citizen and told me he was concerned about being too closely associated with an outspoken activist. He took the only single room on the hall, which didn't bother me. I empathized with his need to avoid attracting the notice of those in authority, although it made me feel a bit guilty about not sharing my true identity with Hernán. I suspected that being a close friend of a son of the Rosenbergs probably placed him at greater risk than rooming with a minor radical student leader in a backwater college would have. But I rationalized that he could use his ignorance of my true identity as a defense. This provided me with a convenient reason for continuing to deceive the person with whom I held my most intimate personal discussions.

At first I was intoxicated by the thrill of not being an incoming freshman. It also was wonderful to be living in a community of kindred spirits. Halls named themselves. We distained the popular sexual double meanings for a name with political connotations by choosing "the Underground." Denizens of the Underground and its intramural sports teams were dubbed "Underdogs."

That first day the pack of us were sky-high just on being together, but within hours the reality of being stuck in Richmond under the thumb of a priggish administration sank in. By the evening of the first day I told Hernán that I would transfer to another college next year.

But in the meantime Hernán and I and our Underdog buddies meant to squeeze whatever life we could out of our time together. Our hall shared an aggressive new ideology. The Underground gave Earlham its first dose of the political, sexual, and psychedelic revolution that was now loose in the nation. Being together emboldened us to attack the system, and the Earlham College administration became our chief target. No longer satisfied with just talking about our beliefs, we confronted the administration repeatedly. We grew our hair, dressed as we pleased, and refused to abide by the administration's social rules that prevented women from visiting men in their dorm rooms. Those who disagreed were uptight fools. I was certain I'd caught the wave of the future.

Confrontation flared almost immediately. Maintenance employees caught Bob, a junior from Chicago who considered himself an anarchist, and several other Underdogs writing "Anarchists Unite" and peace signs in the wet cement on the walk outside the dorm. I went along to provide support when they were summoned to appear before the dean of students.

Dean Curtis was a gentleman with a formal British accent that local Indiana boys probably found intimidating. Tall, reedy, and tweedy, with graying temples, he was almost a caricature of a proper English intellectual. Dean Curtis expected denial or contrition when he laid transgressions at the feet of those hauled before him; our lack of repentance confounded him. Bob said he thought all the sidewalks should be covered with similar graffiti. When we all volunteered to join this campus beautification project, he dismissed us with noises that sounded like the sputtering of the cartoon character Mr. Magoo. The workers had removed the offending symbols from the sidewalk, and the administration did not press the matter.

Other skirmishes followed. That fall several confrontations centered on our fraternizing with women through our dorm's open ground-level windows, and our efforts to bend the gender segregation rules by holding coed hall parties every evening. Each administration effort to control us only attracted more students to us. It helped that we acted with panache and high spirits. The climax that spring was our hosting a regional antiwar conference that included a Saturday-night concert by Phil Ochs, which attracted hundreds of longhaired radicals to the campus from all over the region.

Alarmed by our antics, the administration sought to stem the tide of unruly entering freshmen before things got even more out of hand. They produced a new promotional booklet, *The Earlham View Book*, to be distributed to thousands of high school guidance offices. It included language designed to discourage disruptive applicants. In it someone had written that Earlham did not believe in the "alleged" revolution in sex and drugs, and all those who would be dissatisfied with the "simple Quaker social life" should not bother to apply. At first we peppered the opinion board with protests. With typical tact I wrote: "Whoever wrote that paragraph should be congratulated for attempting to impose his small mind on Earlham College." I learned later that President Bolling had penned it.

But, as always, we were not satisfied with verbal protests. A friend on another hall discovered that the administration had stored almost fourteen thousand of these booklets in the attic of the administration building. This led to the great *View Book* caper. After days of careful planning, we positioned Nick's, Steve's, and Hernán's cars in the lot behind the building on a cool and calm evening. Another friend who was on the student government council left his keys to the building's back door and its service elevator in a place where one of the conspirators could borrow them for the night. I had scouted the campus police patrols and learned that no one checked the building between 3:00 and 4:00 A.M. The deathly quiet of campus at 3:00 A.M. magnified every sound we made. Time slowed with my rising excitement. Don't worry, I told myself, they're too stupid to catch us, and even if they do we'll just pretend it's a prank rather than a politically motivated effort to undermine administration policy. We entered the building at 3:05. The freight elevator was so loud I could have sworn it could be heard across the Ohio line five miles away. I took my perch at the arched attic window and flashed a two-pulse signal to Hernán, the outside lookout, to let him know that things were going according to plan. As inside and outside lookouts, Hernán and I were to give the six haulers fair warning if the cops returned before they were finished. Now time crept as I stared fixedly at the bush where Hernán crouched. I stared so hard that my vision flickered, and I had to look away to rest my eyes before I could focus on him again. An eternity later Nick tapped me on the shoulder, and I signaled Hernán to meet us at the cars. At 3:50 we drove off campus to a safe location with three cars loaded with almost a ton of *View Books*.

I originally wanted to make a bonfire of them in the center of the campus, but cooler heads prevailed. We hid them instead. The administration showed its teeth and tried to intimidate the perpetrators by posting a notice on the opinion board that more than fifty thousand dollars' worth of college property was missing. Ultimately, the administration found the *View Books*, but not before the entire campus was inflamed. Now everyone was discussing the *View Books'* contents, and even some faculty became concerned that President Bolling's characterization of the Earlham community might have a negative impact on the quality of students applying for admission. The administration modified the language the following year. It was too late to stem the tide of student unrest in any event; President Bolling moved on to become head of the Eli Lilly Foundation, and Earlham became a minor breeding ground of political and cultural activism for the next several years.

What befuddled the administration and attracted supporters was our public proclamation of our positions. The impact of openly articulating our beliefs was a revelation to me. I had grown up keeping many of my deeply held beliefs secret from those who did not agree with me. With a few exceptions, Old Left political culture had been driven underground during the McCarthy period. Suddenly the problem with the Old Left seemed obvious: You couldn't convince many people of your beliefs if you did not pronounce them in public.

I had acted on my new attitude of trumpeting my views several months earlier in January. I asked the student run newspaper if I could write a weekly column. The editors of the *Earlham Post* were not particularly liberal and did not want to provide me with a platform for my antiwar views. They told me I could only write columns about campus events. They didn't realize that that was what I wanted all along. I called my column "On a Limb," and used it to attack the administration's rules and student passivity. The opening paragraph of my first article, the first installment of a three-part series on student apathy, got everyone's attention: "Have you ever wondered as you wander around Earlham where everybody is? Have you ever wondered what they are doing? My only answers to these questions are that too many are nowhere and that they are doing nothing."

My columns caused a commotion. I suspect that the main reason the editors did not fire me after the first few weeks was that my weekly diatribes increased readership. Perhaps the administration took no action at first because they had learned that attempts to silence my cohorts and me only gained us converts. But the administration could not ignore what I wrote in one of my final columns:

> *Earlham is controlled by conservatives and conservative Quakers who donate large sums of money to the college. It is this power block which would be shocked and horrified by social experimentation.*
>
> *If we want to gain control over our own lives in an orderly manner, we must shift the economic foundations of this school. We must get rid of conservative money.*

Each trustee of the college received the current issue of the *Earlham Post* and apparently read my article. President Bolling called me into his office a few days later. First he tried to argue with me about the administration's rules. When I argued back he said: "We once had another boy from the suburbs, and things just didn't work out. He transferred to Williams College, and there were no hard feelings."

I had already been accepted as a transfer student at the University of Michigan. But I decided to let President Bolling stew a little longer before he found out that I wouldn't be returning in the fall.

I had another reason for transferring to Michigan. During my sophomore year I indulged my love of nature by taking several natural science courses. In high school I had read books about the evolution of life on earth and had been particularly interested in landforms, the Ice Ages, and human evolution. I took whatever courses Earlham offered in these areas. My increased interest yielded better grades. I decided to major in human evolution and discovered that that line of scientific inquiry was called physical anthropology. Although Earlham did not have an anthropology department, I discovered that the cradle of SDS, the University of Michigan, had an excellent one. My rapidly improving grades, coupled with my ability to articulate a valid academic reason for transferring, probably contributed to my application's success. Hernán also applied to Michigan and was accepted. We looked forward to spending the remainder of our college careers together.

It was easier to find girlfriends when I was a sophomore, but I didn't meet anyone I could compare favorably with Elli. Elli invited me to visit her in Kentucky during the fall, and she returned the favor with a weekend visit to Earlham in the spring. Each visit renewed my hopes, but they were isolated episodes, and she was unwilling to make a commitment to me. I vowed never to have any involvement with Elli again after her spring visit. Given my history of successfully sealing off unpleasant memories, I was surprised at how difficult it was to put her out of my mind.

In August 1967 my father and I drove out to Ann Arbor. Karen, who had worked at Camp Thoreau with me several years earlier, and her husband, Terry, had tried but failed to find me an apartment in Ann Arbor's crowded student ghetto. I settled for a single room in the attic of a run-down house a few blocks off campus. Hernán, still keeping some distance from his radical friend, elected to live in a dorm. Fortunately his roommate never appeared, so I could stay over whenever I wished.

The car ride out to Ann Arbor was one of the last extended periods of time I spent with Abel. I was concerned because he seemed to repeat himself more frequently than he had during our conversations while I stood in his study doorway several years before. I remember thinking, *How could he be losing his memory when he was only in his middle sixties?* I buried this disturbing thought and chose instead to laugh about his parting advice: "Don't take any of that DSL [LSD] stuff." I said I wouldn't, and I never did.

Ann Arbor was a small city of one hundred thousand located forty miles west of Detroit. It was more pleasant to live in and to look at than Richmond. Unlike in Richmond, you could wander off campus without fear of being cursed or beaten up by the locals, Easterners not being an oddity. I was told that the *Blue Front*, a newsstand and pharmacy several blocks south of the campus, was the largest single outlet for the Sunday *New York Times* west of the Appalachians and east of Chicago. Not such a big deal unless you'd spent the last two years in Richmond, where even the *New York Times* raised eyebrows.

There were plenty of cornfields in southeast Lower Michigan, but the countryside around Ann Arbor had modest hills and forested areas. Set where the Huron River Valley intersected glacial moraines, it was just far enough north so that a mixture of maples, birches, oaks, and evergreens replaced Indiana's more uniform oaks.

The campus was dominated by massive stone buildings that reminded me of the buildings on the Capitol Mall in Washington. The Graduate Library, with its imposing columnlike structures, sat at the center of the campus. It was situated on the north edge of a large cement plaza called the "Diag" because diagonal walkways led from it in all directions. The Diag was a favorite spot for demonstrations.

Karen introduced me to her friends in SDS. Although Tom Hayden and other SDS founders had moved on, SDS at Michigan was still a force to be reckoned with. When I arrived in the fall of 1967 the SDS chapter was called Voice Political Party. It fielded a slate of candidates who often won election to student government positions. Connections to the student newspaper the *Michigan Daily* ensured excellent coverage of its activities and plans.

The nondescript glass, steel, and cement Undergraduate Library that I once heard described as having "classic high-Eisenhower architectural style" sat to the left of the Graduate Library. Students appropriately called it the "Ugli." SDS regularly reserved the "Ugli multipurpose" room for its meetings. Some 150 students crammed into this room's deep rectangular space at the first meeting of the semester to plan its fall activity campaign. Karen was elected chapter president, and she nominated me for a position on the steering committee. I declined, citing my recent arrival and lack of familiarity with campus politics. In fact, my old caution when entering a new situation had resurfaced. I craved the political sophistication of one of the nation's hotbeds of student radicalism, but was intimidated now that I'd found it.

Student radicals at Michigan weren't haggling with the administration about having women in the dorms. Instead SDS's first action that fall was to help university service workers who'd gone on strike for the right to join a union. Although many students opposed the strike because they missed their maid service, the Teamster's Union drivers refused to cross the service workers' picket line and stopped delivering food to the dorms. The striking workers did not have enough members to maintain the picket lines at the receiving building throughout the night, and they feared that the university might induce the drivers to make late-night deliveries. In response to the service workers' call, I joined several dozen SDS comrades who prepared to pull a political all-nighter. We sat and sang old union songs on the building's steps. We had a great midnight touch-football game in the parking lot. We even did some picketing. At 2:30 A.M. we learned that the university had caved in, and we held an impromptu celebration. I remember being nervous about what might happen if the Teamsters tried to make a delivery or if the cops had tried to roust us, but neither of these things happened. Instead I felt exhilarated. This was what I had left Earlham to find. I was engaging the real world and helping people to earn a living wage. I had only been on campus a few weeks, and I was already sipping the wine of a student-worker coalition victory.

There were many more radicals than at Earlham, but there were also a lot more factions. The Communists fought with the Trotskyites, and anarchists argued with both. The partisans of these groups could quarrel over the finer points of the Russian Revolution, or debate Rosa Luxemburg's theories. Unlike me, they'd done more than read a couple of books from the Little Lenin Library. There was also a more amorphous mass of issue-oriented new leftists who did not adhere to Old Left formations, but focused instead on antiwar or civil rights activities. A lot of meetings degenerated into procedural wrangling as one group vied with another to have its pet project adopted. I was dismayed that the minute radical activists had even a little power to wield we began to fight over it, and also concerned that this behind-the-scenes manipulation violated the spirit of professed political openness.

I supported the positions taken by Karen and her friends. SDS at Michigan, like most campus SDS chapters, was focused on building the struggle against the war in Vietnam through education and direct nonviolent demonstrations. We also supported antipoverty efforts and the civil rights movement, although we talked, more than acted, on these questions. Unlike many campus chapters, Michigan's SDS's Old Left ties also drew it to organized labor. I was most comfortable with other red-diaper babies who were also children of ex–Communist Party members. I sympathized with some Communist Party positions but never even considered joining the party. I did not openly criticize the Soviet Union, but I viewed that nation as repressive and bureaucratically moribund. The American Communist Party seemed politically timid and stodgy. They supported what I saw as the most conservative antiwar positions of negotiation and gradual withdrawal from Vietnam. I felt it was important for SDS boldly to demand that the United States withdraw from Vietnam immediately and even to voice its sympathy for the Viet Cong, whom I viewed as revolutionary heroes. I respected Old Left politics because I respected Ethel and Julius Rosenberg and Anne and Abel Meeropol, but my heart was with the political openness and social audacity of the New Left. I found, however, that I could maintain friendly relations with all but the most strident members of all the factions. At Earlham you were forced to work with people you disagreed with if you wanted to accomplish anything. I wished that more of my political comrades at Michigan could develop such an ecumenical attitude.

Politics weren't the only exciting thing about Michigan. I loaded up my schedule with physical and cultural anthropology courses. I quickly gravitated to the latter and became a cultural anthropology major. The breadth of human cultural possibility astounded me. Although I believed in revolution, I'd grown up accepting Western cultural norms. Now I saw that our society was not necessarily any better or more advanced than any other. Those who placed the United States at the pinnacle of history and felt it would endure forever demonstrated both their ignorance and lack of imagination.

Michigan also had several SDS-oriented assistant professors. I got course credit for taking "the Sociology of Revolution" with Tom Mayer, and for reading Che Guevara and Régis Debray's *Revolution in the Revolution* for homework.

While I had many political acquaintances, I had few real friends. Although I was glad to be out of Earlham's insular atmosphere, I missed the powerful friendships forged by fighting a common enemy. Hernán and I made the four-hour drive to Earlham twice that fall for visits. When I returned east for Christmas vacation, I arranged to spend New Year's with Hernán and several other Earlhamites in Washington, D.C.

I saw Elli at a party at my old roommate Arthur's parents' house. She invited me to join her and her friend Christi at Elli's parents' house in Bethesda for New Year's Eve. I agreed, despite my never-again vow.

It is easy to overlook the little things that good friends do that can make a massive difference. I felt vulnerable going to Elli's by myself, and asked Hernán to accompany me. He agreed, although I'm sure he had better things to do than play chaperone on New Year's Eve. Perhaps Christi was doing the same for Elli. I doubt that either Christi or Hernán had any interest in each other. I believe that without their support Elli and I would not have gotten together that evening.

That fall a mutual friend had told Elli that I was a son of the Rosenbergs. Although she did not mention this to me, she finally understood what had been troubling her about me, why I seemed so closed, and was willing to give me another chance. I had no idea that our kiss at midnight that New Year's Eve was the start of our enduring partnership.

We spent most of the next few days together before I returned to Ann Arbor for the start of the next semester. Elli had finished her year in Kentucky six months earlier, taken art courses at a D.C. area college over the summer, and spent the fall at California College of Arts and Crafts in Oakland. She didn't have to return for classes for another week and wanted to visit me in Ann Arbor on her way west. "No visit," I said. "If you come you have to stay."

To my surprise she agreed. In a week she collected her stuff, moved out of her Berkeley apartment, and dropped out of yet another college. I'd moved out of my crummy attic room and into a house with three other SDS activists a month earlier. My housemates, two men and a woman, agreed that Elli could join us.

Elli arrived in the midst of a frigid Ann Arbor January. The fronts of my legs froze through my pants in the just-below-zero cold, and icicles hung from my mustache by the end of the mile-long walk from the house to class every morning. After mild California, Elli must have experienced thermal shock hiking across campus, in miniskirt and panty hose, to her new secretarial job at the School of Public Health.

Elli had demonstrated her commitment to me by moving to Michigan. She was working so she could qualify for in-state tuition and transfer to the university's School of Art in the fall. Now it was my turn. Although I was just twenty years old, I was ready to make a lifelong promise. But how could I expect her to reciprocate if she didn't really know what she was getting into? Lying together on the lumpy mattress on the floor in our small room the night she arrived I told her, "I have something to tell you." I took a deep breath and said the words I'd never said out loud to anyone. "I am the son of Ethel and Julius Rosenberg." Letting that barrier down was so stressful that

I can't recall much about the conversation, other than her telling me that she already knew, and how relieved I was to have told her.

Openness became my panacea. There wasn't anything we couldn't reveal. I wanted to share every thought in my mind and every inch of my body with her and explore every thought and inch of hers. I felt embarrassed walking around campus. How could people fail to notice that my mind was enraptured and that I exuded sexual satisfaction? I was so focused on her that I neglected my friends. Elli knew almost no one at Michigan. I couldn't leave her alone even to go to a basketball game with Hernán.

Elli and I did not wish to share our new relationship with several housemates. We found a small dark semibasement studio apartment a block from the School of Public Health and moved in at the beginning of March. We adopted a kitten, named him Catsup, and set up housekeeping. Our first purchases were a $29 cotton double mattress that was comfortable for about a month, and a small black cast-iron cooking pan for $1.95. We left the mattress when we moved out of the apartment that summer, but we still cook eggs in that pan.

Elli is very forthright, and neither of us likes to dawdle. That February while watching Joni Mitchell perform at a small coffeehouse just off campus I made an oblique comment about getting married. She agreed. I suggested August. She said, "Why wait?" We decided to marry when the semester ended in late April.

We each called our parents to announce our wedding plans. Elli spoke with her parents first. Neither set of parents seemed concerned about our living together, but Elli's mother commented logically that Elli, who had worked summers during high school as a clerk-typist for the federal government, would never get another security clearance. They were cordial, though restrained, on the phone with me. I told my parents. When I put Elli on, Abel apparently was so tongue-tied that he started barking. Anne's mortified: "Oh, Abel, stop it!" had no effect. I doubt Abel even heard Elli's "Meow" in response.

We arranged a party in Hastings the weekend after finals ended, a party in Bethesda the next weekend, and in between were married in a civil ceremony at the Rockville, Maryland, County Courthouse with Hernán and Elli's friend Becky as witnesses. Under Maryland law women could marry without parental consent at eighteen, but consent was demanded of men until they were twenty-one. This sexist vestige was declared unconstitutional several years later, but since I was two weeks shy of my twenty-first birthday I had to obtain my parents' notarized permission before we went to the courthouse. Marriage was not the norm for young activists in 1968. I didn't realize it then, but now I believe it was no accident that despite cultural trends both my brother and I married early and presumed we would have families. I must have wanted to re-create the early family life that had been stolen from me.

We stayed in Ann Arbor that summer. Elli had to work at the School of Public Health through July to qualify for in-state tuition in the fall. She'd been accepted into the art school at the university and transferred previous credits so that she'd graduate the following year with me.

I took more anthropology courses in summer school so as to graduate on time in the spring with my anthropology degree. I was particularly interested in Professor Eric Wolf's "Latin American Peasantry" course. Professor Wolf, a renowned anthropologist, was rapidly becoming my academic mentor. He was a Marxist, although he would not yet admit it publicly. When a group of students suggested that he direct an independent study seminar on Marxist anthropology, he suggested that we call it "Materialist Methods."

At the end of the summer we moved to a slightly bigger apartment on the south side of campus, closer to both the art school and the anthropology building. The apartment's saving graces, other than its location, were that it had two walk-in closets and that the large bedroom/living room could also serve as a study. Elli's closet, the larger of the two, even had a window. Once after an argument she put her desk chair in there, closed the door, and looked out the window until she calmed down.

We argued quite a bit. I idolized openness but still held in my hurts until they burst forth in a flood. If something bothered me, Elli wanted me to say so rather than withdraw. If I interrupted her too frequently or didn't pay attention to what she was saying, Elli reacted instantly with outspoken anger that I resented but could not immediately answer. We were like rocks in a streambed during a spring flood. We wore our rough edges smooth as we tumbled and bounced against each other through the white-water rapids of relationship building.

Although SDS laid the groundwork on campus that summer for intensifying its campaign against classified war research, there wasn't as much political activity as during the school year, and Elli and I were more focused on our deepening bond during July and August.

We met Randy and Rayna at a retreat SDS held to plan its fall program just before the start of classes that fall. They were also newly married, and the four of us became close friends almost immediately. Rayna was starting a doctoral program in anthropology, and Randy was beginning a doctoral program in psychology. They had been at Michigan for four years and introduced us to their large circle of friends.

Randy and Rayna came from Old Left families in the New York City area and immediately understood the connection between the names Meeropol and Rosenberg; I didn't have to tell them who I was. Rayna was a short, dark, intense academic star who spoke in machine-gun bursts of language. Randy and Rayna lived in a university-sponsored cooperative house just a couple of blocks from our apartment. We started cooking dinners together, although at first Rayna and Elli did all the cooking while Randy and I played Frisbee and football. Randy had light reddish brown hair and had a facility for coming up with outrageous one-liners that left everyone speechless.

Later that year the four of us went to see the movie *Elvira Madigan*, a popular tearjerker about a nineteenth-century nobleman who fell in love with a circus performer. After the nobleman's family cut off his funds, the star-crossed lovers were reduced to starvation. In the final scene he takes out a gun while she chases butterflies across a flower-filled field. Two shots ring out, the screen goes black, and the credits start to roll. Over the sobs of the audience Randy called out: "My God, he shot the cameraman!"

The late summer SDS retreat took place just after the Democratic National Convention in Chicago. Many liberal antiwar students from Michigan had just returned in disillusionment from the convention, where the Chicago police had beaten Eugene McCarthy's supporters. They were open to SDS critique of liberal electoral reforms, and ripe for our more radical analysis that called for changing the nature of the system.

Elli and I were in Ann Arbor when the Chicago police attacked unarmed students outside the convention hall. We did not go to Chicago because we did not support Eugene McCarthy's candidacy even though he was against the Vietnam War. We viewed him as a reformer who would never institute basic change. We were skeptical of electoral politics in general because we felt the system was rigged so that only candidates with a stake in the status quo would prevail. We felt that electoral politics diverted activists and sapped energy from efforts to build grassroots mass movements for basic social change. We were radicals as opposed to liberals. A liberal was someone who believed the system was unfair to the poor and to blacks, but felt that the United States could be fixed without changing its basic nature. As radicals we knew that American capitalism created the economic inequities that caused poverty, and that it also fanned the flames of racism to pit workers, black and white, and poor people, who should work together, against one another.

SDS did not have a single political line, but many members who thought about it felt that you couldn't end racism and poverty without getting rid of capitalism. SDS's slogan, Let the People Decide, reflected its belief that people should be more powerful than money, while under capitalism money was paramount. I felt that the transformation SDS demanded would ultimately require a violent revolution since capitalists would never give up power without a fight. Some in SDS disagreed. They felt this transformation could be achieved peacefully. Since no one felt that the revolution was at hand, the disagreement remained academic.

After witnessing police brutality on Chicago's streets, many students felt compelled to further action. Just a few days later a local welfare rights organization asked student support for its demand, rejected by the county, to increase the winter clothing allowance for each child from forty to sixty dollars. Michigan winters were cold. A number of students wanted to sit in at the county building to support this demand. I argued against the sit-in. I felt that it was foolish to place ourselves intentionally under the authorities' power. We should demonstrate and be disruptive but leave before we were arrested so we could return to repeat our actions the next day. If they obtained an injunction against demonstrations at that site, we should find another one. If they banned all demonstrations, we should wait until the ban expired and then start them up again. I called this strategy "float like a butterfly, sting like a bee," after Muhammad Ali's fighting style.

But the majority of student protesters wanted to put their bodies on the line immediately. Elli and I sat in with over two hundred other students at the county building on the cool marble floor that warm September day and sang civil rights songs. At first the police tried to wait us out; alternative entrances enabled work to continue as usual. The arrests began because we refused to leave when the building closed at 5:00 P.M. The police firmly hauled the protesters up and walked them into waiting vans. My heart pounded as the arresting officers came closer. I wanted out of there, but fellow demonstrators surrounded me. I could not have left Elli in any event, and she was determined to stay. We were arrested and charged with criminal trespass. This was as calm and polite as a mass arrest could be, and yet I felt panic-stricken. I was in "their" clutches. My panic did not abate until we were released on fifty-dollar bond after our arraignment late that evening.

Legal strategy meetings and court appearances dogged us for the next eight months. Our attorney, Bill Goodman, could do little to prevent our conviction. We were given a fifteen-dollar fine, sentenced to two weeks' community service and, by far the worst, assessed a hundred fifteen dollars each for court costs. Although the welfare clothing allowance was increased to fifty dollars three weeks after the mass arrest, I vowed never to put myself in that position again. At the time I believed in my vehement arguments that civil disobedience resulted in a ridiculous waste of movement resources, but now I think this masked my emotional inability to put myself anywhere near my parents' shoes.

After the sit-in SDS concentrated on attacking university research contracts to develop hi-tech counterinsurgency weapons, which were to be tested in Thailand's jungles. Student government scheduled a November campus-wide referendum to decide if such research should be banned from campus. I made one of my most effective contributions to Ann Arbor radical politics by suggesting that we print buttons in maize and blue, Michigan's colors, that read: GO MICHIGAN BEAT THAILAND. These buttons, which played off of Michigan's fall football fanaticism, were wildly popular. The button was even cited in a *Newsweek* article about campus unrest during the fall of 1968. We set the next meeting to discuss campaign strategy, not realizing that a rebellion was brewing.

Before the next meeting, Elli and I met Karen and Terry in the student center cafeteria for a farewell lunch. They were moving to Seattle, where Terry would enter graduate school. Bill Ayers, a blond young man with a fresh face who exuded enthusiastic charm, joined us. He knew Karen and Terry, though I'd never met him. He described his work at Ann Arbor's new alternative school, but said he was going to get reinvolved with SDS and shake things up. I didn't give this much thought until the next meeting.

Bill led a faction of students who claimed that the referendum campaign was morally bankrupt. He argued that Michigan students had no right to vote on whether Southeast Asian jungles should be destroyed by American ordnance. He said we should begin disrupting this work immediately and continue to disrupt it regardless of what the majority of students voted. The old guard answered that if we won the referendum we could stop the research, something those claiming the moral high ground would never accomplish. The meeting was quickly reduced to chaotic name-calling. We agreed, however, that at next week's meeting each side would make a ten-minute presentation to be followed by a controlled debate and a vote on fall actions.

The old guard called itself the Radical Caucus and asked me to present its position. I reluctantly agreed. Bill would speak for the Jesse James Gang. The Ugli multipurpose room was bursting at the seams when the meeting began. I found it hard to control my breathing before such a large audience. I doggedly outlined a middle position between the reformism of Eugene McCarthy and revolution, which I said was still a long way off. We needed to focus on face-to-face organizing to broaden our base of support, and the referendum would accomplish that end.

Bill spoke in more general terms. He didn't claim to have as many answers as I did, but he said American weapons were pulverizing thousands of Vietnamese every week and we must do more than hold a referendum. He smiled a lot, dropped the *g* from words ending in "ing," and frequently raised the pitch of his voice at the end of a sentence so that statements sounded like questions. This folksy style probably swayed some of the undecided. The gang prevailed by a narrow margin, and the caucus walked out. Each group began meeting separately and went ahead with its plans.

Although I'd given the caucus speech, I was not firmly in their camp. A Trotskyist offshoot called International Socialists (IS) dominated the Radical Caucus. I was uncomfortable with the IS's openly anti-Soviet and anti-Castro stances, as well as its dismissal of Latin American Marxist guerrilla movements as irresponsible ultra-leftist adventures. Soon I was trying to broker reconciliation. I argued we should find common ground and unite against the enemy. At a caucus meeting I said this dispute might have some validity if we were about to seize state power. In that case such strategic disagreements could have a direct impact on thousands, even millions, of people. Unfortunately, since the revolution was not about to happen, we should explore ways to work together. In response, a leader of the caucus contemptuously christened me chairman of the "Mush-Head" SDS. I said that I'd accept being a mush-head if that's what it took to build a coalition. I took a perverse pride in that title; I still think of myself as a member of Mush-Head SDS.

The caucus's counterinsurgency research referendum failed. The caucus hadn't reckoned on a huge turnout from the engineering school overwhelming the liberal bastion of the arts colleges, and the group unraveled. Bill Ayers and other Jesse James Gang members left town to help start the Weatherman faction of the SDS, which would over the next several years chart a more violent course, first advocating street battles with the police and later conducting a bombing campaign. Their followers who remained on campus were quiet that winter and spring.

Other political and social currents rocked our world. Elli and Rayna got involved in a surge of feminist activism that flooded through SDS and the civil rights movement. Radical men, for all our rhetoric about individual freedom and equality, did not treat women as equals. One black power leader, when asked about the position of women in the Student Non-Violent Coordinating Committee (SNCC), replied: "Prone." Although he probably meant supine, this answer reflected rampant sexual discrimination within the civil rights movement. Sexism joined racism and capitalism in the pantheon of oppression, and my world changed. Elli, Rayna, and others called the traditional divisions between men and women into question. Why should they cook while we played? Wouldn't it make more sense to divide all household-related chores equally so that we were all capable of doing all tasks? Why shouldn't women's voices carry as much weight as men's at political meetings?

I was raised in a nontraditional household with a stay-at-home father. Anne Meeropol had a very strong voice in all family decisions. This, coupled with my tendency to empathize with the underdog, led me to understand and accept everything that Elli and Rayna were saying almost immediately. It seemed obvious to me that the arguments men used to scorn "women's lib" were the same ones used by racist whites to denigrate blacks' legitimate claims. Women were no more "girls" than blacks were "boys." Claims that women were more emotional and less rational than men, and therefore unsuited for societal leadership, were convenient concepts designed to perpetuate patriarchy. The almost entirely male leadership of the anti–Vietnam War and black civil rights movements was discovering that the most difficult oppressor to recognize was the one in the mirror.

Elli and Rayna argued that women had an equal right to pursue careers and men were equally obligated to raise children. I found this logic inescapable. And this merging of personal politics with our political beliefs felt like a natural extension of the open and equal way I urged men and women of all ages to act with one another in my Earlham newspaper columns. The four of us discussed how we could banish these divisions from our lives and create a community to nurture our political and personal growth. I had been accepted into the anthropology Ph.D. program and been awarded a National Science Foundation Fellowship for my first two years of graduate study, so Elli and I would remain in Ann Arbor after graduation. We decided to organize a "commune" with Randy and Rayna after the spring 1969 semester ended.

Two other anthropology grad students, Susan and Ed, and Ed's wife, Rene, would also join us. Ed was a bit older. Rene, a social work research assistant, was pregnant and due to deliver that summer. The seven of us frequently ate together and planned long into the night. The strong friendships and our commitment to openness made it possible for me to share my secret with all my future communards. It added an additional layer of comfort and security to have more people in my circle of friends know about my heritage.

The spring of 1969 was alive with unlimited possibilities. New radical movements were emerging, from feminism in Ann Arbor to the Stonewall rebellion in New York's Greenwich Village that sparked the gay liberation movement. And we were embarking on a social adventure to create a loving community.

The seven of us found a sprawling rental house eight miles from campus, in the neighboring town of Ypsilanti, near Eastern Michigan University, and moved in at the beginning of June. Our bedroom had a screened sun porch that was a joy to sleep on in summer. We painted the wall of Ed and Rene's upstairs bedroom green and the ceiling sky blue and called it Sherwood Forest. There were generous communal areas in the large, open living and dining rooms on the ground floor. The house also had a converted garage that became a group study room for the graduate students.

Combined record and book collections, shared TVs, stereos, and kitchen equipment and bulk food purchases decreased our living costs. We postulated that the consumer economy would suffer a tremendous blow if our lifestyle became the norm. We did not, however, even consider reducing the number of vehicles we owned. We shared Randy and Rayna's new subcompact Saab, Susan's VW bug, and Ed and Rene's pitifully underpowered VW bus to get to and from campus. Elli's schedule was less flexible. She regularly drove our huge six-year-old blue Dodge, a wedding present from my parents, to the job she found at the end of the summer working as a teacher in a day-care center run by Karen's mother.

Communal practice did not always match its theory. Some anticipated problems worked themselves out. Our tough male outdoor cat, Catsup, quickly reached an accommodation with Randy and Rayna's tolerant German shepherd, Hibbie, short for "Hibernia," and Ed and Rene's timid mongrel, Daphne.

But people were less flexible. After moving into the house in June, Randy and Rayna departed for two months to do anthropological fieldwork in a peasant village in southern France. Elli and Susan and I were left to take care of Hibbie and set up the house with Ed and Rene, whose son, Jason, was born a month prematurely at the beginning of August. We joyfully welcomed the new generation and declared that all babies born into the commune would be given the middle name "Friend" because that was Susan's middle name and it had a communal ring to it. Elli was particularly enthusiastic about helping with child care. She helped me overcome my fear of injuring the scrawny five-pound infant. Elli and I got up in the middle of every other night to feed Jason. But when Randy and Rayna returned in August, they were not so keen on being communal parents. Jason was a colicky child, and often our best efforts could not quiet him. Most of us had no experience with newborns, and Jason's frequent crying was very difficult in a household of graduate students.

Tension between Ed and Rene, and Randy, Rayna, and Susan built quickly after the fall semester started. Elli and I found ourselves in the middle, very attached to Jason and wanting a solution. But our primary connection was to Randy and Rayna. Ed and Rene moved out of the commune in the beginning of November. The tension in the house subsided, but a somber atmosphere replaced it. Our grand experiment had not gotten off to a good start.

We decided to lift our spirits by hosting a giant communal Thanksgiving feast that included my brother, Michael, his wife, Ann, and their thirteen-month-old daughter, Ivy. Michael was finishing his

Ph.D. in economics at Wisconsin, and Ann was teaching in Madison's public school system. Accustomed to midwestern distances, they were not daunted by the prospect of driving four hundred miles each way for a long weekend through potentially nasty late fall Great Lakes weather.

Ivy was a cherubic blond round-faced child who was just saying her first words and taking her first steps. She divided the world in half, everything was either "bee-bee" (baby) or "duck," but she'd call out "prit-tee" (pretty) with perfect diction when she got excited. After dinner she pointed to Hibbie and piped: "Bee-bee?" When none of us agreed, she continued quizzically: "Duck?" Half a dozen graduate students came to her aid collectively intoning: "No, that's a dog!" To which she responded: "Prit-tee!" Elli and I decided we wanted one of those cute little things before too long.

With Ed and Rene gone, the house was too expensive for the five remaining members. We also discovered that commuting from Ypsilanti was problematic during the Michigan winter. We found a smaller house in Ann Arbor about a mile from campus and moved in January 1970.

The political cauldron had continued to simmer while we bumbled about attempting to live ideal socialist lives. Although I had stopped attending meetings after the split at the end of 1968, I was aware of ongoing SDS activity. During the fall of 1969 a vibrant new version of SDS had resurfaced, dominated by a group of undergraduates whose sympathies lay with the recently formed Weatherman faction of SDS. They were attempting to drive military recruiters and the ROTC off campus with a campaign of confrontation and disruption. They staged angry demonstrations in front of the campus ROTC building, whose windows were repeatedly smashed. I felt odd to be an older outside observer of these SDS activities, which the new leaders called "actions."

The commune attended a meeting to learn more about this new SDS. It appeared more democratic and less sexist. It was organized into subgroups of approximately a half dozen students, called collectives. Each collective took on tasks, such as writing leaflets, or acting as lookouts at an action, and was responsible for the safety of its members during these actions. This collective structure dispersed control and encouraged group participation.

At the end of 1969 the commune decided to become an SDS collective, and we also agreed to apply for grants to do summer anthropology fieldwork connected to Professor Eric Wolf's Mediterranean project. Dr. Wolf and another professor had received a Ford Foundation grant to study the modernization of peasant villages in the Mediterranean basin. Teams of graduate students were given small grants to spend the summer gathering data about life in remote villages throughout the region. Rayna received a grant to return to their village in southern France, and I got one to find and study a similar village in the Spanish province of Catalonia. We divided these funds further so that Susan could also spend the summer doing fieldwork in another Spanish village.

But we would not be departing until May, and by the end of January were caught up in an intense round of campus protests. The campaign against military recruiters and ROTC escalated rapidly. I supported these actions wholeheartedly. We'd been peacefully protesting the war for years. But the American military continued to rain napalm and toxic chemical defoliants on Vietnam, killing hundreds of thousands. Some of us had been beaten and jailed while the majority of Americans did nothing or actually applauded. We were going to stop the war even if we had to take increasingly violent actions. Any violence we engaged in was dwarfed by the reign of terror being waged in our name by our military in the jungles of Southeast Asia. We were going to raise the price of the war for those promoting it. It was time to make the warmongers pay by hitting them in the pocketbook. One tactic was "trashing," damaging property related to the military-industrial complex, such as the university's Social Research Institute, where counterinsurgency programs were being developed against guerrilla fighters in Southeast Asia. Our strengthened commitment and common purpose drew the few hundred most active SDS members together like no other group I'd ever belonged to.

The trashing tactic was supplemented by a more aggressive version of the "float like a butterfly, sting like a bee" strategy. We blockaded the military-industrial complex recruiters inside campus interview rooms, chained the doors, and fled before the cops arrived. By then most job recruits had given up or been scared away. The university began taking pictures of the disrupters, so we took to wearing ski masks. These new SDS actions were different from the earlier large demonstrations. The old SDS style of organizing big demonstrations took weeks of preparation. Their success or failure was measured by the size of the crowd. These new actions were almost daily smaller events that a relative few of the already converted could plan overnight. They made it virtually impossible for the recruiters to conduct any business. I summarized this strategy as "Another day, another action."

We were following the routine script while preventing a GE recruiter from conducting on-campus interviews at the end of February 1970. But it was a surprisingly warm day. Several demonstrators had taken off their ski masks while occupying the stuffy office and were photographed as they fled. As the police arrived, one woman tried to disable the camera. The police tackled her, dragged her through the "engine arch" that separated the Gothic building at the edge of the campus from the street, and threw her in a waiting police wagon. We stormed through the arch to free her, but found a phalanx of police protecting the van. Hundreds of student bystanders quickly surrounded the action. Engineering students hung out the windows of their building cheering the police on.

I watched with fascinated horror as several collectives singled out vulnerable policemen and attacked. Other police rushed to their aid pummeling the street fighters and throwing them in the van. My legs would not obey my brain. At first I dashed around pointlessly like a chicken with its head cut off, and then I stood frozen. Instinct cried, Flee! Don't let "them" get you in their clutches! while loyalty demanded that I join the fray. For an instant it felt as if I had risen outside my body and was looking down on my immobile form. The incongruity of the scene from above assaulted me. Familiar street, bright sun reflecting off parked cars, dirty piles of melting snow covered with cops and SDSers clubbing and kicking one another. Then I snapped back, yelled, and joined others throwing iceballs at the cops. I recognized friends in the human chain that failed to prevent the van carrying a dozen of our comrades from pulling away, but could not join them. Suddenly silence replaced screaming, and everything was still.

None from the commune had been arrested. Elli was at work and didn't even hear about the event until the end of the day. When she got home we were sitting on our downstairs living room couch in shock. The phone rang almost immediately after she arrived, with a call to attend a hastily arranged emergency meeting. The Chicago Seven defendants had been convicted of traveling across state lines to disrupt the Democratic National Convention.

Campuses across the country had been primed to erupt if the defendants, respected antiwar leaders, were convicted. SDS held a meeting just before dinner to plan an evening march to city hall. After the day's street battle, the police were patrolling the campus perimeter with automatic rifles pointing out of open patrol-car windows. It began to rain, and we worried that the demonstration would be small. Some of us at the meeting feared the upcoming confrontation that evening might make that day's street fight seem like a minor skirmish. The confrontation might even turn deadly. I looked around at the 120 of us jammed into the meeting room and wondered which of my comrades might not be alive by morning. I'm sure I wasn't the only one who was frightened, but we were resolute. We planned to parade past the major dormitories just after dinner, gain what support we could, and head downtown.

Despite the weather, students poured out of every dorm in numbers we could not have predicted in our wildest dreams. The rain turned to snow, but more people kept coming. SDS wanted to manage the march to prevent further violence, but the couple of dozen strategically placed collectives could not control the crowd, which had swelled to five thousand. Marchers began smashing the windows of businesses adjacent to campus, and an undisciplined mass surged through the sloppy snow toward city hall. The cops attacked the front of the march in force, but that only transformed a single throng into smaller clusters that could trash at will. The commune collective did not feel that smashing things for fun was a good idea. By that time all we wanted to do was get home in one piece as quickly as possible. While other demonstrators fanned out and headed south through Ann Arbor's unprotected downtown, the commune continued west toward our house and quickly left the demonstration in our wake. In a few minutes we were all catching our breath in our living room, having survived the most intense day of political activity we'd ever experienced.

But the next confrontation was already racing at us. The Black Action Movement (BAM) had been patiently pushing for increased minority enrollment for the entire school year. They finally became fed up with the administration's stalling and set March 17 as "do or die day." If the university would not comply with their demands for increased minority enrollment on that date, they would call a campus-wide strike and shut the university down. SDS enthusiastically supported their demands and started organizing. We canvassed the dorms over the next two weeks, speaking to receptive groups. The BAM rally on the seventeenth was well attended and quickly turned confrontational when the university refused to budge. Some BAM members were arrested.

Elli had planned to quit her job in mid-April in anticipation of our early-May departure for Europe. Instead she left work in March to become Women's Liberation delegate to the BAM strike steering committee, and spent eighteen-hour days involved in planning events and actions. As the "do or die day" rally wound down, Elli and Randy spotted university president Robin Fleming heading for his office. I joined the few SDS collectives that chased and cornered him at the entrance to the administration building. He thought he had escaped with only a tongue-lashing until sometime later, when he discovered that someone had spray-painted a large red stripe down the back of his suit jacket.

Chanting "Open it up or shut it down!" BAM and its allies swarmed the campus for a week of disruption of business as usual. How could a faculty member who wanted to teach what remained of his class do so if teams of strikers burst into his class to argue with him about his racism? Who would stay in classroom buildings that, with the aid of chemistry-student-made stink bombs, now smelled worse than the town dump? How could students hear what the professor was saying with a snaking line of up to eight thousand student strikers singing at the top of their lungs in the corridors?

After a week of effective disruption, the university reached a compromise plan with BAM to increase minority enrollment and develop a black studies program. All charges against BAM members who had been arrested were dropped, and the campus quieted quickly. Except for Susan, who was organizing the first Earth Day protest, which was set for April 1, our small commune began to come down off its two-month adrenaline rush. My weight had dropped below 150, and Elli's below 100, but we had been passionately making the revolution and hardly noticed. We had just helped orchestrate a campaign that brought a major American institution to its knees. Our actions were undermining the military-industrial complex and smashing racism. We felt we were changing the world.

And the commune was working. Randy, Rayna, and Susan had

become our colleagues, comrades, and family. We still had bumpy moments. One evening the five of us decided to play a game of Monopoly. Although my obsession with the game had passed, I still remembered all its details. I anticipated an all-night marathon, but Elli had a string of bad luck and soon had no money to pay even the paltry rental on one of Randy's properties. Rayna cavalierly gave her "cash." I said we should talk about whether we would allow loans. Rayna responded that it was a gift, not a loan. Randy objected, but Rayna declared socialism and offered to pool her money with all who needed it. Susan thought this was an excellent idea, but Randy and I became apoplectic. You're ruining the game, you're missing its point! we cried. No, *you're* missing the point, the women declared; Why should we play by these stupid capitalist pig rules? Randy and I stormed off. Perhaps the bright blue sky of revolution had a few clouds in it, but I was so gung-ho that I couldn't see them.

Michigan's semester ended in late April, and the campus became eerily silent. But protests continued at other campuses not yet on semester break. Four nonviolent student protesters were shot and killed by Ohio National Guardsmen at Kent State University that first week in May, and three more students were killed at Jackson State in Mississippi a few days later. The media focused on the deaths of the four white students. To this day, in most of white America, Kent State remains a dramatic historical event while the black Jackson State victims have been a culturally insignificant afterthought.

Elli and I spent several days visiting my parents in Florida after the semester ended. We were joined by Michael and Ann, their daughter, Ivy, and their recently adopted son, Gregory. My parents were very upset with Elli's and my militancy. At the close of one argument Abel muttered, not quite under his breath: "I'm afraid I'll never see you again." His fears echoed my own, but I did not admit that to him. I was intellectually convinced of the necessity of our increasingly violent tactics. But I was learning how inept I was in violent confrontations, and I doubted I could endure too many of them. It probably allayed both our fears that Elli and I were scheduled to leave for a summer of anthropological fieldwork in Europe the following week.

Elli and I felt we were betraying the revolution by leaving the country to do fieldwork, but we could not let Professor Wolf down. We left what we ruefully called the war zone, and within two weeks Elli and I were ensconced in a Catalan peasant village of three hundred in the foothills of the Pyrenees. Cultural anthropological fieldwork suited me because its participant-observer method of information gathering was in sync with the way I had entered new social situations since I was a child. I grew up being observant and cautious so as not to offend anyone inadvertently, and that meshed well with how cultural anthropologists were supposed to behave when they first encountered the people they planned to study. Elli and I acted as sponges, becoming almost fluent in Spanish, soaking up as much knowledge as possible.

Suddenly so far removed from the SDS life we'd been living, we began to view our actions of the past year with growing detachment and criticism. We walked the lushly forested hills amid birdsong, keeping vigilant eyes out for the tiny brown vipers that lived in the area. Our daily goals shifted from smashing the state to polishing off the liter of potent sherrylike red wine we were served with our midday meal. We talked at length, and within weeks concluded that we had taken a wrong turn politically. We reminisced about how once we laughed and had fun with our politics. Until recently we'd never taken ourselves too seriously and never lost sight of the absurd in the world. But in the past year we'd become deadly serious. Our recent actions had been motivated by responsive anger rather than the joy of creating a better world. We found we could bridge the cultural chasms that separated us from the villagers. We had been doing the opposite at home. We were distancing ourselves from the vast majority of Americans by fighting and throwing rocks at windows. Until the last year we'd done our best to convince those who did not agree with us. We'd had some success, but we'd become frustrated with the pace of our progress. When we switched from demonstrations to actions, we in effect said to hell with those we failed to convince. Now Elli and I realized that we needed to get more Americans to see our point of view, but we'd never succeed if we failed to connect with them. We concluded that we must have been crazy to think we could get increasing numbers of Americans to support our revolutionary outlook by calling them names and smashing windows in our cities. When we rejoined Randy, Rayna, and Susan at the end of the summer, we learned they had had similar realizations.

A chill of fear and frustration cloaked Ann Arbor by the time we returned in September 1970. We could not recapture the spring momentum, and felt powerless, like farmers whose carefully tended crop faced an early killing frost. The core of SDS support remained, but those on the periphery vanished. Five years of growing radicalism were evaporating. Our newfound questions about our previous tactics contributed to our political paralysis.

Fragmentation of a different sort soon plagued the commune. We added a new member that September, and she quickly became a divisive force. Discord was emerging between the couples and single people. "Smash monogamy" had become a New Left cultural slogan, but the two strong couples were unwilling to give up the primacy of their relationships. I remember Randy, in typical fashion, trying to break the tension by banging on the tree in the front yard while chanting, "Smash mahogany!"

Elli got a new job in the fall and found living with graduate students increasingly frustrating. Dropping a hard-earned hourly wage into the communal financial pot was not the same as contributing a government stipend that arrived like monthly manna from heaven. At twenty-two, I had completed my master's degree. I was on a fast track to finish course work, take preliminary examinations in the spring, and start doctoral dissertation research afterward. But my ambivalence toward a life of scholarship resurfaced. Maybe I should live in a "real" American city before I made a career choice I might regret.

Randy and Rayna were moving forward with their Ph.D. plans and prepared to spend an entire year starting the following spring in their French village. We had planned to live together indefinitely, but abruptly it became impossible to build our lives together.

The six of us could not work through the growing tensions and could no longer locate the sense of joy that had bound us together. The commune split up precipitously. Elli and I were living in a small apartment by early 1971. We didn't even have our cat, which we'd found frozen to death by the side of the house a year earlier.

How could things go so wrong so quickly? How could we have failed so utterly? I wanted to go backward, to get a second chance, but time is unyielding. Ann Arbor became haunted with lost possibilities and old friends we avoided meeting on the street. We continued seeing Randy and Rayna, but were constrained with one another. Interacting with constraint was a negation of all we had worked to build, and our time together became melancholy. Political and social depression were hopelessly entwined. Over the last several years we had ardently believed that our social lives had to be consistent with our politics. How could we build a socialist world if we failed so miserably when we tried to collectivize our social lives? Our arrogant but joyful irreverence and commitment had been replaced by sadness and uncertainty. We feared, but refused to believe, that the most exciting time of our lives was behind us. We were desperate to recapture our awareness of purpose and community, but we knew it could not happen in Ann Arbor.

Many in SDS were getting ready to leave town. The plan was to move en masse to a city and transform Students for a Democratic Society into Movement for a Democratic Society. But we could not reach a consensus. Several of us decided to return to our northeastern roots. We sought a small city with diversified industry to do community organizing. Springfield, Massachusetts, met all our criteria, and it carried a special bonus as well. The economics department of Western New England College had recently hired my brother. Michael and Ann's presence in Springfield added a welcome family harbor in an uncertain sea of change.

I did not burn my academic bridges, however. I shifted my focus from European peasant studies to urban anthropology. I pitched my move to Springfield as the first step toward getting a predoctoral dissertation grant from the National Institute of Mental Health (NIMH) to do an urban anthropological field study in a small New England city.

We were handed an unexpected financial boost as well. Earlier that year Anne and Abel told me that the remainder of the trust fund collected for Michael and me as children was ready for distribution. I received almost eight thousand dollars before we left for Europe. With uncharacteristic caution, we had decided to keep these funds for ourselves, at least for the time being. The commune's rapid demise that fall showed the wisdom of that decision. Elli and I put most of it in savings, but spent two thousand dollars on a new robin's egg blue Toyota sedan.

We circled the country from May to July in our little blue Toyota, visiting dispersed friends, mourning lost magic, and contemplating our new lives in Springfield. And we decided it was time to start a family.

CHAPTER 5

Rosenberg Son

———◆◆◆◆◆———

"ROBBY. IT'S YOUR BROTHER ON THE PHONE," ELLI WHISPERED. I'D
been rocking our five-month-old daughter, Jenny, to sleep for the
night. Michael should have known better than to call at this time.
He'd be pissed if I called at bedtime for four-year-old Ivy or three-
year-old Gregory.

"I'm sorry to call now," he said, "but I just got off the phone with
Walter Schneir. That bastard Nizer is reading Mom and Dad's letters
on TV."

"So what?" I gave him my typical nonreaction to disturbing news.

Michael explained that Walter and Miriam Schneir, whom I'd seen
only a couple of times since visiting them during my senior year in high
school, had to obtain permission from the trust that held the copyright to the letters to include them in *Invitation to an Inquest*, their
book about the Rosenberg frame-up. Walter believed Michael and I
held the copyright, since the trust had been dissolved. Walter thought
that if we didn't sue Louis Nizer for stealing our copyright, the letters
would become public domain, rendering our copyright worthless.

We talked a bit more before I said lamely, "I don't know. I need to talk to Elli about this."

I stood frozen at the phone. My right thumb and forefinger toyed with the ends of my curly hair that hung over my ear. Had the time come for Michael and me to come out? What would that mean? I slumped slowly into a nearby chair.

I hadn't yet recovered from the demise of the commune or my political malaise that followed SDS's collapse two years earlier. But we were building a comfortable community in Springfield, and it was a good place to raise a family. I was teaching anthropology part-time at Western New England College, where my brother taught economics. I'd developed an urban anthropology doctoral dissertation project in Springfield, and recently completed a grant application to fund my work. Elli had worked as a preschool teacher in a local Head Start program until Jenny was born, and now was working part-time as a counselor in an abortion clinic. Two part-time jobs enabled us to share child-care responsibilities.

Springfield was an old industrial city of 150,000 situated on the east bank of the Connecticut River, 90 miles west of Boston and 135 miles northeast of New York City. Big towns and small cities flanked the polluted river, but Springfield was almost surrounded by beautifully forested hills. It had been one of the first centers of the industrial revolution in the early nineteenth century, and was ethnically diverse. About 15 percent of its population was black, and its slightly smaller Hispanic population was growing rapidly. A mix of Poles, Italians, Irish, Quebecois, and Portuguese provided its skilled workers and a growing number of professionals. The original Protestant colonizers owned most of its factories, banks, and insurance companies. Springfield was a cultural and political backwater, but its location at the intersection of I-90 and I-91 left most of New England or the New York City area accessible by car within three hours.

Springfield was more liberal than the Midwest, but it retained an

Our family just after Rachel's graduation from law school (2002).

The Meeropol clan, December 2000. *Back row, left to right:* Elli, me, Ann, Michael, and Thomas (the husband of Michael and Ann's daughter, Ivy). *Front row, left to right:* Ivy, Rachel, Jenn, and Greg (Michael and Ann's son).

Reading my lines before an audience of 3,500 at the performance of "Celebrate the Children of Resistance" in Berkeley, California, in 2000. *(Jeffrey Blankfort)*

Talking with Susan Sarandon, one of the RFC's earliest high-profile supporters, at an RFC reception in Manhattan (1993).

Me, in front of the Albuquerque apartment David and Ruth Greenglass rented in 1944 (1993). *(Margaret Randall)*

Answering reporters' questions at the same location. *(Margaret Randall)*

On the road with Marshall Perlin (left), playing with other babies when I can't play with my own (1977).

Rachel is not sure my mixing work with child care is a good idea (1977).

Jenny, age eight, on my lap in our apartment in Berkeley (1980).

Elli, Jenny (to my left), and Rachel in Springfield shortly after our return from Berkeley (1981).

Talking with Ron Kovic, author of *Born on the Fourth of July*, during the United 25th Anniversary Movement rally, June 19, 1978. (© *L. Delevingne 1978*)

I'm speaking about reopening the Rosenberg case (1974).

Me and Michael, 1974. (*Barry Rosenthal*)

Elli, around the time we met, studying in a tree at Earlham (1965).

With my Earlham roommate, Arthur, fooling around during sophmore year (1966).

One of Elli's and my wedding pictures (1968).

On the steps of our apartment in Ann Arbor (1969).

Summer camp, in this instance Camp Woodland, was the high point of my childhood (1959).

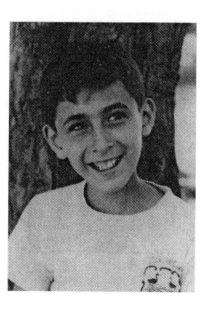

The Meeropol family (I'm on the right) in front of the Hastings house (1963).

Anne and Abel, shortly before Anne's death in 1973.

Anne Meeropol, me, and Michael singing in the living room of the Meeropols' apartment at 149th Street and Riverside Drive (1954).

Me, Abel Meeropol, and Michael playing with Richard Posner's old train set at the 149th Street apartment (1954).

Me, center, wearing my favorite T-shirt while celebrating my tenth birthday at a neighbor's apartment (1959).

When I was two, my mother liked my hair too much to have it cut (1949).

Me and Michael wearing Brooklyn Dodger caps with Grandma Sophie in front of the White House. This demonstration (June 15, 1953) to spare my parents' lives is the only one I remember attending. *(AP/Wide World Photos)*

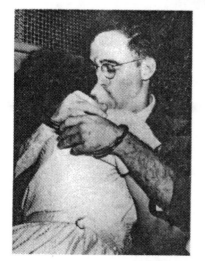

My parents kissing in the prison van after their arraignment (1950). *(Corbis/©)*

element of conservative small-town parochialism not present in the bigger eastern cities. I thought of it as a typical slice of America, New England style.

We lived in the modest second-floor apartment of a triple-decker house in a white working-class neighborhood. Rents were cheap, and we had five small rooms. We slept on a mattress resting on a plywood board mounted on cinder blocks. More blocks and plywood provided low-cost shelving. We purchased old desks, dressers, and chairs at local tag sales for next to nothing. We ate on Elli's parents' old Formica kitchen table. The washing machine and dryer, gifts from both sets of parents on Jenny's birth, were our prize possessions. We'd taped a brightly colored poster of a Vietnamese woman with a baby in her arms and a gun strapped to her shoulder to our bedroom wall. Huey Newton stared at the woman from another wall as he sat regally in a high-backed wicker chair.

"What's the matter?" Elli asked, her annoyance at the interruption of my bedtime duties turning into concern when she saw my expression.

I recounted what Michael had said. Our first thought was for Jenny. We had a critical decision to make that would affect her entire life. I had personal anxiety as well. My brother and I had been living as Michael and Robert Meeropol for almost twenty years. There had been no media stories about our identity since the custody battle in 1954.

I remember being more concerned about emotional discomfort than physical fear. Would people point me out on the street and whisper behind my back, "Do you know who *he* is?" How would it feel to be a curiosity or worse, an object of pity? Would people want to know me or shun me because of my parentage? I imagined walking around town with a neon sign above my head that flashed: ROSENBERG SON.

This was not the first time we'd considered going public. My brother had looked forward to changing his name back to Rosenberg when he reached twenty-one. Anne and Abel persuaded him to wait until *I* was twenty-one. By then he was married and ready to start raising a family; his daughter, Ivy, was born the following fall. By that time we had been living anonymously for fifteen years, and realized how much our lives might change if we reclaimed our birth name. We had repeatedly postponed any decision that might draw public attention.

Now, in April 1973, the publication of a book about our parents' case by the famous trial lawyer Louis Nizer presented a challenge. Even worse than publishing large sections of our parents' prison correspondence without permission, he removed all reference to my brother and me from the letters he reprinted. We felt that he did so to support his thesis that our parents loved communism more than they loved their children. This made my blood boil. I remember ranting at my brother: "They were convicted of conspiracy, not child abuse!" And just as bad, in the concluding paragraphs of the book, he portrayed Michael and me as well-adjusted and productive Americans and implied that this was because we had rejected our parents' values.

Nizer's distortions presented a stark choice: Either we use this opportunity to sue him for copyright violations, correct these hurtful misrepresentations, and abandon the safety afforded by the anonymity of the name "Meeropol," or we remain silent and let all those who read what was predicted to be a bestseller conclude that Nizer's portrayal was accurate.

Elli and I spent many hours over the course of several weeks discussing this fork in the road. We talked with Michael and Ann and with Anne and Abel. The six of us decided that we might file suit against Nizer for copyright violation, but we needed to consult with an attorney. I felt that we had two separate questions to decide. Since I was unwilling to give up our anonymity unless we had a real case, we needed a legal assessment of the viability of our claim before we went further. Second, even if we had a strong case, we might decide that we did not wish to forsake our camouflage in any event. This was a very difficult decision, and I wished to proceed cautiously. I wanted to know if we could file suit and still maintain our anonymity.

Walter and Miriam and Mort Sobell, my parents' codefendant, had tried six months earlier to enlist my brother and me in a campaign to attack Nizer's conclusion that our parents were guilty, but we had refused. The Schneirs and Sobell were already public figures who were engaged in the ongoing political debate that still swirled around my parents' case. At that point we hadn't read the references to us in the Nizer book, didn't know that he had violated our copyright, and did not wish to break our silence simply because one more bad book had been published. But now we knew that this book not only perpetuated lies about our parents; it also misrepresented our relationship with them and implied that we had rejected what they stood for.

Three years previously Mort had been released from prison after serving twenty years, most of them at Alcatraz. Michael contacted Marshall Perlin, who had been Mort's lawyer. We arranged to meet with Perlin to discuss our potential copyright claim with him.

Michael and I took the three-hour drive to Manhattan and met with the lawyer in his midtown office. Marshall Perlin was a bear of a man. I took an immediate liking to him, perhaps because he subliminally reminded me of Manny Bloch. His slicked-back, jet-black hair, high forehead, and prominent chin provided a fitting launching pad for his commanding baritone. He smoked constantly, dined on take-out deli food, and practically lived in his office.

Perlin had entered my parents' defense during the final two days of their lives. He and another attorney made heroic but futile efforts to find a judge to issue a stay of execution after the Supreme Court vacated Douglas's stay. Perlin had also been Mort's attorney for almost twenty years, and he came with Mort's endorsement. Mort assured us that no one intimidated Perlin and no one alive knew the record of my parents' case better.

Perlin advised us that he thought we had a strong copyright claim. We asked if he thought we could pursue this matter while maintaining our anonymity. I now believe that Perlin had a duty to tell us flatly that this was impossible, but at that time his less definitive response left me wishfully believing that anonymity remained a possibility.

Our major concern was the impact the decision to go public would have on our children. We did not want to endanger them or subject them to harassment. But post–Vietnam War and Watergate-absorbed America provided a much safer political landscape for "going public" than had the McCarthy era. The decision that we made—Michael and Ann and Elli and I—was fraught with worry but inevitable. We'd always maintained that we would reclaim our heritage when the time was right. I felt that we might never have a better opportunity, and feared that if we didn't act now we probably never would.

In retrospect I believe the decision we made was very positive for our children. We were on the offensive, first with our suit against Nizer and later with our FOIA suit against various government agencies. Jenny and Rachel, who was born in 1975, heard discussions about their grandparents and the "reopening effort" from their infancy onward. We never sat either one of them down to tell them about their grandparents; they just grew up with it. They can no more tell you when they first heard about the case than they can tell you when they first knew their names. It was who they were.

This relaxed acceptance of their rather remarkable ancestry occasionally generated peculiar incidents. Jenny's third-grade teacher once asked the class if anyone knew what the government did. Jenny eagerly raised her hand and answered that the government had killed her grandparents. The teacher skillfully moved on to more acceptable answers, but telephoned our home that evening with her strong concerns about our daughter's "delusions." This led to a conference at which Elli explained Jenny's answer.

Many years later a *New York Times* article mentioned that a granddaughter of Ethel and Julius Rosenberg would attend Wesleyan University in the fall. Rachel was talking with another freshman at a mixer the first week of school. They noted that their class contained a lot of interesting people, and he said, "I heard the granddaughter of the Rosenbergs is in our class." Rachel's response was matter of fact: "That would be me."

In 1997, a documentary filmmaker interviewed both my children. My daughters reported that the interviewer seemed surprised when they told her that being a granddaughter of the Rosenbergs was more boon than burden. Their pride in their heritage placed them within an international community of support. It was never a dark secret or a source of tension for them. Understanding the choices made by both their grandparents and their parents helped form their worldview and gave them a clear sense of right and wrong. Although I am hardly an objective source, I believe it made them stronger and better people.

It was also a positive step for Michael and me. Although at first we were apprehensive about going public, we anticipated filing suit with growing excitement. We made several trips to Perlin's office that May and June. The six-hour round-trip journey flew by as we mapped out the contents of our complaint and discussed future plans. For as long as I could remember we'd suffered whatever was said about our parents in silence. We had never had the opportunity or the emotional freedom to give voice to our opinions about our parents' trial and execution. Now we had a chance to speak out. And I had a political focus to replace what I'd lost at the end of the 1960s. I might be incapable of engaging cops in pitched street fights, but here was a politically important battle I could wage. We were going to strike back and set the record straight. This was just the start of a campaign that would make "them" sorry they'd ever picked on our family.

We also relished becoming plaintiffs in a multimillion dollar lawsuit. I was naïve: Dollar signs danced before my eyes, and I began spinning scenarios about how we'd spend our winnings. I was just twenty-six, and my brother, who was so much older—almost middle-aged at thirty—was just as naïve. We fantasized about spending the money before we even filed suit. We felt that it would be wrong to keep the money for ourselves; we'd have to do something "good" with it. Michael and I agreed that we would start a foundation in our parents' honor with the money we would win. We didn't know what this foundation would do, but we'd figure it out. We even picked a name: "Rosenberg Children's Fund." Thinking about it now, it isn't clear who was to have benefited from a fund with that name. Perhaps this reflected our ambivalence about parting with what we imagined would be a great deal of money. We claimed damages totaling six million dollars for copyright infringement, invasion of privacy, and defamation of character.

As it happened, this legal action never generated our pot of gold, but the seed that would one day become the Rosenberg Fund for Children nonetheless took root in my mind. I also gained strength from my wholehearted collaboration with Michael. In the past he had pushed me to reclaim our birthright, and I had dragged my feet. I had always believed that one day I would act. Although at the time I resented Nizer's imposing this decision upon us, I have no idea how long I'd have continued to say, "Someday," if it hadn't been for Nizer's book. I didn't dwell on it, but occasionally I felt uncertain that I'd ever have the courage to come out as a Rosenberg son. This led me to suspect that publicly acknowledging my parents would be emotionally beneficial for me. I could only express this in private because Perlin cautioned that even hinting that Nizer had done us a favor would be the death knell of the aspects of our lawsuit proclaiming he had invaded our privacy and defamed us.

In fact Nizer's book did defame our family. While Nizer rejected Judge Kaufman's death sentence as unduly harsh, he nevertheless joined him in condemning Ethel and Julius as parents: "Even [Judge Kaufman's] death sentence did not make [the Rosenbergs] hate him as much as his slur upon them as parents. The reason was that they knew subconsciously, at least, that there was some validity to the accusation. They had failed even before their arrest. Although brimming with love, they had not communicated it sufficiently to Michael and Bobby [*sic*] to prevent their neurotic behavior" (Louis Nizer, *The Implosion Conspiracy* [New York: Doubleday, 1973] p. 367).

There is no evidence that I was "neurotic" before my parents' arrest, and I certainly do not remember feeling unloved. Family members and others report that my brother was overly demanding, not because my parents had difficulty communicating their love to him, but rather because they doted on him and had trouble setting limits.

No evidence supports Nizer's further claim that my parents courted martyrdom. Their lawyers, at their direction, did everything they could think of to forestall that event. They were ecstatic when Justice Douglas stayed the execution because they believed that it might never take place. Their letters, both those apparently written for public consumption and those that they never expected to be published, reflect their love for each other, their children, and for life in general. Nizer concluded that my parents were guilty, and so dismissed their claims that they went to their deaths because they were innocent, or because they would not place others in the same position in which the Greenglasses had placed them. But Nizer's reasoning is circular: In his mind their presumed guilt made martyrdom the only reason possible for their refusal to confess. He never considered that they didn't confess because the government wanted them to confess to things they did not do.

I knew we could not remain silent in the face of these lies, but was unwilling to confront the personal consequences; so I persisted with my irrational belief that we could file suit and still maintain our anonymity even as my excitement over striking back grew. That hope was shattered within hours of our filing the suit on June 19, 1973, the twentieth anniversary of our parents' execution. We were required to list our names and addresses on the complaint Perlin filed in Federal Court in New York City. A reporter from the local paper called both Michael and me at our homes that evening. As planned, we both said that we wished to remain anonymous. The headline in the *Springfield Union* the next morning read: ROSENBERG SONS SHUN PUBLICITY. The article contained our names and addresses.

My potentially cataclysmic secret was out, but my life did not alter dramatically. I endured a few tearful embraces and intense conversations with friends who hadn't known. Such emotional outbursts made me very uncomfortable, but I also felt relief to have the information out in the open.

I'd imagined that investigative reporters seeking the story of what we'd done since 1953 would impose themselves upon us. We gave interviews to *Ramparts* and *University Review*, two left-wing magazines, but the mainstream media left us alone. A filmmaker who was working with the Schneirs on a documentary about our parents' case for PBS television asked to interview us. It was easy to grant him an exclusive because no other TV outlet was interested.

Being on camera for the first time in twenty years did not make me nervous. Michael and I were filmed together in late summer in a park-like backyard of a suburban New York home. There were no crowds, and the filmmakers were very supportive, promising to edit out embarrassing misstatements. We were not presented as experts. We stated our belief in our parents' innocence. I rather inarticulately called for "some sort of" government investigation of our parents' frame-up.

This film (*The Unquiet Death of Julius and Ethel Rosenberg*) raised serious questions about the fairness of my parents' trial. It brought to light for the first time that the key prosecution witnesses, David Greenglass and Harry Gold, originally did not agree that Harry had used the password "I come from Julius" when he introduced himself to David at their supposed meeting in Albuquerque. This one and only meeting between the two most important government witnesses was essential to the prosecution's case. Without proof that this meeting took place and that my father had had a hand in arranging it, the government could not have obtained a conviction against my parents.

The link between Gold and Greenglass was critical because, while Gold testified about frequent contact with KGB agents, he never said he met either of my parents. The Greenglasses, on the other hand, recalled many interactions with my parents, but Greenglass wasn't even sure he'd ever met a Russian. This Albuquerque encounter was the linchpin of the government's conspiracy case because it was the only event that simultaneously linked the alleged key conspirators—Gold, Greenglass, and my father—to the conspiracy. Now for the first time an FBI agent stated on camera that he had suggested to Greenglass after Greenglass was imprisoned that the code phrase contained Julius's name. This undermined the government's claim that my father played a role in facilitating the Gold-Greenglass connection. I took this as further proof of my parents' innocence.

Being plaintiffs in a civil suit was expensive. We would have to raise funds to finance it. With Perlin's aid, Michael and I established the Rosenberg Sons Legal Fund, and so began my fund-raising career. Anne Meeropol had experience in this area and started to raise money for the suit as well. She would be a powerful addition to our organizing effort.

We planned our first fund-raising party in New York City that fall. I was anxious about speaking about my parents' case in public, but this party was set in a very safe environment. Michael and I would be together. Our hosts were people I had known since childhood, and those attending were longtime Rosenberg supporters. The first party went smoothly. My nervousness evaporated once I started speaking. Once my initial secret was out I had nothing more to hide. It felt good to be speaking freely with political allies, and the audiences I addressed were extremely supportive. As the months passed I became more comfortable in similar situations.

• • •

In late September 1973 Anne Meeropol had a massive heart attack and died. Even though we'd known that she had heart disease and that her family had a strong history of heart problems, we were stunned. By the age of twenty-six I had had four parents and already lost three of them. I clutched at positive straws. At least she'd lived to meet our daughter. At least she'd lived to see us go public. Abel told me that raising us had given her a lot of joy.

Michael and I flew down to south Florida immediately and spent several days with Abel. He talked to us about his life more openly than ever before. We learned how proud he was that he and Anne had kept separate last names for two years after they had gotten married in 1929. They felt it was wrong for a woman to give up hers, but the constant hassle this unheard-of behavior generated eventually caused them to give in to tradition. We learned how guilty he felt about preventing Anne from taking a role in a movie while they were in Hollywood because he feared what might happen to their relationship if she became too successful.

Abel seemed lost in the past. He was wrapped up in reviewing his old writing, and puttered around the house filling time with pointless tasks. Anne had been his ambassador to the public sphere. A few months before her death she had expressed her concern to me that Abel's personality was changing, and that he was no longer writing anything new. Now Michael and I feared he would withdraw into a grief-stricken world if we left him alone. We asked him to move to Springfield so that he could live near us, but he stated emphatically that they'd have to carry him out of his house in a body bag. All we could do was keep in contact as much as possible.

A month after Anne died, Emily Alman, who along with her husband, Dave, had founded the National Committee to Secure Justice in the Rosenberg Case more than twenty years before, contacted us about spearheading an effort to reopen the case. She said that a new generation should be given a chance to review the case, and that maybe we could clear their names. She organized a meeting we attended in New York City at which key Rosenberg supporters from the 1950s pointed out that growing awareness of our government's lies and dirty tricks in Vietnam and during the Watergate scandal increased the likelihood of public acceptance that our government might frame people for crimes they did not commit. Morton Sobell disagreed. Although he had supported the idea of suing Nizer, he cautioned against starting a new Rosenberg committee. Since my brother and I had already decided to pursue this course, I didn't even ask why he opposed forming a new committee. Disregarding Mort's advice, we agreed to start the National Committee to Reopen the Rosenberg Case (NCRRC) by organizing a mass meeting in New York City on the twenty-first anniversary of our parents' execution.

The media began to notice us. In January 1974 ABC Television aired Stanley Kramer's dramatization of my parents' trial, starring Brenda Vaccaro as Ethel and Allan Arbus as Julius. Their lines were taken directly from the trial transcript, but some critics attacked the show for being pro-Rosenberg. Vaccaro and Arbus played my parents as honest and heroic. Allen Garfield portrayed David Greenglass as a slimy liar. The show left the impression that something was dreadfully wrong with my parents' trial and execution.

The ABC show was followed a month later by the PBS broadcast of *The Unquiet Death of Julius and Ethel Rosenberg* documentary, raising more questions about my parents' guilt. The *New York Times* and the Associated Press did feature-length interviews with us after the TV shows aired. The Sunday *Times* carried our interview and picture at the bottom of its front page on March 10, 1974, my brother's thirty-first birthday. The AP feature ran in most major Sunday papers the same day.

Once these articles appeared, the media clamored for follow-up stories with us. As the publicity built, we signed a book contract to tell our story. Michael and I dickered with the publisher about the book's contents. They wanted us to reveal what it was like to live in the shadow of the electric chair, and to provide intimate details of our lives since the execution. We wanted them to reprint our parents' prison letters, over a hundred of which had been published in 1952, with Manny Bloch's help to raise funds for the campaign to save their lives. A revised edition of these letters, *The Testament of Julius and Ethel Rosenberg*, was published after their execution to raise funds for our support. But fewer than a quarter of all the letters they had written while in prison had been published. We wanted a larger cross-section of the public to have the opportunity to read as many of the letters as possible. We compromised; our book *We Are Your Sons* contained one hundred letters and snippets of our personal stories.

I was convinced that the dice were rolling our way. I confidently predicted before the twenty-five hundred supporters who packed our initial NCRRC rally at Carnegie Hall on June 19, 1974, the twenty-first anniversary of my parents' execution, that: "In the next year we are going to blow the lid on this case." Such youthful optimism!

Petrified of publicity for two decades, I now learned to welcome media attention. My major frustration with journalists was that they did not give us the opportunity to present the factual basis for our contention that our parents were innocent. One such incident stands out in my mind. Before the Carnegie Hall rally, NBC news reporter Betty Rollin interviewed us for a feature story about the rally to be aired on the NBC evening news. We spent an hour during the interview providing her with factual details to support our position. In preparation for the interview, Michael and I had condensed this material into sound bites so that she could include at least one of them. But none were used. Instead we were shown making a general claim of innocence and, with a packed Carnegie Hall in the background, Rollin wrapped up the segment on camera by saying: "The Rosenberg sons have lots of supporters; now all they need are some facts."

I also remember one newspaper reporter badgering me a few months later about the possibility that my parents were guilty. I responded that anything was possible. I explained further that mathematicians state that in some instances one plus one does not equal two. "So anything is possible," I concluded, "but I believe in my parents' innocence as firmly as I believe that one and one equals two." That journalist included a sentence in his article that the younger son of the Rosenbergs admitted his parents might have been guilty. For the remainder of the 1970s I took even greater pains to proclaim my belief in my parents' innocence.

My new life as a Rosenberg son was now in full swing. The dean at Western New England College informed me that the college would not renew my contract for the fall 1974 semester since I had been teaching part-time for three years in a row. I learned later that the three-year rule was applied only when convenient. I don't know why they applied it to me then. Perhaps it was because I had resisted the chairman of the management department's efforts to teach the kind of anthropology that would help students more effectively market products to other cultures. I doubt that I endeared myself to him when I said that I would not help American businessmen sell Coca-Cola to the natives because I had taken a firm stand against tooth decay. I suspect, however, that the college was willing to have one Rosenberg son on the faculty but felt uncomfortable with two.

In any event I was already planning to divide my time between the reopening effort and my child-care responsibilities. The NCRRC set up an office in New York City and hired a staff of one. An executive committee, composed mostly of veterans from the previous Rosenberg and Sobell committees, Michael, and me, set NCRRC policy. We had already augmented the legal team by adding veteran progressive lawyers Max Millman and Sam Gruber, and although they generously contributed some of their time, the legal bills grew. Our plan was relatively simple: First, use the funds generated by the Carnegie Hall rally to pay initial legal expenses and for an office that would develop a national mailing list of donors. Next, the office would organize a series of fund-raising receptions and public events and start an annual round of fund-raising mailings to feed funds into an FOIA suit we would file the following year.

In the wake of the Watergate scandal, Congress passed a strengthened FOIA, which was to take effect in February 1975. We planned to make our administrative request immediately after it went into effect, and to follow that up with a court case if necessary. Ultimately we expected to use the dirt we dug up to file a wrongful death action that we hoped would one day clear our parents' names.

Michael and I were supposed to generate publicity, speak at parties, public events, and colleges to produce more funds, and to hold personal meetings with potential major donors. Because I was no longer teaching, the committee assumed that I would engage in these activities full-time. My brother agreed to take a year's leave of absence in 1975 from his work so he could join me on the road in January.

Elli had focused on feminist issues since our move to Springfield. She'd helped found the Springfield Women's Center and later the Springfield Women's Union, which developed programs to meet women's educational, health, child-care, and political needs. She'd been active in a reproductive rights group and in a modern underground railroad of sorts that facilitated women's trips to New York, where abortion was legal. After *Roe* v. *Wade*, she worked as an abortion counselor for Springfield's first abortion clinic.

With other members of the Women's Union, Elli worked to start an antisexist child-care center. In 1974 Elli and I joined with three other families who had preschool-age children to form an informal playgroup while we navigated the bureaucratic red tape needed to open Mudpie Childcare Cooperative. Although the play group provided Elli and me with some child care, I couldn't travel for long periods of time without contravening our strongly held beliefs that both parents should be equally involved in childrearing. Committee members, most of whom were activists from my parents' generation, took for granted that our wives would understand why they should stay home with our children while we changed the world. Most of them presumed that Michael and I would expect this. But both of our wives worked, and neither Michael nor I wanted to be absentee fathers.

Being an involved father wasn't just an ideological matter for me. I loved hanging out with Jenny and the other little kids. I didn't hesitate to get down on the floor, be a horsy, play with building blocks, read books, or engage in never-ending absurd word games with this group of verbal two- and three-year-olds. It delighted Jenny to be called Jennifer, juniper, conifer, aquifer. (I knew Lucifer also fit, but I omitted it.) It was exhausting but joyful work.

I told the committee that I would only travel ten days a month. In response committee members offered to hire a baby-sitter so I could travel more. I spurned this offer. They just didn't understand how I felt about leaving my two-year-old. My parents had been taken from me when I was three, and I'd be damned if I was going to abandon my child in an effort to show the world how wrong that had been.

Starting in the fall of 1974 my pattern of travel was more like a yo-yo than a tour. The four-day trip I took to St. Louis that October was typical. I spoke at Washington University, held a fund-raising reception, met with the editors of the *St. Louis Post-Dispatch*, and did local TV and radio interviews and talk shows. All the funds generated, including the honoraria, went to the NCRRC, and I returned home exhausted.

The transitions to home were rarely smooth. I was tired and distracted. Elli, who had been a single parent while I was away, wanted to jump back into her adult life. By the time things settled down I was getting ready to leave for the next trip, and the cycle would repeat. Instead of sharing childrearing tasks on a daily basis, I was either trying to be completely available or I was gone. Over the long haul I did plenty of child care, but Elli, who was the more consistent presence, became the primary parent. Neither of us was happy with this deviation from our ideal division of labor, and managing it from day to day strained our relationship.

It would have been easier if I had been able to focus on home life without outside distractions while I was home. But there were long legal and committee meetings to attend in New York City, final revisions to make on the book, and interviews that were too important to put off. Each trip required debriefing and generated future organizing leads to pursue. The pressure from the committee and from Perlin to be more involved was unrelenting, and I was not good at saying no.

Being a Rosenberg son in public no longer terrified me, but it was still problematic. In some ways the fund-raising receptions that started with the Nizer suit were the most difficult. They were emotionally charged events staged in private homes. Many of those who came had fought to save my parents' lives. Before my presentation at these parties, local performers or personalities often read a selection of my parents' prison correspondence. I felt exposed sitting before audiences of fifty or one hundred people while my parents' last words were read. I didn't like receiving applause and special attention simply because I was the son. Sometimes I'd return home after several days of this and feel like I needed to take a shower to wash off layers of emotional residue that clung to me like stale cologne.

Speaking to older audiences invited the kind of response from listeners that caused me difficulty. Invariably someone would tearfully tell me their experience on the evening of my parents' execution. Although these declarations have been a part of my life for almost thirty years, I'm still not comfortable responding to them. I know it is reasonable for people to want to share these experiences with me, but they make me self-conscious, and I fear my body language is giving away my discomfort. I try to be as understanding and responsive as possible, but I don't know how well I succeed.

While I didn't relish the prospect of speaking to crowds of hundreds or thousands, I was told that I was an effective speaker, and I was usually well received. Having performed in the classroom for the past three years helped enormously. I was more comfortable interacting with college-age people than I was with my parents' generation, who frequently referred to me as one of the boys. It was weird: The older adults who attended the receptions treated me as a child, while the students at my lectures treated me as a historical figure.

I reread the major books on the Rosenberg case, and the entire trial transcript. From this I created a college-oriented lecture I called "The Emperor's New Clothes." First I gave students the flavor of the McCarthy period. Next I outlined the government's case against my parents, the key points of testimony, and the major pieces of evidence. I pointed out that because my parents were charged with conspiracy, the government did not need to produce tangible evidence that anyone had stolen anything or had given it to anybody. All they had to do was show that two or more people planned to commit espionage and took one act in furtherance of their plan. I explained that David and Ruth Greenglass, my mother's brother and sister-in-law, testified that my father, Julius Rosenberg, with my mother's help, recruited David into the atomic spy ring in the fall of 1944. David was an army sergeant who had been assigned to work as a machinist at the secret scientific base in Los Alamos, New Mexico, where the first A-bomb was being built. David and Ruth swore that at my father's request David snooped around and gathered data that enabled him to draw two sketches. David and Ruth testified that David gave one sketch, a cross-section of the bomb, to my father at the Rosenberg apartment while he was on leave in September 1945. They stated that Ethel was present at this meeting and typed up the notes David made to explain the sketch. David also swore that he gave a second sketch, the triggering mechanism of the bomb, to Harry Gold when he presented himself at the Greenglasses' Albuquerque apartment. Greenglass testified that Gold used the code phrase "I come from Julius," and matched his cut Jell-O boxtop half with the half Greenglass said my father had cut and had given Greenglass to use as a further recognition signal. The Greenglasses also testified that they had taken passport photographs so they could flee the country, that they deposited the money Gold gave them for one of the sketches in their bank account, and that my parents' console table had been converted into a piece of spy equipment.

Harry Gold took the stand and testified about his lengthy career as a spy courier. He swore that he regularly transported information from atomic scientist Klaus Fuchs to the Soviet Consulate in New York. He corroborated the Greenglasses' story by stating that on one occasion he received information from Greenglass, instead of from Fuchs, after introducing himself to Greenglass with the code phrase and the Jell-O boxtop half. That was the gist of the government's case.

In preparation I'd already written seven key pieces of evidence on a blackboard behind me:

1. I come from Julius.
2. Hotel card
3. Atom sketches
4. Jell-O boxtop
5. Passport photos
6. $400
7. Console table

Then I'd review what researchers had uncovered about this testimony and evidence in the last twenty years.

1. The FBI suggested this password.
2. The hotel card couldn't prove that Harry Gold was in Albuquerque when he supposedly met Greenglass because it had the wrong date, the original had been destroyed, and a handwriting expert said Harry Gold's signature on it was a forgery.

3. Atomic scientists said the sketches were worthless.
4. Since Greenglass cut the Jell-O box in the courtroom during the trial, it provided no independent proof that it was used to identify Gold to Greenglass.
5. The "passport" photos did not show that the Greenglasses planned to flee the country, because they were actually family snapshots.
6. The Greenglasses had several secret bank accounts into which they deposited money on a regular basis and appeared to be involved in black marketeering rather than espionage.
7. My parents purchased the table at Macy's. It had not been hollowed out to convert it into a piece of spy equipment as the Greenglasses had testified.

I'd cross out each item as I refuted it, and when I was finished, no "evidence" was left. I'd conclude by connecting the case to current political issues: National security had been used as a smokescreen to cover up government misconduct for more than twenty years. Since this misconduct grew out of McCarthy-era abuses of power, exposing the wrongs committed against my parents would get to the root of the political skulduggery that produced the Watergate scandal. That was why our FOIA suit was still vitally important in 1975.

Audiences were very receptive to this analysis. And I emphasized that while I believed my parents were innocent, the most important thing was to open all the secret files, expose everything to public scrutiny, and let the chips fall where they may.

Although leaving home caused problems, I enjoyed being on the road and seeing new cities. My hosts were usually local activists whom I enjoyed getting to know. In Louisville I stayed with Carl and Anne Braden, whose *Southern Patriot* newspaper had been the model for the *Northern Patriot* I'd helped produce in the eighth grade. The state had charged them with sedition in retaliation for their efforts to integrate suburban neighborhoods around Louisville during the 1950s. In Chicago I stayed with Evelyn Eldridge, who described how the FBI had rifled through her trash during the 1950s because she was one of the leaders of the Chicago chapter of the Committee to Secure Justice in the Rosenberg Case. It was a thrill to be hosted by my heroes, people from every corner of the country who had resisted during the McCarthy period. As an extra treat, old friends appeared on almost every trip. I saw my eighth-grade girlfriend Ronnie for the first time in more than a decade at a book-signing reception in Los Angeles in 1975. Mark, the friend I'd played ball with on the evening my parents were killed, reintroduced himself to me after a speech I gave in 1993. I stay at my old sociology professor, Tom Mayer's, house, whenever I speak in Boulder or Denver.

But the benefits did not outweigh my being away from Elli and Jenny. Elli and I fervently hoped that 1975 would be better because Michael would be on academic leave and split the travel responsibilities with me. Once Mudpie opened in March 1975 our child-care arrangements also improved. But this was soon offset by increased travel demands. Michael and I went on tour in May and June, after *We Are Your Sons* was published. We filed a massive FOIA suit against seven government agencies in July. That cost more money, necessitated more meetings, and increased media coverage and speaking requests. I had hoped to cut my travel in half my splitting it with Michael, but instead the workload doubled, and I was back where I started. Mudpie helped, but Elli, who was now pregnant with our second child, was becoming increasingly unhappy with travel demands that stretched indefinitely into the future.

Elli and I began to bicker with Michael and Ann about who should be traveling more. We felt that Michael should do the lion's share of the travel in late 1975, when our baby was due. His academic leave would be over at the end of the year, and he would be much less available in 1976. They felt, however, Michael was already at his limit, and if I needed to cut back I should. We divided up travel responsibilities like siblings squabbling over whose turn it was to take out the garbage.

By the fall of 1975 being a public figure and a stay-at-home dad was becoming a double existence. One week I'd be at home spending one or two mornings working at Mudpie, playing with a dozen pre-school-aged children. I'd dress in old jeans and T-shirts with faint spit-up stains. I'd get some reopening work done on the mornings I wasn't working at Mudpie or during Jenny's afternoon nap. I'd spend the remainder of the afternoon with Jenny and close her day with our bedtime ritual of reading and songs. By the time she was asleep I was in a semivegetative state and had energy only to park myself in front of the TV.

One evening I told Elli over a cup of tea how surprised I was that I didn't have any intellectual energy left after a day of child care. She sprayed tea all over the kitchen table. After she stopped laughing she congratulated me on finally figuring out what women all over the world know.

After Rachel was born, in December 1975, child care became even more all-consuming. The adults I interacted with saw only a stay-at-home father. I remember how much I resented one Mudpie mother's comment that of course I could spend more time with my kids than her husband could because I didn't work.

After a week at home I'd be back on the TV talk-show circuit dressed in jackets and slacks discussing childhood memories or making political pronouncements to college students about national security, government secrecy, and civil liberties. While I was on only a couple of national network shows during that period, I made dozens of local TV talk-show appearances. The people I interacted with while on the road saw the dutiful son working to vindicate his parents or the crusading activist fighting governmental abuses of power, and thought that they knew who I was and what I cared about. I was working toward these goals, but it was equally important to me to engage in routine family responsibilities. Most people I met while traveling gave me puzzled looks if I mentioned these everyday concerns.

"They" apparently took note of my brother's and my media exposure. The Justice Department followed a two-prong strategy. The first was to make us fight for every document. Dragging out the suit could bankrupt us, and the public did not have a long attention span. The second was to release documents that might embarrass us. In the fall of 1975 the FBI made its first release of several hundred pages. The press seized on the fact that the documents contained statements made by Jerome Eugene Tartakow, a jailhouse informer imprisoned with my father in New York City before my father was sent to Sing Sing. Tartakow reported to the FBI that my father confessed that he had led a substantial spy ring. My brother and I laughed at the absurdity of his claims that our father, who went to his death proclaiming his innocence, had boasted about his spying exploits to someone who was imprisoned for passing bad checks. The media reported that my brother and I did not believe Tartakow, but did not report the reasons for our disbelief. Other files eventually revealed that the Justice Department decided that much of what Tartakow said was unreliable.

Michael and I had considered and rejected the possibility that our quest might reveal information that would point to our father's guilt. A few months earlier we heard about a story James Weinstein told of a mysterious car ride and visit my father made to Weinstein's apartment in Ithaca in late 1949. Weinstein, the founder of the progressive newsweekly *In These Times*, was a progressive historian, and we had no reason to doubt his honesty. Michael and I took this information to Perlin. Perlin dismissed it, saying it proved nothing.

While we knew it didn't prove anything, we were concerned about what it might imply. Michael reviewed the trial transcript and discovered that my father testified that he took a trip to Ithaca to borrow money. We concluded that this might have explained my father's behavior, or alternatively that he might have been involved in laying the groundwork for the Communist Party's underground network that was put into operation a couple of years later. I wasn't troubled by either the Weinstein or Tartakow stories. There had to be an innocent explanation. How could someone who believed in his parents' innocence as strongly as he believed that one plus one equals two take these stories seriously?

But we were troubled by an emerging pattern of media coverage. They wanted to produce what my brother termed "hearts and flowers stories" based on what we remembered of those times. They reported our belief in our parents' innocence, but never the factual basis of those beliefs. We were cast as interested parties rather than as experts, even though by that time I doubt there were more than a dozen people on earth who knew more about our parents' case than we did. We felt that the message the media was feeding the public was, Don't take them seriously; what would you expect children to say about their parents?

We tried to counteract this image by focusing on the facts, but then we were attacked as nitpickers who spouted evidentiary minutia while ignoring the overwhelming evidence against our parents. Michael and I fumed that "there is nothing left to the government's case once you pick all the nits." We also noted that the press devoted extensive coverage to the Tartakow story that pointed to my father's guilt, but ignored files released that fall showing that the prosecutors arrested my mother even though they had no evidence against her.

In late 1975 we received an astounding set of documents relating to the conduct of Irving R. Kaufman, the trial judge. After months of analysis by our attorneys and researchers, we released a set of two dozen documents we entitled "The Kaufman Papers" at a press conference in June 1976. They showed that Kaufman lied from the bench when he claimed he had consulted with no one about whether to impose the death sentence. One file reported that he had secretly consulted with prosecuting attorneys about what sentences he should impose. In addition Kaufman had privately indicated to Justice Department officials while the trial was in progress, but before the jury verdict, that he would impose the death sentence. Other files revealed that Kaufman had used the Justice Department and FBI to intercede with the Appeals Court and the Supreme Court to expedite the appeals process and ensure a more rapid execution. This supposedly impartial judge had actually acted as a member of the prosecution team.

Revelations about the Supreme Court had more serious implications. The files revealed what actually happened during the eleventh-hour appeals I fantasized about as a child. On Tuesday, June 16, 1953, Justice Douglas agreed to postpone his vacation one day to consider a new appeal. The next morning, before going on vacation, he stayed the execution so that the entire Court could consider it. One FBI file stated that on Tuesday evening, as Douglas was considering the request, Attorney General Herbert Brownell met secretly with Supreme Court Chief Justice Fred Vinson. The file concluded that at that meeting Chief Justice Vinson "said that if a stay is granted he will call the full Court into session Thursday morning to vacate it."

Researchers found this memo, dated June 17, 1953, from FBI official A. H. Belmont to another FBI official, named Ladd, in Julius Rosenberg's FBI headquarters' file number 1823. It provides documentary evidence that the attorney general, one of our nation's top executive officers, conspired with the chief judicial officer of the United States to vacate a stay of execution authored by another sitting Supreme Court justice before they had read the legal reasons for the stay. They couldn't have known the legal basis of the stay because it wasn't written until the next morning. In other words, this file is evidence that the Chief Justice of the Supreme Court and the attorney general of the United States engaged in a conspiracy to obstruct justice. That is a felony.

This revelation should have been a bombshell, in the parlance of the times a judicial Watergate.

When we released this material to the press, Judge Kaufman was the chief judge of the United States Circuit Court of Appeals for the Second Circuit. In the statement we released at the press conference, our attorneys accused Kaufman, one of the most powerful judges in the country, of actions that constituted "criminal conduct, a violation of the Canons of Judicial Ethics, his oath of office, [and] abuse of the judicial processes." And we had FBI documents that supported our charges.

Nat Hentoff wrote a feature about this in the *Village Voice* entitled: "Rosenberg Sons Nail Judge Who Made Them Orphans," but for the most part the press ignored us. I recall arguing with Fred Graham, CBS-TV's chief legal correspondent, immediately after the press conference at which we released the Kaufman papers. First he used the line of Judge Kaufman's defenders, that this was thirdhand courtroom scuttlebutt that proved nothing. Not so, I said, these are FBI documents, not rumors. There are names, dates, quotes, and what happened during the last week of my parents' lives dovetails perfectly with what they record. I'll never forget what he said in response: "We're not going to pillory an aging ex–attorney general and a revered deceased former Chief Justice with this stuff."

This was followed in the fall of 1976 by the release of what may be the single document most destructive to the government's case against my father. It reports a meeting prosecutors arranged between Harry Gold and David Greenglass on December 28, 1950, many months after their imprisonment, but more than two months before the trial began. Both had been imprisoned and fully cooperating with the FBI for more than six months, but apparently they couldn't get their story straight on what happened when they supposedly met in Albuquerque five years earlier. Greenglass said Gold introduced himself as "Dave from Pittsburgh," but Gold said he told Greenglass he brought "greetings from Ben." Michael and I already knew that in the documentary *The Unquiet Death of Julius and Ethel Rosenberg*, an FBI agent said on camera that he suggested the code phrase: "I come from Julius."

This newly released file gave the story a slightly different twist, reporting that on December 28, 1950, Greenglass suggested to Gold that code phrase could have contained the word "Julius." The memo concluded that Gold said that might be right, but he wasn't sure about it. Ten weeks later at the trial they both swore that the code was "I come from Julius," thus providing the key evidence that linked Gold, Greenglass, and my father together in the conspiracy. This was as close to a smoking gun as we could get, short of finding a memo from J. Edgar Hoover that read: "Nice job on the frame-up, boys!" Although this discovery was reported on the front page of the *Los Angeles Times*, no wire service picked it up, and it received no national media attention.

The progress we were making with exposing my parents' wrongful conviction did not ease tensions at home. Elli left her job at the abortion clinic when her pregnancy began to show over the summer of 1975. We agreed that after Rachel's birth she would stay home with the girls while I traveled extensively until the end of the summer of 1976, and then in the fall I would limit travel to a couple of days a month while she started nursing school. Our finances would be tight, but my portion of the book advance provided money to live on while Elli completed her two-year program. But this plan did not mean that either of us was happy with my current absences.

Elli's unhappiness had become more pronounced since an incident that took place at an NCRRC rally held at the Santa Monica Civil Auditorium in February 1975. The Civil Auditorium is a large, modern, oblong box–shaped hall that seats about twenty-five hundred. National television audiences know it as the former site of the Academy Award ceremonies. The Los Angeles chapter of the NCRRC had worked very effectively to gather a stellar cast to read my parents' letters and dramatize the current revelations. Of course Michael and

I were included on the program, but Henry Fonda, Martin Sheen, and the other stars were the real draw. I was sitting backstage before the performance when a young volunteer cruised through giving out passes to enable the performers to move freely between the front and backstage. She confronted me saying, "Are you somebody?" I tried to turn my visceral negative reaction into a joke by parroting the words of a rock song, "Everybody is a star." She missed my point, rolled her eyes, and handed me a pass. My unease at placing too much importance on being a star was part of the reason why I stayed backstage and missed the chance to rub shoulders with the stars when they finished rehearsing. Anyway, I was having too much fun singing "Changes" and other songs with Phil Ochs and my brother in the greenroom.

An hour later the house was packed, and master of ceremonies Roscoe Lee Browne had just welcomed people when there was a loud popping noise in the hall. Despite his cultured air, Roscoe was streetwise enough to seek cover instantly behind the podium. After a moment I saw him tentatively peek out and say: "*Qu'est-ce que c'est que ça?*" Suddenly tear gas enveloped the audience.

The hall was evacuated without incident. Michael and Phil played guitar for the majority of the crowd in the parking lot. Despite the pouring rain, most of the crowd refused to leave for almost two hours, until they could return to the hall to see a truncated version of the program. Performers had to wipe streaming eyes because of the tear gas residue.

Two days later, when I returned to Springfield, I received a call from one of our organizers who told me the police had found an unexploded pipe bomb on the roof of the building where I'd met with local committee members the day after the debacle. We learned later of a pattern of attacks against left-wing groups in Southern California, carried out by a neo-Nazi cell that had stolen munitions from a military depot in the area. Although I never received official confirmation that the attack on our program and the attempted pipe bombing were carried out by the neo-Nazis, I have assumed that they were.

Now Elli began to fear for my safety whenever I went on the road, and flatly stated that she didn't want me to return to Los Angeles. I'd dealt with the issue of danger by denying its existence. I was frequently asked at receptions and on college campuses if I had been threatened or if the government had harassed either my brother or me. I explained that I did not fear government harassment because any action they took would draw sympathetic attention to us.

The government's primary tactic had been to ignore or dismiss us. Ironically, I reasoned, this offered us a degree of protection from bureaucratic harassment and physical violence. But I also had to acknowledge that America was a violent society, and anyone who stuck his or her head above the crowd faced the danger of someone trying to lop it off. While I paid lip service to the danger, I refused to believe that I might be attacked. I wasn't brave enough to admit the danger to myself and still go about my business. I did not deny Elli's fear and did not return to Los Angeles again for many years, but I put what had happened in Santa Monica into a box and didn't think about it.

Elli started a two-year registered nurse educational program after Labor Day in 1976. Jenny was almost four, and Rachel would celebrate her first birthday in December. Mudpie was licensed as an infant and preschool center, and now both our children attended from 9:00 A.M. to 1:00 P.M. I worked at Mudpie one morning a week. I'd bring the kids home when Mudpie was over, take an already-sleeping Rachel out of her car seat, and put her in her crib for the rest of her nap. I'd play quietly with Jenny until Rachel woke up and we could go pick up Elli at class or the hospital.

A few months before Rachel was born we moved into the bottom half of a Boston duplex at the edge of Springfield's Forest Park neighborhood. This area of stately turn-of-the-century houses sat on the bluffs that overlooked the floodplain of the Connecticut River a mile south of downtown. It was built around a large Frederick Law Olmsted–designed park. Forest Park, a great destination for the kids, was an easy four-block walk from our apartment. Mudpie, although a little farther away, was still in walking distance.

During our first year there several young men rented the upstairs apartment, but in the summer of 1976, with Abel's help, we bought the house with another Mudpie family. Larry and Sherry's son, Eli, was just a couple of months older than Rachel. Our two families ate together once a week and set up an intercom system so that we could baby-sit for each other without leaving our apartments. The extended Mudpie community provided many opportunities for the kids to visit back and forth. Parents had adult company or could do adult work or chores while their children played with their best friends. I entered a world of child care and household chores with interludes of family-oriented talk in neighborhood kitchens while sipping an ever-expanding variety of teas.

Mudpie families often spent weekend time together as well. We frequently shared large communal meals. The kids became so familiar with their friends' parents that we often behaved as an extended family. I'd played with Frank and Juanita's daughter, Maria, at Mudpie for many hours, and even taught her how to tie her shoes. She treated me more like an uncle than a friend's father. I can't think of a more care-free time than those unstructured hours I spent with the Mudpie community.

But I was equally involved in the reopening effort and that part of my life was far from carefree. Although I warned both Perlin and the committee months in advance that I would cut back on travel to take care of my daughters, I don't think they really believed me and apparently felt betrayed when I refused to spend more than two or three days a month away from home in late 1976. From my current middle-aged perspective, three years of almost complete devotion to the reopening effort does not seem that long, but at age twenty-nine it seemed I'd been doing it forever.

I'd set my final limit, and I was going to stick to it. This decision had some unanticipated consequences. As 1977 progressed, a rift developed between the NCRRC Executive Committee and the lawyers. In part this was due to a drop in income that resulted when my brother and I stopped speaking on college campuses. I worked from home on the phone and wrote letters to raise funds from individual donors, but had a hard time generating as much income as when I was on the road. The lawyers complained that the NCRRC absorbed too great a percentage of the funds raised. The NCRRC felt it was addressing important political questions and should be more than a fund-raising vehicle for a lawsuit.

My relationship to the NCRRC was complex. Initially it was composed mostly of Old Left radicals of the 1930s generation who were primarily interested in clearing my parents' names. But partly due to Michael's and my efforts the NCRRC also included increasing numbers of 1960s new leftists. They felt the case illuminated post-Watergate debates about creating a more open government and should always be connected to current struggles. While I agreed politically with the New Left group, I often deferred to the older activists. Michael and I were more than figureheads of the reopening effort, but we were not in control of the lawsuit or the NCRRC political agenda.

Michael and I were particularly loyal to Perlin, whom we viewed as our champion. As his clients we felt that it was our duty to supply him with sufficient funds to continue the effort, especially in light of the tens of thousands of dollars of his own money he told us he had contributed to the lawsuit. In 1977 we backed Perlin's demand that if the NCRRC could not meet the lawsuit's financial needs, we would shift our support from the NCRRC to a new organization, the Fund for Open Information and Accountability (FOIA), to fund the lawsuit. When the NCRRC balked, we acted on our ultimatum.

I regret that I did not have the political maturity to realize that this was a dreadful mistake. The younger NCRRC members were solidly against us, and I lost some valued political comrades. My brother and

I were probably the only people who could have forced both sides to cooperate. Instead we let our loyalty to Perlin cloud our judgment. I had no say in how much money Perlin and the other attorneys spent. I had no idea of the NCRRC's income and expenses. I didn't even know how many tens of thousands of dollars my efforts had generated for the NCRRC and the lawyers. I followed Perlin's lead blindly.

Although I stretched my travel limits and did several fund-raising parties to help jump-start FOIA in the fall of 1977, this did not succeed in substantially increasing the flow of funds into the lawsuit. The growing debt FOIA owed Perlin for the lawsuit dogged us. And since the NCRRC continued its political work, we had to confront the chaos caused by having two committees. Michael and I tried to raise funds for the lawsuit without attacking the NCRRC. I remembered how no one gained from the SDS split at Michigan, and ruefully recalled Mort Sobell's warning not to start another committee. The only good thing that came out of this experience was that it solidified my belief that splits were almost always worse than compromises.

Despite increased travel, I continued to work at Mudpie. The co-op rented the spacious upstairs auditorium in a neighborhood church with a large fenced-in backyard. The high ceiling and large windows provided a sense of sun-filled openness and helped hold down the din generated by fifteen young children. The parents built a six-foot-square two-story structure in the center of the room. It had a downstairs playhouse and an open upstairs area. The kids could nest in the downstairs area, climb the ladder to the top, hang out on the railed second floor at adult eye level or slide back down. Mudpie also rented a smaller downstairs room that was stocked with cribs, changing tables, and toys suitable for infants.

Mudpie was a parent-run cooperative. The fees, which covered rent, supplies, and a full-time head teacher, were calculated on a sliding scale according to family income. One adult member of each participating family was responsible for working one 9:00 A.M.-to-1:00 P.M. shift each week. Typically three parents and the teacher took care of twelve to fifteen kids on any given day.

The group put a lot of thought into encouraging the kids' sharing and cooperation as well as cognitive skills. At first I did the more custodial work with the babies in the small downstairs room, but once I started working upstairs in the big room I enjoyed planning several projects each week. In addition to building block cities, supervising Play-doh art projects or nature experiments to watch water evaporate or seedlings sprout, I liked reading with the kids and dramatizing the stories. One of my favorites was "Caps for Sale," the story of a salesman who walked through the jungle with dozens of hats on his head calling: "Caps for sale!" Naturally he got tired of carrying his wares in this manner and fell asleep under a tree. He awoke to find a troupe of monkeys, each wearing one of his hats, sitting on various branches. Ultimately the man throws his own hat on the ground in frustration at being unable to get the monkeys to return his hats, and the monkeys copy him.

After a read-through, we'd dramatize the story using the climber. I'd gather up all the dress-up hats, put them on my head, and walk around the room calling: "Caps for sale! Caps for sale!" A giggling group of kids would watch from the top of the climber as I staggered over and fell asleep against it. They'd quietly remove the hats, I'd "awaken," and we'd act out the rest of the story. But it seemed that no matter how many ideas I came up with, kids started and completed them with breathtaking speed. The thought and effort it took to plan and implement an hour or two of meaningful activity that would engage a dozen two-, three-, and four-year-olds astounded me. I gained an abiding respect for all who were devoted to this challenging and important work.

Mudpie was a feminist project, but relatively undogmatic. Springfield's progressive community was so small and diverse that any group that insisted on imposing its dogma on anyone quickly found that they had no one to talk to. Feminism at Mudpie meant exposing all the children to a broad range of human possibilities. Three-year-old Graham dancing around in a tutu while wearing heavy corrective shoes caused suppressed chuckles but didn't raise eyebrows.

Although almost all the parents were left of center, we didn't spoon-feed the kids radical politics. Most of us believed that children should be free to be children, and not have the cares of the adult world imposed upon them. Occasionally we did expose the kids to civic issues, such as when we learned that President Ford was planning a brief stop in town. It was during an economic slump, and progressive activists and organized labor formed the Coalition to Lay Off Ford. We took the older Mudpie kids to stand amid Springfield's few high-rise buildings. The kids and a hundred adults yelled slogans as his limousine glided by. Four of the oldest Mudpie girls chanted an age-appropriate expression of disapproval: "Yucka yucka poo, noodles on your head!"

My child-oriented life sometimes spilled over into my public work. In several interviews I stated that I thought the world would be a better place if the world's leaders were expected to spend one morning a week working in a day-care center. Many people thought I was fooling, but I was serious. I still think it would be an excellent idea, though I'm not sure it would be fair to the children.

In the spring of 1978 FOIA's leaders, concerned that the reopening effort was floundering, decided to stage a mass outdoor rally on the twenty-fifth anniversary of my parents' execution. FOIA worked with more than a dozen groups to hold an event in New York City's Union Square, where ten thousand people had stood vigil during the last moments of my parents' lives in 1953. We hoped that a strong turnout and good media coverage would increase the pressure on the Justice Department to release a final flood of files and bring our lawsuit to a victorious conclusion.

The seven thousand people who gathered in Union Square for the five-hour event on that June 1978 evening reflected what had become a constellation of broad-based progressive support for our efforts. The rally evoked emotional déjà-vu for those supporters who had stood near the same spot in similar heat and humidity twenty-five years earlier. But I was moved more by the number of people of my generation who attended, and the ethnic and political diversity of the crowd. Civil libertarians stood side by side with feminists, labor organizers, Trotskyites, and Communists. Supporters of gay rights, the Black Panthers, the American Indian Movement, and Puerto Rican Nationalists flanked them. Speeches by disabled Vietnam War veteran Ron Kovic and American Indian leader Russell Means alternated with music by Holly Near and others, and as always, Ossie Davis and Pete Seeger were there.

That rally, I now realize, was also my brother's and my farewell to the reopening effort. More than five years had passed since we decided to go public. The event had been partially successful in goosing the government to release more files, but the suit could drag out for several more years. Perlin had pumped $25,000 of his own money into the effort, and none of the lawyers had been paid for their time. But the United States Treasury soon gave us the break we needed. The court found we had "substantially prevailed" in the lawsuit, a finding that obligated the government to pay our attorneys' fees. On August 18, 1978, the government cut a check payable to Michael and me for $195,802.50 for our attorneys' fees. I still have a copy of the check taped to my office wall.

For the first time in several years we no longer owed Perlin money. We arranged to meet with him and another member of the legal team at my house in September to discuss our plans for the future. At the meeting they insisted that Michael and I should take advantage of the momentum the twenty-fifth-anniversary event generated by returning to the road. They were shocked by our response. We told them that we would no longer accept responsibility for funding the suit. We would remain as the named plaintiffs so they could continue the action if they wished, but that was their choice. We were going to get on with our lives. Michael wanted to focus on his academic career. I might travel a bit for FOIA, but Elli had found a full-time job as an RN after completing nursing school in May 1978, and I planned to be the primary caretaker for my children while I decided what to do next.

At first Perlin insisted that we were obliged to continue. But he backed off once I told him, "I want you to be my Freedom of Information Act attorney, not my divorce lawyer."

Elli and I were nowhere near divorcing, but Perlin finally understood that family had to take priority over the reopening effort. I didn't know how my birth parents would have felt about the choice we were making. Placing family before politics may seem at odds with their choice. It may even seem more in line with the choice Uncle David made when he abandoned his integrity and sold his sister to the executioner in order to gain leniency for himself. I did not see it that way. Perhaps I was rationalizing, but I felt that my birth parents' refusal to toe the government's line was at least in part to benefit their sons. I did not believe we could have grown up to be decent human beings if they had mimicked the Greenglasses' betrayal. I concluded that my birth parents would have supported our decision.

It was painful to desert Perlin in this fashion. I did some traveling to raise funds for the lawsuit that fall. But the crowds at speaking engagements and receptions were dwindling, and my heart wasn't in it. Post-Watergate public support for a more open government and exposing abuses of power was fading. Reaganism was waiting in the wings. I felt that pursuing the reopening effort was becoming an exercise in futility.

Elli's and my sense of political staleness in Springfield matched my disengagement from the reopening effort. While we were comfortable with the Mudpie community, it provided us with no new political inspiration.

In October I was only half serious when I commented during a phone conversation with our Berkeley friends, Jim and Diane, that if they found me a job, we'd move there. They had become very close friends, although they lived on the other side of the continent. Jim was the older brother of my camp friend Ellen from long ago. Elli and I both knew Diane from Michigan. Their daughter, Rebecca, was Jenny's age, and their son, Jesse, was a few months younger than Rachel.

We began to look longingly to the Bay Area as a place where we might find a family-oriented community of political kindred spirits. We might even recapture the joyful excitement of the late sixties by building a new multifamily commune with Jim and Diane. We were particularly concerned about passing our values on to our children. We felt the best way to do that was by living in a vital progressive community that embodied those values most explicitly. We hoped to find that in the Bay Area.

So when Diane, who was a member of the *Socialist Review (SR)* editorial collective, called back in November 1978 to ask if I would apply for its managing editor job, Elli and I responded positively. Elli had been working as a pediatric nurse and was confident about finding a job in the Bay Area. During the job application process I realized how valuable the skills I had developed might be to progressive institutions. Many groups had more than adequate numbers of spokespeople, theorists, and organizers, but few had staff members with business skills. During my work for the reopening effort, I had learned about fund-raising, mass mail campaigns, promotion, and publicity. I'd always enjoyed working with numbers. I discovered that I had facility with fund-raising and a good sense of what kinds of promotions worked. I mused to Elli that if I'd been raised in an apolitical environment I might have become a Madison Avenue ad man.

The job offer came in early 1979. Elli and I decided we'd move to Berkeley in July, and I'd start at *SR* on August 1. We looked forward to the move but regretted leaving our many friends in Springfield. We had a compatible house-sharing arrangement with Larry and Sherry. And our good friends Fred and Betsy had bought a house across the street a few years earlier. I enjoyed having friends close by and valued the informality of spur-of-the-moment visits for no particular reason. And, of course, we'd be on the other side of the continent from my brother, Michael, and Ann and their children. We decided to play it safe. I made a two-year commitment to *SR*, but we rented our portion of the house to friends, so we'd have the house to return to in Springfield if Berkeley didn't work out as planned.

I felt mostly positive about what the reopening effort had accomplished. Publicly acknowledging my heritage, confronting my fears, and making this effort was personally powerful for me. I have never regretted that decision. I could smile before falling asleep at night about forcing the government to release files showing that my parents' trial had been unfair and that critical testimony against them had been tainted. Then I could laugh to myself as I drifted off about making the government pay our legal costs for causing them all that trouble. I saw no contradiction between my need to make a clean break from the reopening effort and the response I would have given if someone had asked me what I'd like to do in the best of all possible worlds. I would have answered without hesitation that I wanted to create and run a foundation in my parents' name.

But we had not won a clear-cut victory. The government still withheld more than one hundred thousand pages and refuses to this day to make all Rosenberg-case-related files public. We never obtained from the Supreme Court the declaration I dreamed about, vindicating my parents. But our efforts had had an impact in the court of public opinion. While relatively few people agreed that Julius and

Ethel Rosenberg were innocent, my brother and I had played a critical role in convincing a significant percentage of the population that something was wrong with the way they were treated by the government. I was proud of our efforts, even as I acknowledged sadly that it was unlikely that I'd ever realize my dream of clearing their names.

CHAPTER 6

Denial and Defeat

---◆·►·◄·◆---

WE ARRIVED IN BERKELEY WITH EXPECTATIONS OF RECAPTURING THE
political magic and personal connections of the 1960s. The Bay Area
contained one of the largest concentrations of progressive people in
the country, with many left-wing organizations and activities, but
quantity did not translate into the more tightly knit progressive community we craved. Our friends from the 1960s generation had aged
ten years, were living mostly in family units, and focused on raising
children and pursuing their careers.

Jenny was in public school, but Rachel was still in day care our first
year there. We became close to several other parents whose children
attended Pickwick West and have continued those friendships to this
day. The woman who directed Pickwick had been my brother's girlfriend at summer camp in 1958. Everyone called her "Sudy,"
although her birth name was Susan. "Sudy Coo," the nickname I gave
her back in 1958, had stuck.

Our work life in Berkeley was consuming. Elli was working three
nights a week as an RN in the pediatric intensive care unit of Oakland

Children's Hospital. Working with deathly ill and critically injured children took a lot of guts, especially for someone with two small children of her own. Her job was particularly hard during the first six months when she lacked seniority and could not work a regular schedule. The sleep deprivation lessened once she earned a regular rotation of three nights on, two nights off, three nights on, and six nights off. Elli worked from 11:00 P.M. to 7:00 A.M., so the kids saw her in the evenings. Although she was zombielike during the period when she worked six of eight nights, that was followed by almost a week of uninterrupted home time.

When I arrived *SR* was like a car careening down a mountain road with two of its wheels already over the edge of a financial cliff. When I was interviewed for the job I was told that the magazine was $25,000 in debt but not that it owed its vendors an additional $25,000. The first week on the job I had to beg several of my reopening effort supporters for $2,000 to induce *SR*'s printer to release the journal's next issue.

Asking for funds does not mortify me. I enjoy the instant gratification generated by gathering funds to support politically exciting projects. But I've never liked desperation fund-raising. At the start of each workday I sat quietly for a few minutes taking deep breaths to dissipate excess nervous energy until I became calm enough to focus on the day's first task. I returned home from work at dinnertime utterly drained. I was a nervous wreck during the first year because money was so tight I was not certain of either the magazine's survival or my paycheck.

I joked that being managing editor of *SR* meant that I never managed to edit. Rather, I acted as its publisher and production manager. I interacted with donors, creditors, designers, typesetters, printers, mailers, and advertisers as I learned the tasks needed to produce and market a magazine. I had done some similar work during the reopening effort, but I hadn't worked in an office as part of a staff and had not been in charge of managing these tasks. During my first year at

SR I developed and instituted a fund-raising and promotional plan; the plan's success helped ease the tension during my second year.

I had relatively little input into the magazine's contents, which was controlled by *SR*'s editorial collective. It was my job to ensure the journal had enough money to operate and was published on time. Regularizing the magazine's schedule was critical to its financial health, since subscription renewals were its greatest source of income. The editorial collective, composed primarily of social science graduate students working on their dissertations, was more concerned about the magazine's contents than its schedule. I nagged relentlessly to ensure its timely publication. My compulsiveness paid off in the second year, when the journal came out punctually for the first time since 1970, its first year of publication.

SR was dedicated to promoting democratic socialist and feminist politics. It occupied the political space to the right of Old Left formations like the American Communist Party and to the left of the Democratic Party. It published groundbreaking articles by left-wing feminist and gay-rights theoreticians while attempting to straddle the line between theory and activism. It tilted too much to the former for my taste, but for the most part I found its politics and mission compatible with my beliefs.

I had worked amicably with Old and New Left groups during the reopening effort. I was still a "Mush-Head," following a policy of no enemies on the Left. But *SR* was firmly in the New Left camp and attacked the Old Left as authoritarian. This put the magazine at odds with Leninist, Maoist, and clandestine revolutionary cells, all of which followed a strict party line and believed a small group could lead (or drag, depending on your perspective) the masses into a revolutionary transformation.

I sprang from that party-line tradition. I had respect and admiration for the dedication and passion of many of its adherents and would not attack these people. I still view many old leftists who grew up in the 1930s as the best people of their generation. But being surrounded by dedicated radicals who supported democratic ideals reinforced my faith in the principle of democracy. I believed in democracy because I simply did not trust any small group, whether the president's cabinet, the board of directors of General Electric, or a revolutionary cell, to make policy decisions that controlled society at large.

Despite my strong belief in democracy, I wanted to include the entire Left spectrum in my political community. Several members of the *SR* collective disagreed, and this important difference was brought home during my first fall at the magazine. On November 3, 1979, the Ku Klux Klan shot and killed four members and one sympathizer of the Communist Workers Party (CWP) at an anti-Klan demonstration in Greensboro, North Carolina. I was horrified by this event, which became known as the Greensboro massacre. I was almost as shocked by the reaction of a fellow staff member.

The CWP had mounted an organizing effort to unionize black and white workers in area cotton mills. When the Klan threatened the organizers, they fought back by verbally attacking the Klan. CWP members chanted "Death to the Klan!" at rallies, and wrote leaflets with the slogan Kill the Klan. My colleague reacted as if these tactics justified the Klan's attack. He argued that the CWP had brought death upon themselves with vitriolic sloganeering and by openly proclaiming their Communist politics in North Carolina.

I felt that the CWP's provocative tactics were foolhardy, but I identified with the organizers whom the Klan had gunned down while engaging in labor and civil rights work. We might disagree with the CWP's tactics, but we should support them as our comrades.

Perhaps I felt so strongly about my colleague's reaction because I felt similarly about progressive people who did not support my parents. During the McCarthy period you either stood with those who were attacked, ran for cover, or joined the chorus of condemnation. I admit to measuring my friends by this standard. Throughout my life I have considered which of my friends would have stood up for my parents or would stand by me if I had to face the inquisitor. I felt more comfortable working at *SR* after that staff member left.

My efforts to save *SR* from financial ruin might have failed had it not been for the arrival of a significant bequest. A generous soul had left *SR* $12,500 in his will. While this was not an enormous sum, its impending arrival was used first to forestall creditors, and was then apportioned among them.

The impact of this person's bequest impressed me. I reflected on the wealth in the Bay Area and the many progressive people who lived there in relative comfort. In the long term these people could have a dramatic positive effect on many politically Left projects simply by including them in their wills. But there were few left-wing professionals with the technical skills to advise progressives how to do this effectively, and almost no progressive projects engaged in long-term planning. The bequest to *SR* had made a tremendous short-term difference, but wouldn't it have been wiser to set some of it aside as a reserve against future crises, or even to start a fledgling endowment fund with it?

I merged this realization about the power of bequests with my reopening-effort experience. I considered attending law school in order to become a left-wing estate planner and encourage clients to make bequests to progressive organizations. I might make a major contribution to such causes with this combination of political commitment and technical skills. Obtaining estate-planning expertise might even help me create the foundation I had vaguely dreamed of starting to honor my parents.

After nine months in Berkeley we quietly made the decision to return to western Massachusetts when my two-year commitment to *SR* ended. I didn't realize that western Massachusetts had become home until we moved away. Once we had gone, I recognized the strength of my attachment to the Connecticut River Valley. I find its landscape most visually satisfying. I enjoyed the Bay Area's dramatic beauty, but felt in awe rather than in tune with it. New England's erratic weather is the baseline against which I measure other climes. Folks in California were more casual and friendly than New Englanders, who are known for their reserve, but I still felt most in tune with how New Englanders dress, look, and act.

In addition to our sense that Springfield was just "home," the Bay Area was impossibly expensive. And as we observed our thirteen- and fourteen-year-old babysitters growing up in the fast lane, Elli and I felt more comfortable raising our daughters in the relative social backwater setting of Springfield. Springfield even had a law school I could attend, part of Western New England College. (In fact, some of its professors were Mudpie parents.)

I was a bit chagrined that I might be repeating my parents' decision to pull me out of Elisabeth Irwin High School. I hoped that recognizing that I might be mimicking Abel and Anne would enable me to improve on their actions. We involved Jenny and Rachel in our discussions and our decision to return to Massachusetts. Jenny never acclimated to Berkeley and was pleased about this. Rachel had adjusted most quickly to California and I believe would have been happy to remain, but at five years old she followed our lead.

Once the choice was made, another development lent urgency to our return. Abel had never recovered from Anne's death. I do not know when depression ended and Alzheimer's disease began, but even before my family left for California, Michael and I had been wondering how long Abel could remain in his house. Michael and I began spending several days with him almost every month. The flight from Berkeley to Miami was long, but because Michael and I took turns during Elli's and my first eighteen months in California, I only made the trip about a half dozen times. We enlisted increasing housekeeping help and personal care for him, but our arrangements barely kept pace with his deterioration. In the spring of 1981 we made the difficult decision, and the painful task of moving Abel to a Springfield-area nursing home fell to Michael.

In retrospect we may have waited too long. It was difficult for Michael and me to accept Abel's decline as an inexorable process. I hoped for a magic solution to reverse his degeneration. For a decade after his death, I occasionally awoke from a dream in which I had a joyful conversation with Abel after his miraculous recovery. Each time Michael or I departed Miami, we felt that we'd left Abel with an adequate support system, but we both repeatedly failed to anticipate the next regression. During his last few months in Florida, Abel could easily have wandered off and disappeared. Still, he'd made clear his intense desire to remain in his house, and we wanted to help him stay there for as long as possible. I looked forward to returning to Springfield at the end of July 1981, not only to return home but also so I could see Abel frequently.

When we returned to Springfield, Elli and I found it impossible to restart where we left off. Our kids were no longer in Mudpie, and that community had lost its hub because the children were not in school together. We did, however, pick up the threads of some relationships, and our family friendship networks soon spread to encompass the college towns of Northampton and Amherst, twenty miles to the north, and the countercultural center of Greenfield, fifteen miles farther up the Connecticut River Valley.

The Left's political priorities in the valley's three counties reflected their distinct activist communities. The Left in Hampden County, centered in Springfield, was the most traditional, focusing on labor, civil, and poor people's rights. The Hampshire County towns of Northampton, Amherst, and South Hadley are home to five colleges, including the massive University of Massachusetts. Peace, gay and lesbian rights, and radical student politics predominated in this area. Franklin County's small hill towns, with Greenfield at their heart, had attracted a large contingent of ecology-focused and alternative lifestyle folks active in the antinuclear power movement and other environmental concerns.

One foggy April morning, four months before I left the Bay Area, a magazine published in Greenfield, called *New Roots for the Northeast*, arrived in *SR*'s mail. Stuck inside was a note from its editor, Rob Okun, asking for an exchange subscription. I spent the next hour devouring articles about New England's antinuke and green politics. I became nostalgic for my Connecticut Valley home as I read advertisements for woodstoves and solar panels. I brought it to Elli that night, and she had the same reaction. I wrote Rob back the next day that I was returning to western Massachusetts, had business-oriented magazine experience, and might be interested in working there in the fall.

Within days of our return to Springfield in July 1981, Elli found an RN job at Shriners Hospital working with children with orthopedic conditions. It took me longer, but soon I was commuting three days a week to a part-time consulting job at *New Roots*. *New Roots* was in worse financial shape than *SR*, and our combined efforts only staved off the inevitable for several months. But in the process Elli and I were introduced to a new activist community and a new group of friends.

I had applied and been accepted at Springfield's Western New England College School of Law (WNEC), but classes didn't begin until the following August. Through contacts at *New Roots* I learned about a temporary job at a new public foundation, the Peace Development Fund (PDF). PDF was looking for someone to sustain its forward momentum while its executive director was on maternity leave. They needed a person with fund-raising and production-management experience who would depart after six months. I had eight months left before law school and wanted to gain work experience that would contribute to my secret dream of running my own foundation. PDF was based in Amherst, and so I became connected with a number of activists in its large antiwar community.

• • •

Although law school is an ordeal for many, I found it enjoyable. Many of the professors at WNEC were approximately my age and treated me as a peer rather than as a student. Several of them were Mudpie parents. Some I had not known previously because our kids did not overlap at Mudpie. Now they became my friends. John Egnal, a Mudpie father who taught civil procedure, had advised Marshall Perlin on procedural matters for our ongoing FOIA suit. I agreed about many political questions with Bruce Miller, another Mudpie father, who taught constitutional law. The frequent contact I had with several of my law professors sped my understanding of legal concepts. I treated law school as a nine-to-five job, studied in the library between classes, and came home to Elli and the kids at night.

My friends expected me to take courses that would lead me to the predictable left-oriented criminal or constitutional law career. They were skeptical of my plans to become a left-wing estate planner, and incredulous that I took so many business- and tax-law classes. Some may have felt that I was turning my back on my heritage.

I felt I wanted to move beyond rather than turn away from my legacy. But in law school there were reminders that made this difficult. I took an intellectual property class because Michael and I were managing Abel's copyrights. *Meeropol* v. *Nizer* was included in the textbook. In that case the Appellate Court ruled that since my brother and I were public figures we had to demonstrate "actual malice" on Nizer's part in order to prevail with the defamation count of our suit. Proving actual malice rather than negligence is very difficult, and although the Appeals Court did not dismiss our suit, we lost that portion of it. After the appeal in 1980, we agreed to a sealed settlement with Nizer rather than proceed to a trial we could not afford.

Law school classes focus on analyzing appellate decisions. The accuracy of the factual background of a case presented at the beginning of each decision is presumed. It was fascinating to have inside information about the real facts of a case. In *Meeropol v. Nizer*, the court repeated what was common knowledge. The Rosenberg case generated enormous publicity. Pictures of Michael and me had been published worldwide: Of course we were public figures. That our names had been changed, that we lived anonymously, and that the press had not published one word about our whereabouts for almost twenty years were conveniently ignored. This was just one of many examples I encountered in law school that indicated the fallibility of our judicial system.

This realization of judicial imprecision gradually altered my position on the death penalty. Although the thrill of actually striking back during the reopening effort in the 1970s had replaced my revenge fantasies of the 1960s, before entering law school I still retained my childhood belief that those who had orchestrated my parents' legal lynching should face execution. But encountering so many questionable court decisions in law school led me to conclude that our judiciary could not be trusted with life-and-death matters. This was not a radical position. Most law students were familiar with the statistical studies that demonstrated that nonwhites and the poor faced the executioner in disproportionate numbers. Even the Supreme Court had ruled, in 1972, that the arbitrary and capricious nature of our court system's enforcement of the death penalty was unconstitutional.

Although my views evolved slowly, attending law school also had a profound impact on my views of my parents' case. The publication of *The Rosenberg File* by Joyce Milton and Ronald Radosh in 1982, which concluded that my father was guilty and that my mother aided him, did not sway my belief in my parents' innocence. *The Rosenberg File* is still touted as the definitive proof of my parents' guilt, but from my knowledge of the trial transcript and FBI files, I recognized its serious errors and omissions. Michael persuaded me that we had to respond to the misinformation in *The Rosenberg File*. In 1983 and early 1984, we wrote three chapters that were included in the second edition of *We Are Your Sons*, although it was not published until 1986. I provided a written version of my typical 1970s college-lecture-circuit speech in the first new chapter. Michael wrote the second chapter, about the provocative findings in *The Kaufman Papers*, and was primarily responsible for the last chapter that refuted *The Rosenberg File*. I believe my brother demolished its scholarship so effectively that nobody would take *The Rosenberg File* seriously if his text were to receive the media attention it deserves.

By the time I completed law school in 1985, however, I realized that the evidence we had amassed did not actually prove my parents' innocence but rather only demonstrated that they had been framed. This may seem like hair-splitting, but it is a crucially important distinction. What *if* Gold and Greenglass *had* met in Albuquerque, and my father *had* played some role in arranging that meeting, but the government had no proof that this was the case. The prosecutors could have planted the code phrase "I come from Julius," as reported in the FBI file I described earlier, and forged Gold's hotel registration card in order to create proof. I came to realize that even if you proved defendants were framed by showing that the evidence necessary to their conviction was fabricated, they might still be guilty.

This uncomfortable realization forced me to reevaluate my position. What did I really know? By 1985 I had read and reread the trial transcript. I knew that my parents had not received a fair trial. *The Kaufman Papers* proved that. As a student attorney I knew that defendants convicted with tainted evidence in an unfair trial are entitled to a new trial at which they are, once again, presumed innocent. From a legal standpoint I concluded that my parents should be presumed innocent. But the public debate that still raged over my parents' guilt or innocence had gone beyond the courtroom.

• • •

Dr. Henry Linschitz was the scientist who had headed the part of the atomic bomb project in which David Greenglass had worked. I remembered something he'd said to me one summer evening in the late 1970s. I was speaking about my parents' case in Woods Hole, Massachusetts. The hall was packed with scientists who spent their summers working at the world-famous Oceanographic Institute. Dr. Linschitz took me aside after my talk and offered gentle criticism. "The question is not whether they were guilty," he said. "The question is guilty of what." I said something noncommittal like, "That's interesting," but I didn't get his point.

I had learned from affidavits sworn by Dr. Linschitz and other atomic scientists that the material Greenglass testified about at my parents' trial had little or no scientific value. Government attorneys admitted as much during a hearing to free my parents' codefendant Morton Sobell during the 1960s. But it took me until 1985 to understand Dr. Linschitz's point. I knew that there was no credible scientific evidence that Ethel and Julius Rosenberg had conspired to steal the secret of the atomic bomb. That proved they did not commit the act for which they were executed, but it did not prove them innocent of conspiracy to commit espionage.

I discussed this with Michael. In 1986, armed with my recent legal training and these new insights, I expressed my doubts to Perlin during a visit to his office. I asked how he could proclaim we had proved my parents' innocence when we had not? I was floored when he responded: "I never say they were innocent." He continued: "The trial was a travesty. The sentence was an atrocity. The government's witnesses committed perjury, and government agents suborned that perjury. This is why I always talk about the trial and the evidence. Let others draw conclusions."

I racked my brain trying to remember one instance in which Perlin had said my parents were innocent, and could think of none. But I thought that he had let me be one of those drawing conclusions. I bet almost everyone who had been involved with our reopening effort thought Perlin believed in my parents' innocence. So I asked him point-blank if he thought my parents were innocent. He said, "How could I know?" And I realized that I didn't either.

But I was not about to proclaim my insight that we had not proved my parents' innocence from the rooftops. My new position was uncertain and complicated. Given the propensity of the media to distort what I said when my position was clear-cut, I couldn't begin to imagine how they would mangle my newfound skepticism. Instead I resolved to follow Perlin's lead to let others draw conclusions, not talk about innocence, and state my continuing belief that my parents did not conspire to steal the secret of the atomic bomb. I thought it was just as well that I was no longer speaking publicly about the case, because I would have felt uncomfortable about such temporizing. I did not wish to frame my remarks in a manner that might mislead, even if what I said was technically accurate.

Although for the first time in my life I was not engaged in organized political activity, I did not abandon all work related to my parents' case. I became quite friendly with Rob Okun, who had edited *New Roots*. Drinking iced tea in our kitchen on a steamy summer afternoon in 1983, Rob shared an ambitious plan with Elli and me. He dreamed of gathering together works of art inspired by my parents' case, inviting artists to create new ones, and combining the best of both into a traveling art exhibit. His excitement was infectious, and I thought it was a terrific idea. And so the Rosenberg Era Art Project (REAP) was born, and Rob became its executive director.

Rob knew how to make things happen and didn't need much help. I became his occasional unpaid consultant. I helped him network with those who could find the art and steered him to people who might provide financial support. For the next several years he gave me progress reports as he doggedly tracked down art and scouted potential venues. Although I was pleased with his progress, I was relieved that the project was his responsibility and not mine. While I wished to remain involved in progressive efforts related to my parents' case, I did not wish to be at their heart. As long as I remained in the background, I would not have to voice my doubts about my parents' case publicly, and I could develop a life that moved beyond being their son.

I clung to my plan to do left-wing estate work as the end of law school approached. I was a bit concerned that at thirty-seven I was still trying to figure out what I was going to do when I grew up. Two years in Berkeley, one year of interim work, three years of law school, and I still wasn't exactly sure where it was leading.

The many lawyers I knew who seemed anxious to leave their profession reinforced my uncertainty. They described it as a venal and cutthroat existence that rewarded workaholics and nastiness. I did not seem temperamentally suited to the profession. I thought my experience would be different because I planned to do work that was technically challenging and politically meaningful. My problem was figuring out how to get there. There weren't any left-wing estate-planning law firms in the Springfield area looking to hire an apprentice attorney. After graduation, in the fall of 1985, I started a judicial clerkship with the chief justice of the Massachusetts Appeals Court. The clerkship allowed me to postpone for another year a decision about finding the right job.

The strangeness of working for the court system did not escape me. Even though the federal, not the Massachusetts, court system had been responsible for my parents' death, it took a healthy dose of denial to ignore the irony. I was working for the state system responsible for wrongfully executing Sacco and Vanzetti in the 1920s, the political case most frequently associated with my parents' case. I would have found it emotionally impossible to work on a capital case, but I knew I would not have to because Massachusetts had abolished the death penalty.

I enjoyed working for the court. Cases presented a wide range of civil disputes and criminal appeals. Writing a proposed solution for my judge was like putting an intellectual jigsaw puzzle together. I was fortunate that the judge I worked for was smart, diligent, and an excellent teacher. I didn't agree with his middle-of-the-road politics, but I respected his integrity. I followed his directions and learned what I could.

The reasonable hours of the work left me time to visit Abel, whose nursing home was just over two miles from our home. During his first couple of years there we often took him back to our house or out to a restaurant, but by the time I graduated law school our visits had to be confined to the nursing home. I found it distressing to spend extended periods of time with him. It was devastating to visit the shell of such a remarkable man. His creativity must have been at the core of his being; the last things he appeared to recognize were the words and music to his most famous songs, "Strange Fruit" and "The House I Live In."

I wanted to make him as happy as possible, but I had no idea if my father gained anything from my visits. Abel had expended enormous energy and time caring for his senile mother when we lived in Hastings. When I was a teenager, he repeatedly exhorted me not to let him be a similar burden when he got old. I was very grateful that he granted me this permission, and I knew he would have supported my choice to make my visits with him frequent but short. He died in October 1986.

By early 1986 the United States had endured six years of the Reagan-led conservative revolution of selfishness, and left-wing activity seemed increasingly ineffective. But I felt a political void in my life. Elli and I became involved in the Springfield Area Central America Project (SACAP), a CISPES (Committee in Solidarity with the People of El Salvador) chapter in Springfield.

The United States funded and equipped the contras' terrorist campaign to overthrow the Sandanista government in Nicaragua, and was supporting the military dictatorship and death squads that were fighting left-wing guerrillas in El Salvador. SACAP organized public protests against this policy, lobbied Congress to cut off funding for

U.S.-supported efforts, and raised funds to send humanitarian aid to the victims of Central American wars. I found SACAP's broad-based progressive coalition appealing. Supporters ranged from mainstream church-oriented liberals galvanized into action by the murder of Catholic priests, nuns, and Protestant missionaries, to revolutionaries who believed some of CISPES's "humanitarian aid" helped arm the guerrillas.

Although Elli and I had only limited time, we soon became key members. We were also excited to be working together on a political project for the first time since we had left Michigan. SACAP's leaflets and posters benefited from Elli's writing, editing, and artistic skills. Her sensitivity to group dynamics also made her an excellent facilitator at meetings. I helped with SACAP's fund-raising, the production of materials, and public relations. My ease with public speaking and media experience was also a plus.

We played major supporting roles and were content that neither of us was the group's principal leader. We had time to devote only an evening or two a week, and to attend an occasional Saturday-afternoon rally. Our daughters often joined us. They no longer needed baby-sitters and especially enjoyed SACAP's annual October fund-raising walkathons. For the next five years SACAP became our major extracurricular political project.

Meanwhile our FOIA suit sputtered along. In 1983 the district court in Washington, D.C., declared that the government had done enough after it agreed to release a total of 300,000 pages even though it was still withholding up to 100,000 more. Perlin wanted to appeal this decision to the D.C. District Court of Appeals. For the first time I injected myself into the lawyers' legal strategy sessions. I argued that the courts, almost never our friends, were becoming more conservative and hostile to FOIA actions. Our appeal was likely to fail, and the higher court's ruling might establish bad precedent for other FOIA plaintiffs. But Perlin would not give up, and I did not wish to stand in the way of what had become his life's work.

In 1985 the Court of Appeals denied our appeal. This was hardly surprising since the three justices who heard the case included the ultraconservative Robert Bork and Antonin Scalia. Michael and I flatly refused when Perlin suggested further appeals, and the suit ended.

In September 1986, after my one-year clerkship ended, I took a position as an associate lawyer in a financially successful downtown law firm that focused on business planning and tax and estate work. Though I did not intend to become a corporate lawyer, I felt that this was the best way to gain the kind of experience I'd need to pursue my goals. During the late 1960s the law firms' principal partners had started their careers as legal services attorneys. More than a decade before I'd joined them, these lawyers left public service to build a more lucrative business practice, but I hoped that their liberal background would provide a congenial setting for me. If I could develop a nonprofit and progressive estate-oriented practice within the firm, perhaps I could remain indefinitely. When I heard Holly Near's political songs playing in the office of one of the partners one evening, while I worked late during my first month at the firm, I congratulated myself on having made a good choice.

I delayed starting my work for the firm until September 15 to give myself a vacation after my clerkship ended. On Wednesday, September 10, after I sent the kids off to school, I drove into the Berkshires and headed north on back roads into the southern Green Mountains of Vermont. I stopped at the edge of a secluded field and sat on a low stone wall at the side of the road. Densely blooming goldenrod bordered the wall and clusters of delicate purple New England asters sprouted from its cracks. The subtly sweet smell of decaying vegetation from the forest floor mingled with the blooming flowers. Only a few swamp maples had started to turn a rusty red color. The remainder of the deciduous trees on the hillside beyond the field retained their deep green. The warm September sun, lower in the sky even at midday, cast shadows in the hazy oblique light. The faint hum of bees moving among the flowers was hypnotic. As I took out my sandwich, two does and a half-grown young deer stepped out of the forest to nibble the grasses in the shade at the far end of the field.

Organized religion and the concept of a self-conscious God who governs the universe had never made sense to me, but since moving to Massachusetts in 1970 I'd felt a growing connection with nature. The chemicals that in combination make up our bodies are drawn from the earth and will return to it in a geological instant. The idea that human beings are apart from, and live in opposition to, natural forces strikes me as absurd. As I sat on my stone perch I could feel the boundaries between the world and myself dissipate. My molecules seemed in tune with my surroundings. I suppose some would call this experience spiritual or even religious. Whatever you term it, it was for me a cherished moment.

I felt that this natural world was infinitely more important than the work I was about to submerge myself in. *Submerge* was the right word. I was going back under cover. The partners might know my lineage and have liberal backgrounds, but they served businessmen who tended to be conservative. As a corporate lawyer in training I'd have to keep my beliefs under wraps, just as I had in high school. I thought back to the time I'd joined Springfield's Junior Chamber of Commerce in 1972 in preparation for my proposed urban anthropology dissertation about the impact of businessmen's decision-making networks on public policy. Where did my recurring desire to burrow into the bowels of American business come from? Was there something about what happened to my parents that made me want to spy on my enemy and learn his tricks? Could I really pull this off? My plan seemed so clever in theory, but now that I was about to venture into unknown territory I doubted its viability.

I finished my sandwich. The deer perhaps heard the crinkle of my paper bag and bounded into the forest. A yellowjacket hunting for crumbs started to harass me, and I retreated to the car. I'd made my job choice and felt there was no turning back. I put my doubts into my well-used childhood box and refused to think about them. This field and many others like it would be here if I needed to return to it. I drove home to greet the girls after school with the somber feeling of someone forced to leave good times behind to confront an unpleasant but necessary task.

I joined the law firm just as dozens of business clients began clambering to have the firm take the legal steps necessary for their businesses and families to adjust to sweeping tax-law changes. The partner I worked with most frequently at the firm called the Tax Reform Act of 1986 the tax lawyers' employment act. These changes generated tens of thousands of dollars in legal fees for the firm, but had the potential for saving clients more than ten times as much. The 1986 act was a major step in the current trend that shifts the tax burden away from the wealthy and onto the shoulders of those with more modest incomes.

I was quickly engulfed by paperwork and twelve-hour workdays. I entered the law firm like a swimmer poised at the edge of a river with the objective of swimming across. Once I plunged into the current it was all I could do to avoid inhaling a lungful of water as I stroked forward. I lost sight of my goal, and I had to keep swimming even as I began to tire.

For the first time in my life I was working primarily for a paycheck. I got used to more frequent haircuts and choosing from my expanding wardrobe of suits and ties. I lived for my diminished time with family and stolen moments for SACAP. But the paycheck was comforting as college loomed on the temporal horizon. Our increased financial security also enabled Elli to work part-time for two years while she obtained an advanced nursing degree at the University of Massachusetts. It seemed that at any given time one of us was in school or changing careers.

At first the work was engaging, and the days flew by. I learned valuable lessons at the firm that had little to do with the technical aspects of practicing law. One partner represented businessmen who were either starting businesses or buying them. He thought many new business owners fail because they lack a long-term plan and sufficient capitalization. These neophytes focused too much on the day-to-day activities of running the business. I felt this insight applied equally to progressive projects. The visionaries who start them react to events and usually have neither time nor interest in developing long-term strategic or financial plans. They see such activities as impediments rather than facilitators of their real work. They forge ahead until they run out of funds and energy. I vowed not to make these mistakes if I ever got around to starting my own foundation.

This same partner also pointed out that people usually are or become good at things they like doing. A good owner knows a little bit about many aspects of his business, but focuses on the tasks he likes and develops a management team of people who also like their specialties.

I thought about the times I had forced myself to give out leaflets on street corners or scream chants at demonstrations. I didn't like confronting people on the street, and I doubt I was very good at it. I thought about groups that impose a uniform mold of activities upon their members. There is so much good work to do, why not let members focus on what they like doing? Of course there are tasks no one wants to do. Still, I determined to match those who wanted to help my fantasy foundation with the kinds of things they enjoyed doing most.

Although I was quick to note the mistakes others made when they embarked on projects, I refused to see that working in a business-oriented law firm was not the proper context for me. This caught up with me before long.

At the beginning of 1988 the partners decided that I was ready to deal more directly with clients and assume greater responsibility for closing business deals. The objectives of creating the legal papers to document a transfer of business ownership are deceptively simple. When we represented someone selling a business, we tried to sell it for more than it was worth and protect our client from all potential claims generated by problems the buyer discovered after the sale was completed. When we represented the buyer we wanted to pay less than the business's value and keep the prior owner on the hook for any problems the new owner did not discover until afterward. I wasn't responsible for negotiating the financial terms of the deal, but before long I was put in charge of organizing and drafting the terms of dozens of legal documents that had to be formalized before or at the closing so the transaction could take place.

Any home buyer has suffered through signing a seemingly endless stream of documents at the closing. Many of those documents are standard forms, but the parties have bargained over some of the terms. Imagine many more documents, most of which were subject to intense negotiation. My job was to ensure that these papers accurately reflected our client's view of the agreement. Aggressive entrepreneurs, with equally combative attorneys as well as bankers and other lenders, postured, haggled, dissembled, and backstabbed one another; and it was all in a day's work.

I disliked the whole process and some of the clients. I remember saying to a friend that I gained no satisfaction from having my businessman get the better of the other attorney's businessman. But it was worse than that. While I already knew the objective of corporate law in theory, seeing it in practice brought home that the primary purpose of corporate law was to protect owners, lenders, and investors from the public. The same businessmen who'd scream bloody murder about welfare recipients not acting responsibly had with court support evolved elaborate formalities that enabled owners and investors to escape personal responsibility for much of the harm caused by their businesses and investments. I drafted documents designed to minimize the personal liability of the owner if his or her business caused monetary harm, personal injury, or environmental damage. Our nation's largest corporations did this on a mind-boggling scale. The Ford Motor Corporation was ultimately forced to pay over one hundred million dollars to compensate victims and their families for the deaths and serious injuries caused by its defectively designed Pinto. The plaintiffs prevailed in their civil actions because they showed that top Ford officials knew that the Pinto was unsafe but determined the profits they'd reap from selling these deathtraps would outweigh the cost of compensating the victims. But none of Ford's corporate criminals spent a day in jail or lost a penny of personal income. The kind of asset protection provided by the documents I drafted did not involve such deadly circumstances, but I still found their implications very disturbing.

I could not admit my basic distaste for the nature of my work. Instead I would wake up at 4:00 A.M. worrying that there were imperfections in the documents I'd produced. I obsessed about all that could go wrong, and became convinced that I would be blamed when it did. I could not purge these thoughts that continuously scrolled through my brain like the trailer at the bottom of a TV screen. Sleep eluded me, and exhaustion fueled my anxiety.

My heart would pound at the slightest hint of trouble with any deal, and problems with deals were frequent. I tried to calm myself by coming into the office earlier each morning to repeatedly recheck everything I did. It wasn't difficult to get up early when I couldn't sleep. But I was so jumpy that I couldn't process what I was reviewing.

I couldn't eat. One of the other attorneys I occasionally had lunch with teased that I always ate the blandest foods. I love exotic and spicy foods, but white bread was about all I could stomach while working at the firm. This reminded me of how I reacted each time I tried to solve all of my father's problems in a three-day visit during his last year in Miami. I compensated for how much his deterioration upset me by worrying that I was missing something that could have dire consequences for him. I got so wound up that I stopped eating while I was there. Now I suffered the same loss of appetite, but it was chronic rather than episodic.

Elli encouraged me to seek counseling. Except for a few visits to Dr. Frederick Wertham when I was six and seven years old, I'd never seen a therapist. But I did not hesitate to contact the therapist provided by our HMO. It was helpful to have someone to share my fears with. He quickly zeroed in on my childhood experiences. He understood that there was a relationship between what I had gone through as a small boy and how I was unraveling now, but I don't think he grasped why my current situation set me off. I didn't either at that point. The therapist consulted with a psychiatrist, who prescribed antianxiety medications. I took Xanax during the day and Halcyon so I could sleep at night.

The drugs relieved the worst symptoms but did nothing to resolve the underlying problem. I lived one week at a time that interminable spring. I hung on until Friday so I'd have two weekend days to recuperate. Friday evening was a miracle of relaxation. I took comfort in my family. I'd almost feel like my old self until Sunday afternoon, when the tension would swell. I tried to get used to it, but in honest moments I felt I could not survive such a high level of anxiety for very long.

The first major crisis came in July 1988, when I was supposed to help close the purchase of a business. The partner in charge went on vacation and left me to keep things moving forward until he returned a few days before the closing. The opposing attorney dug in his heels over a seemingly inconsequential matter. Rather than confront him or go to other partners for help, I froze. When the partner returned I'd made no progress, and we both had to scramble to close the deal. The partner could not understand why I had been unable to act. No one at the firm knew what I was going through, and until that point none had any complaints about my work. Fortunately I had just two weeks left until our family's two-week vacation. I counted down those days like someone whose lungs were about to burst holding his breath for a few more seconds.

I didn't want to worry the kids and ruin our vacation with Elli's family on the North Carolina shore, so Elli and I had only limited discussions of my worsening predicament. I refused to admit that I couldn't continue, and Elli did not press her belief that I should leave the firm; she felt I had to reach that conclusion on my own. In any event, I calmed down enough during the vacation so that it took several more weeks at work before my downward spiral resumed.

That autumn quickly degenerated into a haze of therapy sessions, uneaten meals, and snatches of drug-induced sleep. I got through each week by imagining a mathematical model in which each work-week was an eight-hour day. If I worked forty-eight hours in any given week, then each six-hour period was the equivalent of one hour in an eight-hour day. According to my model it was 9:00 A.M. when I arrived for work on Monday, and all I had to do was survive until 5:00 P.M. That meant it was the equivalent of 3:24 in the afternoon when I left for the day on Thursday. All I had to do was to get through another hour and thirty-six minutes without screwing up too badly and I'd be home free for the weekend.

I talked to almost no one but Elli about my growing problem. Our friends Marc and Nancy visited from New York during the middle of the July crisis, and I could not avoid describing my problem. They were supportive, but what could they do? My brother was the next person I told, but that was not until mid-September. He'd been an economics professor for almost twenty years. I doubted he had much understanding of what working in a business law firm was like. He and Ann invited me to join them at a Red Sox game to provide a respite. This kind of support was helpful but temporary.

If practicing law made me crazy, what else could I do? Jenny was a junior in high school. How could we afford to pay for her college without my salary? Elli told me she thought that my body was rebelling because my mind refused to acknowledge the deep revulsion I felt for what I was doing. I thought she might be right, but I was unwilling to leave because I felt I'd run out of options. So I tried to put the thought of leaving my job in a box. But my familiar way of dealing with situations I couldn't confront did not help, because this time *I* was in the box.

Soon my work-related anxiety metastasized into other aspects of my life. Routine matters like paying bills became insurmountable tasks. One weekend I balked at driving the car into Boston. Someone could run into us at any intersection. How could I drive ninety miles each way without making at least one potentially fatal mistake?

Family was my only refuge. Elli, Jenny, and Rachel were a joy to be around. Family time was bittersweet, however, because I was failing them.

While I was falling apart, Rob Okun was putting the finishing touches on REAP. It had taken five years, but the exhibit of art inspired by my parents' case opened at its first venue in New York in September 1988. I had shared Rob's excitement as he tracked down, commissioned, and assembled the works that made up the exhibit, but I did not feel capable of speaking at the opening. I developed a prior commitment that kept me from attending.

I promised Rob that I'd speak instead at the Boston opening in November, and then I had no choice. As the day drew near, I worried about my ability to function at all, let alone stand before an audience and give a speech relating to my parents' case for the first time in almost a decade. I was also apprehensive about speaking immediately after seeing what I feared would be a visual assault. I had seen slides of the work, so I knew the exhibit contained an installation of an electric chair and deeply disturbing images of executions. I arranged with Rob to spend a couple of hours alone with the exhibit before my talk so I could keep my initial reactions private.

Those hours were a revelation. The gallery walls reverberated with the energy of dozens of artists. I sat in solitude on a backless stone bench amid the vast silence of an empty museum surrounded by these images. I pondered why my parents' death ignited such a sustained outpouring of creativity. That they were unjustly executed was not a sufficient explanation. Injustice was—and is—rampant. Killing, judicially sanctioned and otherwise, remains commonplace.

My parents' resistance must have been the catalyst. Although aware that the U.S. government was bent on either breaking or killing them, they refused to acquiesce, and with their letters to each other provided mutual support and helped galvanize the worldwide effort to save them.

I realized that they had not been powerful people—until they resisted. I reflected on Nelson Mandela (then still imprisoned), who gained power over his captors by choosing to remain in prison rather than renounce his advocacy of his people's right to fight for their freedom. Leonard Peltier* might also have appeared powerless at that time; he'd already served fourteen years in prison. But in that museum I felt that his power would outlast that of the police agents, guards, wardens, and judges who kept him unjustly confined. My parents had become powerful because they resisted, and this exhibit was a testament to that resistance. The artwork was acting as a conduit, infusing me with their power thirty-five years later.

As I spoke to the crowd that attended the opening that evening, I felt as if the clouds that filled my life's sky parted to reveal brilliant blue. A shaft of hope pierced November's darkness.

That evening I resolved to leave the firm. I told Elli I wanted to get out of there, but I had no viable alternative. Elli and the kids had also been at the opening, and we stayed overnight in the Boston area before attending a wedding the next day. We sat at a table with Michael and Ann at the wedding. I confided in my brother how precarious my mental state had become. I can't recall my comment, but he says I told him I feared he'd soon see the headline ROSENBERG SON CRACKS UP.

---

*Leonard Peltier, as leader of the American Indian Movement, was wrongfully convicted of killing two FBI agents during the Wounded Knee Occupation in 1973. He is serving a term of life imprisonment.

Afterward I became so tense, dreading Monday in the office, that I couldn't drive home. I survived the week but accomplished next to nothing. The thought of quitting was like jumping off a cliff into a bottomless black pit, but by the next weekend I felt I had no choice. Elli was right. My body was screaming, You will not eat and you will not sleep until you get out of there! My therapist disagreed. He believed that leaving would make me worse.

The following Saturday Elli and I discussed at length whether I should quit my job. Regaining a sense of proportion had to be my first priority. Obsessing about what I could do next while in a constant state of panic was absurd. I decided I had to leave immediately. We explained my decision to the kids. Jenny, then a high school junior focused on college, voiced her concern that we'd lack the money to pay for one of the expensive private colleges that were her top choices. This was precisely what I feared. With characteristic forth-rightness Elli told Jenny we'd pay what we could for the college of her choice, but preventing me from having a heart attack took prece-dence. Jenny had no trouble accepting this priority.

That Sunday we played many games of Clue into the evening to enjoy one another and break the tension. On Monday morning I was so frightened and doped up that I needed Elli to accompany me when I walked into the office of the partner I worked with most frequently and told him I could not continue to work there. While I felt it was humiliating for my wife to hold my hand, I required her support.

The partner's response surprised me. He called a couple of other attorneys I worked with into the office and asked if any clients had complained about my work. When they responded that none had, he said I should take two weeks off and return in early December. This can be a rough business and maybe you just need a little time, he said. I jumped at the reprieve.

I've never felt more relieved than I did on the walk back to my reserved parking spot. Thanksgiving was Thursday, and for the first time since summer vacation I was able to put work-related worries aside, at least for that first week. I was only home alone for the next two days. I kept busy cleaning house and doing other preholiday chores, so I did not brood about my future. But my predicament returned with renewed force the following Monday.

Now I began to share my troubles with more of my friends. I told them that I had lost confidence that I could accomplish any job at all. I was skeptical when they disagreed, but still took solace from their encouragement and generosity. Rob Okun said I could get more involved with REAP. Bruce Miller said maybe I could teach an evening class at the law school. But I knew I needed a long-term solution.

That week an entirely different sort of experience floored me. My Northampton attorney friend, Bill Newman, invited me to hear his client Pat talk about the "Ohio Seven" trial that was taking place at the Federal Courthouse in Springfield. Pat, her husband Ray, and five other defendants were each charged with three counts of seditious conspiracy to overthrow the government of the United States. The three couples and one single person had been members of a revolutionary underground cell. At a previous trial they had been convicted of carrying out bombings against multinational corporations that invested in apartheid South Africa during the late 1970s and early 1980s, and of robbing banks to support their clandestine lifestyle. Even though all except Pat, who had been convicted only of harboring a fugitive (her husband), were serving multidecade sentences, Attorney General Edwin Meese decided to charge them with seditious conspiracy and have them retried. All faced an additional sixty years in prison.

Since the imprisoned defendants had no money, the government was paying for both the prosecution *and* the defense. The trial was originally slated for Boston but had been moved to Springfield for security reasons. Pat, recently paroled into Bill's custody, gave a presentation to explain the trial to the progressive community in Springfield. Afterward she told me that each of the three married couples had three children. When two of her codefendants, Tom and Carol, were arrested in 1985, the authorities seized their three children, then aged eleven, five, and three, and held them incommunicado for several weeks. The oldest was repeatedly interrogated without any supportive adult present. During this period the FBI told the parents that the children would not be released to their relatives until the parents cooperated.

Perhaps it was the drugs or my unstable state, but Pat's revelation coursed through me like an electric shock. Bad as my childhood had been, I had never been interrogated. The authorities had used these children to extort cooperation from Tom and Carol, the same way they had used my brother and me to pressure our parents. But what hit me hardest was that I hadn't even known about it. While I'd been helping businessmen make more money, these kids with whom I felt such a kinship had been terrorized. I added this to my growing list of failures, and returned to work the following Monday.

I was assigned the simplest tasks—standard forms that I could have completed in my sleep a year earlier. By the fourth day back, when I couldn't even figure out how to adjust these templates to the particular needs of the client in question, I gave up.

This time I walked into the partner's office by myself. He surprised me even more when he told me to take two months off before I made my final decision. Although I could no longer stomach the business, I had to admit the firm was treating me fairly and humanely. I agreed, although I was almost certain that I would feel the same way in February.

The next Monday morning Elli went to work, the kids went to school, and I sat in a chair near the front door staring at dust motes suspended in a shaft of sunlight. I had only the cat for company. At that moment she seemed a lot more useful than I was. The mornings during that week were the worst; nervous energy that felt like perpetual pins and needles prickled my limbs. I got up and walked around the neighborhood. The only other idle guys I saw on the street were the recovering drug addicts standing around drinking coffee outside "Serenity House," several blocks away. Welcome to your new world, I told myself. I couldn't wait for the school holidays to start. At least when I went to the supermarket in the middle of the day people could think I was a teacher on vacation rather than a do-nothing loser.

I saw the therapist toward the end of the week. He told me that I had to dig into the core of my childhood experiences, confront what I had always avoided there, and remake my personality from the inside out. Was he right? I reviewed my history. I never finished my Ph.D. I abandoned the reopening effort. I didn't stick it out at *SR*. I couldn't handle working at the law firm. I was forty-one years old, and I felt that I had not successfully completed anything. Perhaps my realization so many years ago, during those two terrible weeks in eighth grade, that I was avoiding my true self had been correct.

Maybe the therapist was right; maybe not. But I'll never forget what he told me next. He said I was unable to function at the law firm because I feared I'd fail my clients just as my parents' attorney, Manny Bloch, had failed to save their lives.

CHAPTER 7

Realizing the Dream

MY FIRST ASSIGNMENT FOR 1989 WAS TO GET WELL. I'VE TAKEN
assignments seriously since college and set about completing them in
an organized, even mechanical, fashion. Despite my dysfunctional
mental state I organized the recovery process intuitively. My most
immediate task was to decide whether to follow the therapist's advice
to begin deep therapy with him. I could not make an intelligent decision about such an important matter with my brain in a drug-induced
fog. So I stopped taking Xanax and Halcyon.

I might have avoided the incredibly vivid and bizarre nightmares I
suffered that week if my panic hadn't prevented me from taking Elli's
advice of tapering off the drugs. I went cold turkey. One dream I still
remember was probably triggered by a book I read that week. My typical diversion of reading science fiction had failed me in the previous
year, so I read one of Elli's mystery novels. It was about a detective in
the decaying Soviet Union trying to solve a murder. The trail took
him from Moscow to Siberia and back. The night after I finished the
book, a huge bright-orange Siberian tiger cornered me. Instead of

devouring me he lectured me about how to solve mysteries with the supercilious air of the Cheshire cat in *Alice in Wonderland*. My conviction that the tiger would eat me at any moment spawned an eerie emotional combination of hilarity and dread. I awoke drenched in sweat with lightning strikes of color etched behind my eyelids.

A week after I stopped the medications, my anxiety attacks were subsiding and I was drug-free, but my nagging feeling that the therapist was missing what really sparked my breakdown persisted. I was reluctant to attempt to unravel and reconstruct my personality with someone whose perspective I didn't quite trust. I decided to get a second opinion from a good friend whose judgment I respected. Lydia Nettler was also a therapist. She told me that I didn't need such drastic measures as extreme therapy. She said she'd had many clients go through similar crises, and they all got better. She felt the situation I'd been in had caused my problems and now that I had removed myself from it I would improve. In effect she told me that my problem was not who I was but what I had been doing. Maybe it was being drug-free or the skillful way she put this analysis together, but I believed her. I talked with her a few more times over the next month, and I will forever be grateful for her lasting positive impact.

I've spent a lot of time since then thinking about what went wrong. The therapist correctly concluded that my paralysis at work was caused by a conflict between who I was and what I was doing. My childhood experience had fostered a political ethic that was at the core of my being. I had developed a plan to function within the system and manipulate it for radical purposes, but it was subverting me rather than vice versa. My parents' experience taught me that it was dangerous to be at war with the most powerful forces of your society, and my life had demonstrated how tiring and frustrating it was to perpetually swim against the current. That's why joining or serving "them" could be so seductive. But I wanted to oppose them, *and* I wanted it to be easy. The therapist's solution might have permitted me to change who I was and join them, but my immediate acceptance of Lydia's analysis showed that despite everything, I refused to abandon my principal values.

But it wasn't until very recently, when I read Jeff Schmidt's *Disciplined Minds* about the brainwashing of professionals, that I comprehended fully what had happened to me, and the source of the therapist's diagnosis. Schmidt points out that the unspoken politics behind almost all professional training and work are designed to give professionals only sufficient intellectual leeway to function effectively within the framework of the status quo. Since many professionals are satisfied with the way things are, they would probably consider the last sentence I wrote delusional. Thus my therapist found a neurotic individual who could not function within the institution of his choice, and only considered adjusting my personality to fit the institution. He apparently never considered that my employer's social function might have caused my problem. This is not surprising, since the typical mental health professional's primary role is to help people function within the system. In Schmidt's words, a therapist is "not about to turn the troubled into troublemakers, no matter how healthful that may be." Lydia, who shared my radical critique of society, saw instantly that I needed to be a troublemaker.

It was not just a matter of perspective. The therapist's remark about my fear of failure was wrong. I didn't fear I would fail my clients the way Manny had failed my parents. I don't hold Manny responsible for my parents' deaths. I knew Manny cared deeply for my parents. I needed to care for the people I served just as strongly. My problem was that I didn't respect my clients' goals and so came to despise myself for working for them. My parents died for their ideals; I could not tolerate betraying my own. I could not function at the law firm because I was helping businessmen take advantage of the same system that killed my parents. I feared failing myself.

At the end of January I had no trouble telling the firm that my decision was irrevocable. I was still fragile, however, and remained unsure of my next step. I took friends' advice and cobbled several part-time projects together. I agreed to teach a night school course at the law school, "Buying and Selling a Closely Held Business," the following fall and snickered at the cliché "Those who can, do. Those who can't, teach." The Ohio Seven defense team hired me as a part-time legal researcher. I also spoke at a forum that complemented the REAP exhibit at one venue, and did some paid fund-raising work to help complete production of *Unknown Secrets*, a short documentary film about the art show.

In early 1988 I had been interviewed for *Unknown Secrets*. In 1989 I saw the finished product several times in connection with the talks I gave at a couple of the exhibit's venues. I didn't think twice about my on-camera comments. When I saw the film again ten years later at the Northampton Film Festival, I was shocked that the first words out of my mouth proclaimed my parents' innocence! I knew that by the time I had given the interview for the film I no longer had such a definitive position, but I evidently didn't feel ready to state that in public.

I began to search for more permanent work. I considered teaching at the law school, and applied for work as an attorney for the Massachusetts Commission Against Discrimination. I met with the judge I had clerked for, and he responded positively when I inquired about doing another clerkship at the Appeals Court starting in the fall. By April that was set. This gained me time to figure out where I was headed, as well as gave us more money to live on. In those early spring days of 1989, starting my own foundation didn't cross my mind even though I'd dreamed about doing so for years.

I'd never taken seriously cartoon pictures of ideas turning on like lightbulbs over people's heads, but several weeks later a cerebral switch was thrown and my brain was rewired. I snapped awake in bed at 4:00 A.M. knowing the mission of my foundation. It would help Pat's kids and Tom and Carol's. It would help kids who are experiencing the same nightmare my brother and I experienced as children.

Pat's story must have been percolating for four months. I wanted to tell Elli immediately, but I knew it would be unfair to wake her. Instead I tingled with excitement while squirming in bed until the alarm went off a couple of hours later.

During those hours I wondered why this idea had surfaced now. Why hadn't I thought of it ten years earlier? Was it just that I hadn't known about the nine kids of the Ohio Seven defendants, or did enduring the purgatory of the law firm have something to do with it? Had the pain of that experience created my desperate need to find a way to fulfill my dream? Could it be that discarding old plans and being forced to consider all possibilities finally brought this to the surface? I realized that my nightmare experiences more than thirty-five years earlier set the scene for this revelation, but finding the foundation's mission took such a long time.

Our alarm was set to ring just after 6:00 A.M. on weekdays even though the kids didn't get up for another half hour, and Elli didn't leave for work until after seven. My post–law firm ritual was to wake Elli up with freshly brewed coffee that we sipped in bed while reading the morning paper. I had resolved never again to become so frantic about my work that I would not relax over a morning cup of coffee with the daily newspaper. But I couldn't contain myself any longer. I handed her a cup of coffee and blurted that I'd finally figured out what the foundation was going to do. Elli was the only person with whom I'd shared this more-than-ten-year-old dream, and she knew exactly what I meant. She thought the idea was perfect. As she left for work she suggested that I mention it to the Ohio Seven lawyers over lunch.

The idea of discussing this half-baked idea with others gave me pause. Where was the money going to come from? I had neither paid work nor money to give away. I had no financing or plan of action. I decided not to discuss so unrefined a plan with anyone. I might have had a great idea, but it wasn't very practical. Perhaps if I'd been more self-confident I would not have given up on something I'd been so excited about only a few hours earlier. Elli, on the other hand, didn't give up on it.

A couple of weeks later, without my knowledge, she discussed it with Pat at our friends Bob and Jan Winston's annual May Day "left-wing chicken barbecue." Their invitation announced they'd cook "Rhode Island Reds, with only left wings and no rednecks." Pat thought the foundation was a terrific idea, which stiffened Elli's resolve to pursue the matter.

Our Berkeley friends visited us that Memorial Day weekend. Dan Scharlin, who is about fifteen years older than I am, has a rare combination of left-wing politics and business expertise. He had provided an excellent sounding board for me to discuss SR's business problems with during our Berkeley years. Dan and I were getting ready to venture out Sunday morning to "slay the wild bagel," when his wife, Harriet, said she wanted to pick up some pastries at the bagel place. Elli asked Dan to stay and help her with other brunch preparations. It seemed as if I was being set up for something, but I couldn't imagine what, since my birthday had passed two weeks before.

I found out when we were sitting in our living room after gorging ourselves. Dan said that Elli had told him about my idea and its financial impediments. He asked me how many years I thought I'd need to make the foundation self-sustaining, and how much money I'd need annually to operate an office and pay myself a minimal salary. I told him three years, and $50,000 each year ($24,000 for me and $26,000 for the office). Dan sketched out a rough business plan for me. Since your time frame probably contains an element of wishful thinking, he began, let's say it will take you four years. So you need $200,000 over four years. Write up a proposal for your project, circulate it to your fund-raising contacts, and find twenty people who'll pledge $2,500 each year for four years. He cut off my objections, saying that since I had more than three months before my one-year job started, I had plenty of time to draft and circulate a proposal.

He reminded me that I'd told him the night before that the clerk-ship was not all-consuming work, so I'd have evening and weekend time to pursue the plan further. He concluded that I couldn't have put myself in a more ideal position if I'd planned it because I had fifteen months to get this off the ground. This would provide an excellent test. If I couldn't line up backers during that time, then the idea prob-ably wasn't viable, but if I could find an initial group of supporters, I'd most likely be able to interest a broader constituency as well. By the time Harriet and Dan left that afternoon, I was wavering but inclined to give it a try.

I ate lunch with the Ohio Seven attorneys several times a week. I particularly enjoyed talking with Liz Fink, the lead attorney on the case. Liz was an almost legendary figure among those working to defend America's political prisoners. In 1991 her efforts would lead to a new trial and the ultimate release of a Black Panther Party member wrongfully imprisoned for almost twenty years. She was also the lead attorney for the "Attica Brothers" civil suit against the State of New York. The Attica Brothers were inmates who had been slaughtered, maimed, and tortured in retaliation for taking over New York's maximum-security prison almost twenty years earlier. Liz and several others would not let the case go despite its seeming futility. It took her another ten years to gain a trial victory and an inadequate but sub-stantial financial settlement from the New York State government.

With growing admiration I'd watched Liz in action during the court proceedings. She told me my parents' case had been a formative experience for her. She said our opponents were very powerful. We couldn't stop them from executing Julius and Ethel for conspiracy (she usually referred to my parents by their first names although she was just a child when they were executed). She told me: "They can get away with doing a lot of terrible things, but if we can't stop them we can make them pay." Her objectives seemed worth emulating.

I observed the way she fought both the prosecutors and the judge during the trial; I saw how she was making them pay. I told Liz over lunch during that last week in May 1989 that I was going to build a foundation that would help the children of political prisoners grow up with a positive connection to their parents. This was my way of making "them" pay. Liz liked the idea, but I could tell that she was skeptical about my ability to pull it off.

I doubted it myself, but now that my dream had found its focus I devoted myself to it. First the foundation needed a name. I discarded the old title, "Rosenberg Children's Fund," because I didn't want people to think I was fund-raising for myself, and settled on "The Rosenberg Fund for Children" or RFC.

I needed to learn more about these children, and if I were going to circulate a proposal I would also have to flesh out the project's objectives. I was startled to learn how many children today were vulnerable to the same kind of nightmares I endured after my parents' arrest. I learned that our country held over more than one hundred political prisoners (Black Panthers, American Indian Movement members, Puerto Rican Nationalists, and white revolutionaries like the Ohio Seven), and my initial survey indicated that among them they had at least seventy children. I still knew next to nothing about the specifics of these children's lives. But my experiences, coupled with those of Tom and Carol's kids, led me to believe that many of these children desperately needed help.

I also gathered stories of progressive activists nationwide who, rather than being imprisoned, had been fired, blacklisted, harassed, physically attacked, or even killed because of their progressive organizing. There were more stories than I expected. During the 1980s the death of Karen Silkwood, the nuclear power plant whistle-blower, had been in the news a lot. She'd been killed, not imprisoned. If she had children it would be ridiculous to deny them support just because she had not been jailed.

I realized that Karen Silkwood's case was exceptional only because of how well publicized it was. The progressive community was unaware of the grim situations faced by many other targeted activists and their children. Lack of publicity in the mainstream media was only partly to blame. By the late 1980s the civil rights and antiwar mass movements of the 1960s had fragmented into myriad projects and minuscule multi-issue parties. In many instances the partisans of one project or formation were unaware, or even suspicious, of the activities of other groups. There was little sense of community among activists. Those working to help political prisoners were unlikely to pay much attention to an attack on an environmental activist and vice versa. Activists' tendency to focus on the targeted individual and his or her cause rather than on his or her children isolated the children even further.

I realized that including a broader range of activists whose children were potential RFC beneficiaries would not only broaden our base of support but might also help to build common bonds among different sets of activists. The core mission of the RFC became to meet the needs of children in this country who were suffering because of the targeting of their progressive activist parents.

Our nation professes to encourage a politically involved citizenry, but those who fight racism, injustice, financial exploitation, and environmental depredation may pay heavily for their service to society. If they have children, activists must often choose between waging these struggles and protecting their families. I realized that the RFC could help these families, and by connecting their children to a support network, we could facilitate the development of progressive community. I included the following paragraphs in my five-page proposal:

> *Regardless of tactical and political differences we may have with these activist parents, their fate is the result of political action they took to transform our society into one that values all people equally, places people before profits, and recognizes the ecological limits of growth. Their children are completely innocent. When*

stand why an endowment was necessary and why it should be for granting, not everyday operating expenses. As a child I had been moved from place to place and never knew what was coming next. Our beneficiaries needed the security of a dependable source of multiyear support. I knew that without an endowment we could not guarantee such support and would risk becoming another source of uncertainty in these children's lives. I explained to potential supporters that without a granting fund endowment we'd risk becoming part of the problem rather than part of the solution for these children. I decided to ignore the advice of those fund-raising experts and go with my gut feeling that this would work.

My proposal established general objectives for our first four years, but the key goals were to provide one hundred thousand dollars of annual support for at least one hundred children and develop a one million dollar granting fund endowment. These goals were based on guesswork, and the RFC didn't come close to achieving them. In 1993, at the end of our third year, I developed a numerical model to predict our future growth based on our track record until that point and projected we'd achieve these goals by the end of the decade. We made it by early 1999.

Raising the start-up funds wasn't easy. I began circulating the proposal in July and continued to pursue leads in my spare time once my second clerkship started in September 1989. As always, I quantified my progress. Each person or couple who made a $2,500-a-year pledge brought me 5 percent closer to my goal. The first 25 percent came pretty quickly. First I asked the people I expected to say yes, and they did not disappoint me. I believe some of them did so only to support me, not because they believed I'd find nineteen others, or even if I did that the RFC would ever achieve its goals. But my search slowed in the fall and it got messier. Several people pledged $1,250 annually, or $1,000, or $500. It would be stupid to turn down this support, but I knew I would not be able to maintain the personal contact needed to ensure that almost everyone would honor their pledges for the entire period if my operating fund campaign program ballooned to more than a few dozen participants.

As New England entered winter I felt as if I was clawing my way up an icy cliff a percentage or two at a time, but I made enough progress to persist. At the end of February, when I passed the 50 percent mark, I decided to go ahead with my plan. I reasoned that if I'd secured more than half the funds needed and still had six months to prospect in my spare time, I'd be approaching my goal by the time I opened an office in September and would raise the rest more quickly once I could devote full-time work to the fund. I'd better be right, because Jenny had been accepted at one of the most expensive colleges in the country, and we'd need every penny of my budgeted $24,000 salary.

I began spreading the word among the circles of people who might benefit from the fund. This brought me back in contact with Bill Ayres, who had given the speech for the Jesse James Gang in Ann Arbor twenty years before. He and his wife, Bernardine Dohrn, had become leaders in Weatherman, spent years underground, and resurfaced several years earlier. They lived in the Hyde Park section of Chicago and were raising their two sons along with the son of imprisoned former comrades. They offered to host a fund-raising reception at their home. The reception would provide the first test of my ability to raise funds for the RFC's granting fund. I couldn't actually collect money for the RFC since it did not exist yet. I would leave the party with an address list and a bunch of pledges.

I had more than one reason to visit Chicago. Several potential operating fund donors lived there, and I felt that personal visits would increase the chance of their saying yes. So I took a day off from work and flew to Chicago for a long weekend to see these potential donors and to attend the reception.

It was cool and rainy that Friday morning in early May 1990. Droplets beaded freshly opened forsythia along the gated fence at the end of the driveway that led past the aging mansion to the carriage house Bill and Bernardine were renting. Hyde Park is a beautiful old neighborhood of stately homes surrounding the University of Chicago campus. It is the only prosperous integrated neighborhood in Chicago and was home to the type of people who were most likely to support my project. In fact, I only had to walk a couple of blocks to visit one potential major contributor. His pledge of one thousand dollars a year started my trip off on the right foot.

An hour afterward I met another potential supporter for a late lunch at the Drake Hotel, an elegant landmark that stands between Michigan Avenue and the lakefront. The enthusiastic response I received here raised my spirits even further. After my lunch at the Drake I was 70 percent of the way toward obtaining fifty thousand dollars in annual pledges, and for the first time was confident of the foundation's ultimate success. I left the hotel and emerged into brilliant sunshine. A breeze billowed brightly colored banners that proclaimed a spring shopping spree at the upscale stores lining Michigan Avenue's "Magnificent Mile." Thousands of office workers appeared to have left work with spring fever by midafternoon and had joined throngs of shoppers. I flowed with them toward the Loop feeling a tremendous surge of potential induced by good news and a perfect spring day. My first full day on the road for the RFC had been cathartic. If this was a foretaste of my RFC work life I was a lucky man indeed. I looked forward to the next day's party with growing excitement.

Bill and Bernardine were good organizers and well connected to Chicago's progressive community. I expected a big crowd and was not disappointed. I told the story of what happened to me in the wake of my parents' arrest, recounted my plan to start the RFC, and asked for pledges of financial support. My pitch was quite successful, but I had special help. The eight-year-old son of two political prisoners Bill and Bernardine were raising sat at my feet. When I was finished, he commented loudly: "Boy, his life was just like mine, only worse!"

In September 1990 I moved into a one-room office donated by a friend's law firm and became the executive director (and only employee) of the RFC. Over the summer Elli and I, along with a small group that evolved into the RFC's initial board of directors, planned to launch our granting fund. We arranged a "Kick-off Benefit Concert" that was scheduled to take place on October 12. Elli and Lydia Nettler had organized a successful Pete Seeger concert at Smith College's John M. Greene Hall five years earlier to benefit both a Northampton day-care program and a documentary film about the Communist Party, entitled *Seeing Reds*. They formed the core of the concert organizing committee along with Bob Winston, the left-wing chicken host; Rob Okun of REAP; and Bill Newman, Pat's lawyer. Collectively we had a wealth of expertise and connections to almost every progressive network in the valley's three counties. I utilized my national contacts to line up Pete Seeger, Richie Havens, "Country Joe" MacDonald, and Jane Sapp, a powerful local singer, as our performers.

My first stab at being an executive producer went reasonably well, even though there were many things that had to coalesce at the last moment. Ironically, I believe I benefited enormously from my experience at the law firm organizing complex closings. I also felt my anxiety level rising just as it had at the firm, and became keenly attuned to my stress barometer as the date approached. Even though so much that was out of my control could go wrong, unlike at the law firm I had ultimate control over the underlying organization of the event. Perhaps most important, the stress was worth it because I was initiating work I believed in. But I also learned that I had a limited tolerance for this kind of work, and so resolved to stage these major events only occasionally.

The concert wasn't sold out, but we came close enough so that almost no one noticed. It seemed almost absurd to dub the $12,500 we cleared an endowment, but we were not deterred. The RFC made its first awards seven months later on May 10, 1991. Two grants, each for $402.50, enabled Tom and Carol's children, terrorized by the federal authorities six years earlier, to attend a two-week session at Maine Friends Camp. When we made that first grant the RFC had fewer than one thousand supporters, less than $20,000 in its granting fund endowment, and only $50,000 in annual pledges stood between it and institutional extinction.

But I went to work every morning marveling at how lucky I was to have found my life's calling. I traveled the country speaking at dozens of receptions over the next few years, raising money and scouting out potential beneficiaries for the fund. My talks were simple; I'd tell the story of what happened to my brother and me after our parents' arrest, explain how I wanted to help children today who were enduring similar turmoil, and conclude by describing the circumstances of a few of our beneficiary families. I'd talk about Judi Bari and her two daughters. Judi, an organizer of the 1989 Redwood Summer campaign to save thousand-year-old redwoods from timber companies, suffered serious permanent injury when her car was bombed. I asked reception guests to imagine the traumatic impact of this event on her two daughters, aged four and nine. I met Judi at a conference in 1992. She told me that for more than a year after the bombing her older daughter was terrified every time Judi left the house fearing she'd never see her mother alive again. Judi said that RFC support that paid for her daughter's piano lessons might seem trivial, but the lessons were therapeutic and provided the girl with a source of solace. I also told the story of a teenage RFC beneficiary who, along with his parents, had been harassed since he was twelve because of his parents' antiracist activity. He had been suspended from school in Alabama without cause, tried for truancy despite proof of medical necessity, and told in court that he would be taken from his parents. The family fled to California to avoid losing their son. The RFC paid for therapy to help him overcome his ordeal. Most guests were shocked by these stories, and were very supportive of my efforts.

The RFC grew steadily. Many people thanked me for the work I was doing. They acted as if I had made some great sacrifice to embark on this course, but I didn't see it that way. I got tremendous personal satisfaction out of helping children with whom I identified so strongly. I felt privileged to do this work.

One key to the RFC's success was our ability to build a project that provided concrete benefits to children and families while also being firmly grounded in activism. When I spoke to groups of supporters, I reminded people of the two most recent periods of mass progressive activity. The 1930s and the 1960s were different in many ways, but they had one similarity so basic that it is often overlooked: Large numbers of youth between the ages of fifteen and twenty-five energized the activism of both periods. This age group often combines new insights with the energy, idealism, and willingness to take chances needed to confront entrenched authority. When I first promoted the RFC concept, I urged older progressives to devote more resources to working with young people, as youth would initiate the next mass progressive movement. In fact, the last several years have seen an explosion of youth activism. This activism has many sources, but we should not discount the positive impact of child-oriented progressive providers who nurtured the next generation of activists.

All the pieces had come together for me. From a dream of honoring my parents' memory, the RFC grew into a viable project to build on their legacy. I believe that this growth demonstrates the inspirational nature of resistance. My parents' resistance inspired a movement. That inspiration survived their execution. My experience suggested that as long as community nurtures resistance and inspiration, a movement might suffer disastrous defeats but would not be obliterated. Compare my parents' refusal to lie with the Greenglasses' acceptance of the deal offered by the government: I doubt the public would support a Greenglass Fund for Children.

Now, when people tearfully confronted me with tales of how they fought to save my parents' lives and failed, I finally had the response I had longed for but could not previously articulate. Although these sympathizers didn't save my parents, they were part of the community of resistance that saved Michael and me. I am convinced that there never would have been an RFC if all of these good people had not acted in the 1950s. I believe the RFC is not only a testament to Ethel and Julius Rosenberg's resistance but also a tribute to all who fought to save them.

And history was far from finished with my parents' case. In retrospect, it was only once I'd started working full-time for the RFC that I began to consistently articulate my new understanding of what happened to my parents. I returned to the college lecture circuit to raise additional funds for the RFC. When I talked about my parents' case I went out of my way not only to demonstrate that they were framed but also to state that I had not proved them completely innocent. In fact, I dramatically (I hope) argued that I had proved that: (1) my parents had not stolen the secret of the atomic bomb; (2) they had not committed the act they were killed for; (3) the government knew this and executed them anyway; and (4) I could not prove that neither one of them ever had any contact with the KGB between their marriage in 1939 and arrest in 1950.

Some who continued to proclaim my parents' pristine innocence were very uncomfortable with my new approach. They warned that the press would distort my position and report that I thought my parents were guilty. This has not been the case. The press regularly asked me if I sought my parents' vindication. Although I'd answered that question affirmatively in the 1970s, by the 1990s I was saying no. My goal was to force both the American and Russian governments to release all their secret files and let the chips fall where they may. I'd tell reporters that I had a massive credibility problem because I was my parents' son, and that no one would take me seriously if vindication were my goal. But their articles still tended to be headlined: ROSENBERG SON SEEKS PARENTS' VINDICATION.

As long as I was certain of both my parents' innocence there was no point in considering the case against each of them separately. My analysis changed once I began to address the possibility that my father had had some contact with the KGB. By the late 1970s, I knew from the FBI files that long after he agreed to cooperate with the FBI, David Greenglass maintained my mother was not involved in spying. I also knew from the files that just weeks before the trial, in a secret meeting, government officials acknowledged the weakness of the case against my mother, and that, shortly afterward, first Ruth and then David Greenglass gave the FBI a new version of what had happened. They swore to this new version at trial, maintaining that my mother was present at their espionage meetings and typed up David's handwritten notes describing the atomic bomb. These statements became the key testimony against my mother. I would tell audiences in the 1990s: "So even if one hundred percent of the evidence presented against my mother were true, the government of the United States executed my mother for typing!"

But the Greenglass statement about the typing was a lie. The FBI files support this conclusion, and although it took until December 5, 2001, Greenglass finally admitted during a nationally televised interview on *Sixty Minutes II* that he had lied under oath when he stated during the trial that he remembered my mother typing his handwritten notes. Greenglass's televised admission is the capstone of an overwhelming body of evidence indicating that my mother was never an espionage agent. But, more important, FBI director J. Edgar Hoover, some of his top assistants, including Special Agent Robert Lamphere, as well as chief government prosecutor Irving Saypol and his assistant Roy Cohn, all of whom orchestrated my mother's imprisonment and ultimate execution, knew from the moment of her arrest that she was not an espionage agent.

My expanded understanding of my parents' case also helped me handle the steady stream of new revelations about it that have surfaced since 1990. Since I no longer had the answer that they were innocent, I was able to evaluate each new piece of information without trying to jam it into a preconceived framework. And since the sources of this material were suspect (that is, the CIA, KGB, and FBI), I treated every one with skepticism while comparing each with the known record.

Some answers were easy. For instance, it was simple to dismiss a book published in 1990, containing transcripts of what were purported to be tape-recordings of former Soviet premier Nikita Khrushchev stating that, before he died, Stalin said my parents provided "very significant help" to the Soviet atom bomb project (Jerrold L. Schecter and Vyacheslav V. Luchkov, *Khrushchev Remembers: The Glasnot Tapes* [Boston: Little, Brown, 1990], pp. 193–94). I already knew from sworn statements of scientists who had built the bomb at Los Alamos that no matter what Khrushchev had said, neither of my parents was directly or even indirectly involved in the transmission of valuable atomic secrets. Sure enough, within months, information surfaced showing that the quality of the tape was so poor that the same voiceprint expert who had been used to verify other Khrushchev recordings refused to certify that the voice on these portions of the tape was actually Khrushchev's.

With the fall of the Soviet Union, murmurs of former KGB agents began to surface in the Western press. Although their statements were not consistent, they shared some points of convergence. The gist was that Ethel and Julius Rosenberg had not been atomic spies, but that Julius had coordinated a group that supplied the Soviet Union with nonatomic military/industrial information. While the KGB files remained closed, former KGB agents appeared to be selling their stories to the highest bidders. Despite the fact that KGB agents could hardly be considered paragons of honesty, I felt that we had to plan for the possibility that more definitive proof of this scenario would emerge in the near future.

I was concerned that we would be ill prepared for the media frenzy that would accompany any major new proof that either of our parents had done anything illegal. I was particularly worried that proponents of the government position would gain exclusive control of interpreting the meaning of any forthcoming proof. In 1992 I suggested to Michael that we preempt this possibility by holding a press conference in which we would explore the scenario that our father *had* helped supply the Soviet Union with nonatomic information. We would explain, however, that if that was true it would prove that the United States government executed our parents for something they did not do, that is, give the secret of the atom bomb to the Soviet Union. Michael was not certain that this was a good idea, but I decided to present my plan to Marshall Perlin at a meeting I had arranged to discuss another matter.

Predictably Perlin thought it was a terrible notion. First, the press would mangle whatever we said. Second, like a senior attorney lecturing the most junior associate, he listed all the reasons why we should never accept anything said by KGB, CIA, or FBI agents at face value. But the core of his argument was that we should not concede anything unless we absolutely had to. I found this line of reasoning very disturbing, not only because it might ignore the truth, but also because my experience on college campuses had taught me that being publicly open to the possibility that my parents might not be entirely innocent was essential to the effective presentation of our position to a new generation. I remember thinking that Perlin was still fighting the battles of the 1950s, and was woefully out of touch with how to wage today's ideological struggles. But what I said was more visceral: "I'm my parents' son, not their lawyer."

Perlin sat up straighter and impaled me with a piercing stare but said nothing. I'm not sure what his look meant. Was he assessing my trustworthiness? Had I become a loose cannon in his eyes? I'm sure he understood that I was saying it was more important for me honestly to appraise what had actually happened than to defend whatever position my parents and their supporters had staked out in 1953. Regardless, Perlin's adamant reaction, coupled with Michael's and my uncertainty, caused me to drop the idea. Events that unfolded several years later made me regret my decision.

CHAPTER 8

On David Greenglass's Doorstep

———◆◆◗◆◆———

RFC WORK EVENTUALLY LED ME TO A PLACE I'D BEEN AVOIDING ALL my life—my uncle David Greenglass's doorstep. At my parents' trial the government presented evidence that David Greenglass gave critical atom bomb secrets to Harry Gold at his apartment at 209 North High Street in Albuquerque, New Mexico, on June 3, 1945. At the trial Harry Gold testified that he checked into the Albuquerque Hilton Hotel and then walked uphill from the central business district to the Greenglass apartment less than a mile away. While David worked on the secret atom bomb project located in nearby Los Alamos, David and Ruth had rented an apartment on the second floor of a house. In his summation to the jury at the close of my parents' trial, chief prosecutor Saypol stated that Gold and Greenglass's matching testimony about this meeting provided the key evidence necessary to support their conviction.

I never went to Albuquerque during the reopening effort. Perhaps this was because Albuquerque was not fertile ground for building the NCRRC. It is also possible that I felt queasy about returning to the scene of the crime that sent my parents to their deaths. Maybe I remembered the uneasy feeling I had while driving through Los Alamos years earlier; in 1970 Elli and I had pitched our pup tent at Bandolier National Monument, not far from Albuquerque and Los Alamos, while traveling across the country in our blue Toyota before moving to Springfield.

I did not set foot within the city limits of Albuquerque until 1993, when the annual conference of the National Network of Grantmakers (NNG) gave me a professional reason to do so. The NNG, an association of liberal and change-oriented foundations, held its annual conference in Albuquerque that year. As the executive director of the RFC, I am a member of the NNG.

I decided to hold a press conference at the hotel described by Harry Gold at my parents' trial. I hoped this would attract significant media attention and generate publicity for the RFC. My plan was to read a short statement at the press conference at the hotel and then hike with reporters to the Greenglass apartment, where I had agreed to answer their questions.

I wasn't sure how this would feel. People still ask me questions in a tentative way that indicates they assume that my childhood experiences left me emotionally fragile. I answer, perhaps somewhat glibly, that I wouldn't engage in so much public activity related to my parents' case if answering personal questions about it were traumatic. Still, I felt it prudent to visit the site of the Greenglasses' apartment in advance. An hour before the scheduled start of the press conference, I drove my rental car down North High Street, parked around the corner, and walked back to the house. I squinted against the almost painfully bright sun on that surprisingly mild early November morning. The house was located in the middle of a shady tree-lined block of small but well-kept 1920s vintage dwellings. I stopped at the address and peered up at the outside stairway that led to several second floor apartments, one of which David and Ruth Greenglass had occupied on that fatal day almost fifty years before. I felt almost nothing. It was, after all, an ordinary-looking house, and I had no memories connected to it. Satisfied that returning to the house with reporters would not be a problem I walked the route I'd soon retrace in reverse to gain a little familiarity with it. I hoped to be answering questions and trying to respond amicably to photographers' requests on the walk with the press to the Greenglass apartment. I wanted to minimize my chances of creating photo opportunities of my stumbling or disrupting traffic.

The press conference was well attended. I left the hotel with several media people in tow. I answered that, yes, I realized that I was probably retracing Harry Gold's route, although I pointed out that you'd have to take Gold's word for it. Since Gold admitted under oath that he created a fantasy life and "lied so often it's a wonder steam didn't come out of my ears," his word was suspect. But my reenactment began to feel a bit weird. It got a little hot in my jacket and tie in the rapidly warming morning, and I remembered Gold's testimony that he began to sweat as he walked up the hill in the late afternoon June sunshine. We arrived at the house and I dutifully pointed out the stairs to the Greenglass apartment for the television crews.

I think I did a good job of covering the nervousness generated by an idea that had occurred to me as we turned onto North High Street. I recalled that the Greenglasses' landlady had lived downstairs in 1945. She had been interviewed by the FBI after my parents' arrests in 1950, but did not remember a man fitting Harry Gold's description coming to the Greenglass apartment. Walter and Miriam Schneir also interviewed her in the 1960s when they were writing *Invitation to an Inquest*. Their probing questions failed to spark her memory as well. I'd read a lengthy article in the *Albuquerque Journal*, published five months earlier to coincide with the fortieth anniversary of my parents' execution, and was surprised to discover that the same woman, now almost ninety years old, still lived downstairs. She was interviewed for the article and told the reporter she remembered

Gold's visit quite clearly. This memory was almost certainly nothing more than wishful thinking, but what if she came out of the house to find out what all the commotion was about and again insisted she saw Gold that evening? It would be easy to demolish this old woman's credibility, but no good would come of it. Fortunately she did not appear, and the event ended without incident.

But the image of the Greenglasses' doorstep didn't fade. It provoked thoughts about my uncle's family. Since 1950 I have had absolutely no connection with David and Ruth Greenglass or with their children, my first cousins, who are approximately my age. I have no childhood memories of any of them. The latter is not surprising since I was only three when I last saw them. When I returned home, I asked my brother what he remembered about David and Ruth and was caught unawares when he answered that other than very general impressions he also had no childhood memories of them. I found this intriguing because he was seven when he last saw them and remembers a lot of detail about his last couple of years with our parents.

Of course, I had thought quite a bit about David and Ruth Greenglass over the years. But I had given little thought to their two children and possible grandchildren. I knew that David was released from prison in 1960. I had learned that he and Ruth changed their last name, lived anonymously in the New York City area, and raised two children. I'd never lifted a finger to contact them. While I was on the college lecture circuit in the 1970s, people often asked two questions about David Greenglass; I still faced the same questions in 1993: How could Greenglass send his sister to her death, and why hadn't I tried to contact him?

My answer to the first question may have sounded to some like a defense of David Greenglass's actions. I suggested to these college students, who (I presumed) could not conceive of what David Greenglass faced:

Imagine that you were imprisoned by the most powerful political entity on earth, and its jailers threatened you with evidence that would result in your conviction and execution. Imagine that they threatened to arrest your wife and do the same to her. Imagine that you believed these were not idle threats, and that they would indeed do this. Then these jailers gave you a way out. All you had to do was say that your sister and brother-in-law instigated your actions. We'd all like to think that we wouldn't cave in to such pressure, but how can we know how we'd react until we are placed in a similar situation? After all, David Greenglass could say that his brother-in-law and sister would be offered the same choice of informing on someone else, and so they, not Greenglass, were ultimately responsible for their fate.

My brother and I have had some indirect contact with the Greenglass family through other cousins, the children of my mother's other brothers, Bernard and Sam. During the 1970s a close family friend of my brother reported to him several conversations she had with one of these cousins. This cousin recounted that according to Greenglass family lore the Rosenbergs *and* the Greenglasses had acted heroically. Julius and Ethel Rosenberg were heroes because they held true to their beliefs, and David Greenglass heroically did what he had to do to protect his wife and children. Although I find this a somewhat nauseating rationale, perhaps over the years David and Ruth Greenglass have come to believe it.

I'd answer the second question, about why I hadn't contacted David Greenglass, by responding that I saw no point in meeting him. Even if I could get him to admit that he perjured himself, there would be little I could do with the confession. The government could claim that Greenglass was making such an admission to get back at them for imprisoning him for ten years and for executing his sister. Moreover, the problem with getting someone to admit that he or she lied under oath is that once the person does so, you can't trust anything he or she says.

But I wasn't entirely satisfied with my rationale. A couple of incidents from the 1970s and later indicate that my gut, rather than my brain, dictated why I wanted to keep my distance from Uncle David. One occurred when I had just finished speaking at American University in Washington, D.C., in 1977. As often happened, several students lingered to ask questions informally. One young man hung back until everyone else had gone, approached somewhat timidly, and said: "I hope you won't think poorly of me, because my uncle is Irving Saypol."

"Why should that bother me?" I unhesitatingly fired back. "My uncle's David Greenglass!" More than a decade later I saw a Woody Allen movie, in which the protagonist, played by Allen, sarcastically quipped: "I love him like a brother—David Greenglass." This reference to Greenglass's repulsive behavior resonated deeply. I was pleased that this villain of my childhood had become a negative cultural icon.

The Albuquerque visit, a few years after the above incidents took place, started me thinking about what happened to the Greenglass children. I knew almost nothing about their lives. Remarkably, in 1994, only a few months later, I met a man who claimed to know Greenglass's children. He said that both of them were married and that one had a son. This grandchild, he continued, did not know his grandfather's true identity. I trusted the man's word, although until the 2001 publication of Sam Roberts's book *The Brother*, about David Greenglass, I had no corroboration that the grandchild did not know his grandfather's identity. Still, I tried to imagine what it would be like to have such a skeleton in the family closet. Sooner or later the grandson would find out. The impact of this knowledge and the fact that it had been kept secret would probably be devastating. I believe that a functional family is based on love, sharing, and trust. I feel fortunate that I didn't have to keep such secrets from my children.

I know little about David and Ruth Greenglass's life, but I believe that from 1950 onward, the lurking presence of their most fundamental betrayal of family and community must have infected their family existence—a feeling that may be a vestige of my adolescent desire for revenge. I imagine their isolation to have been, and to remain, monumental. The fear of being discovered and despised for their actions must have clung.

I grew up with a big secret: I grew up afraid that the wrong people would find out about my secret and devastate my life. Fortunately, as far as I know, the wrong people never discovered who I was. Those who knew my secret, led by Abel and Anne Meeropol, created an emotionally safe and intellectually challenging childhood for me, built on the moral certitude that Julius and Ethel Rosenberg were very good people. I suspect that the children in the Greenglass household had an entirely different childhood experience. I was told in 1994 that they tried not to talk about it.

I'm no saint. I derive some satisfaction from hearing that David and Ruth Greenglass have had to live with a secret that is so terrible that even after fifty years one of their children can't share it with even their grandchild. Perhaps this is David and Ruth's final punishment. While this punishment may be fitting for David and Ruth, their children and grandchild deserve better.

Thinking about the all-encompassing multigenerational impact of Greenglass's betrayal, I understood the real reason why I will never contact David Greenglass. David and Ruth Greenglass's decision in 1950 set off a cascade of consequences that sent the Greenglass and Rosenberg/Meeropol families on divergent courses. David Greenglass survived by trampling on the personal and political values I hold most dear. I can't undo the damage he did. However, I can do my best to avoid saying a word to him. Sometimes religious Jews mourn the "death" of someone who has committed an unforgivable act, going so far as to sit shiva for him. What Greenglass did is unforgivable, and I've removed him from my life with similar finality. Although I frequently address his actions intellectually when I discuss my parents' case, on a personal level he is dead to me. Perhaps my aunt Ruth, who made up the story that my mother typed David's notes, is even more culpable than David. Though I do not mean to let her off the hook, maybe I focus on David because, except for my brother Michael and his son, Gregory, he is my closest living male relative.

On the most basic level I define myself as someone who is not David Greenglass. David Greenglass refused to accept responsibility for his actions. He did not have to lie about my mother's typing to protect his wife and children; he'd already secured them with his prior cooperation. David Greenglass sought to shorten his sentence by lying to satisfy the prosecution's strategy of convicting my mother in order to pressure my father. He was protecting no one but himself, and his children and grandchild have suffered, not benefited, from his actions. My life, and the way in which Elli and I have tried to raise our children, is the antithesis of the "David Greenglass story." Perhaps others feel it would be right, or even good, for me to confront him, but I am disgusted by the thought. He will receive nothing, not even venom, in person from me.

My visit to Albuquerque gave me no fresh insights into the case against my parents. I still don't know if David Greenglass met Harry Gold at his apartment that warm June day in 1945, and if he did, what actually happened there. But I learned something important about myself on David Greenglass's doorstep.

In the summer of 1995, more than eighteen months after my trip to Albuquerque, my daughter Rachel had a summer job working in Provincetown after her freshman year at college. Elli and I visited her the weekend of July 9 but returned to Springfield early that Sunday so I could speak at a rally on the Amherst town common against the execution of Mumia Abu-Jamal. We had time for only a quick change of clothes at home before continuing to the rally. There was a message on our answering machine asking me to call a reporter at NBC News.

I never respond to messages from reporters at home and had a bad feeling about this one. The mainstream media's pattern of contacting my brother and me only when apparently incriminating information about our parents surfaced was well established. This was particularly true of New York City–based media. The Khrushchev revelations in 1990 merited headlines in New York City newspapers, but information that demonstrated their inaccuracy went unreported. Another example of this lopsided coverage occurred when in August 1993 the American Bar Association staged a mock retrial of my parents' case in New York City. I did not attend the event because our family was on vacation while it took place, but I tracked its progress through reports in the *New York Times* and *Boston Globe*. I dragged Elli out early to pick up those papers the day the verdict would be reported. When I found nothing in the *Times* I exclaimed excitedly to Elli: "We won!" I explained that we *must* have won because the *Times* would have reported it if we lost. She was skeptical of this analysis, but sure enough the *Globe* reported that the jury had unanimously voted for acquittal.

I kept this in mind while I considered answering the message when we returned home that evening. I couldn't consult with Michael because he was in England. I decided not to ruin a good night's sleep, and put off responding until I got to the office the next morning. When I arrived at work there were several messages from news outlets, so I knew something big was brewing. I called NBC back, and discovered that the National Security Agency (NSA) and the CIA were about to hold a joint press conference to release what these agencies called the "Venona" transcriptions. According to the reporter, this material, kept in utmost secrecy for almost fifty years, proved my parents' guilt. He asked for my comments. I told him I could not comment on them before I had seen them. By the time he faxed the dozen "most incriminating" sheets to me, I learned that a team of local television reporters would be at my doorstep to interview me in less than an hour.

I tried to digest the material quickly. The NSA claimed that its top-secret project, code-named Venona, intercepted and decrypted KGB electronic transmissions sent from the Soviet consulate in New York to Moscow in 1944 and 1945. The NSA maintained that this laborious process had borne some fruit by 1948, and that what they discovered led to my parents' arrest. By the time the TV film crew arrived I had all eighty pages of material that the government claimed proved my parents' guilt. As I scanned the material I realized that it was both controlled and generated by U.S. government spy agencies that had a stake in my parents' guilt. Standing on their own, they appeared at first glance to add nothing to the government's case. They certainly weren't independent corroboration. The material also seemed scanty, and there was nothing connecting atomic secrets to my parents in any of it. Until I had more time that was all I could say. I repeatedly told various news outlets over the next several days that I questioned the accuracy of this material and that it was not independent proof of my parents' guilt.

But major newspapers and television and radio networks not only accepted every word contained in the material at face value, they also repeated the government's spin that it proved my parents' guilt. The USA Today headline SOVIET DOCUMENTS INCRIMINATE ROSENBERGS was typical. Never mind that these were not Soviet documents.

By the time the weekend arrived four days later, I'd felt as if I'd been run over by a mass media steamroller. My comments had been dismissed as those of a dutiful son unwilling to accept reality. I was also furious with myself for backing down after my meeting with Perlin in 1992. If we had acted then to explore the possibility that my father might have been involved in nonatomic espionage, we'd be in a much stronger position to respond to this new onslaught. We could have pointed out that while the Venona transcriptions, if accurate, indicated my father's nonatomic involvement, they also were proof that my parents did not steal the secret of the atom bomb.

By the time Michael returned from England two weeks later I had

had time to review the material thoroughly. We began to assess its meaning and the media's analysis of it. We realized that the mass media were merely renewing prior conclusions that our parents were guilty. After analyzing the pages that related to my parents' case Michael and I thought we understood why they had not been released previously and why it was so important to have the press parrot the government's spin on it. The government had succeeded in diverting attention from the fact that the transcriptions did not point to our parents' involvement in atomic espionage. Julius is never mentioned by name, and the spy code-named Antenna and, later, Liberal, whom the government claims was Julius Rosenberg, was engaged in military-industrial rather than atomic espionage. Even more remarkably, the key reference to Liberal's wife states that she was not an espionage agent! Regardless of the *USA Today* headline, this material exonerated rather than incriminated Ethel Rosenberg.

And we discovered another fact that no mainstream media outlet has reported to this day. Each transcription has a "reissue" date printed on it. All documents relating to our parents' case had been "reissued" in 1975 and 1976. Michael and I discussed this at length. Why would the NSA update this material over twenty years after my parents' execution? It could have been in response to the FOIA request we made in February 1975. How tantalizing: Material that government spy agencies assumed would remain under wraps forever is reviewed and perhaps reworked when the possibility arises that it may be forced into the public eye. That September the NSA refused Marshall Perlin's request for the prior versions of this material. It seemed to my brother and me that the validity of the contents of this repeatedly reworked secret government material remained open to question. But while the material warrants suspicion, I must also consider the possibility that some or all of it is accurate.

My brother and I concluded that even if every word of these transcriptions were true, the following summary remained accurate: Neither Julius nor Ethel Rosenberg was a member of an atomic spy ring that stole the secret of the atom bomb. Neither committed the act for which he and she were executed. And the U.S. government knew all along that Ethel Rosenberg was not an espionage agent of any kind.

Amid this harrowing reassessment, I enjoyed a few moments of comic relief watching authors who already had the answers maneuver to fit new developments into their theses. For instance, in 1990 Ronald Radosh, the coauthor of *The Rosenberg File*, had claimed that the Khrushchev revelations stating that both my parents provided valuable atomic information validated his thesis concerning my parents' guilt. Now Radosh claimed the Venona transcriptions, stating that one of my parents was a nonatomic espionage agent, did the same. Much more recently Jacob Weisberg wrote a feature article published in the *New York Times Magazine* in which he accepted the validity of the transcriptions, even though they report my mother was not a spy, but nonetheless wrote in the same article that believing in either of my parents' innocence was the left wing's version of creation science (Jacob Weisberg, "Cold War Without End," *New York Times Magazine*, November 28, 1999, pp. 119, 156). These promoters of my parents' guilt are evidently so eager to seize upon material to support their conclusions that they ignore the contradictory implications presented by that evidence.

Unfortunately I realized that similar attacks could be mounted against those who claimed my parents were innocent. How could the virtually impossible task of proving someone did *not* engage in a secret conspiracy be accomplished? The best proponents of my parents' total innocence could do was to show that no credible evidence existed that my parents ever had any contact with the KGB. Thus the Venona material that implicated my father could be responded to only with a claim that any reference to him was government-inserted disinformation. While the falsification of government files is possible, concluding definitively that it has happened without providing any direct proof seems indefensible. I believe it is unreasonable to claim more than that the Venona transcriptions *might* contain government-inserted disinformation.

I find it astonishing that the strongest argument for accepting that the transcriptions contain some validity is the fact that they contradict, rather than support, the core of the government's case against my parents. They point to my father's noninvolvement in stealing valuable atomic secrets, and to my mother's innocence. The inclusion of material that hurts the government's case could result from incredible sloppiness on the part of these secret police bureaucracies, but one has to expect that any disinformation they created would bolster rather than challenge their own case.

Throughout the fall of 1995 this last thought kept gnawing at me. The Venona transcriptions are not very long, and I repeatedly reviewed every word. I zeroed in on the file that stated Liberal's wife "didn't work," and the NSA chief decoder's note that this meant she was not an espionage agent. If this were accurate then the government knew before they arrested my mother that she never worked for the KGB. But why would the government create this smoking gun that proved it knowingly executed my mother for a crime she did not commit?

I must have read one particular line dozens of times before I grasped its significance. The author discusses Liberal's knowledge of the atom bomb project: "referring to his ignorance of the problem, [Liberal] expresses the wish that our man [apparently another spy] should meet 'Kalibr,' [the government claims that this was David Greenglass's code name] and interrogate him personally." At first I hated these lines because they implicated Liberal in Kalibr's work—something I did not want to be true. But I was dumbfounded when I finally grasped its implications. No wonder the government refused to release this material for so long! According to this page, the man they executed for being a master atomic spy didn't know squat about the atom bomb project. But once again, the same material that appeared to clear my parents of the act for which they were killed seemed to implicate my father in a lesser crime.

I thought of an analogy. What if rather than executing my parents for stealing the secret of the atom bomb the government had executed them instead for being serial murderers? What if a national debate raged over their guilt for decades after their execution? And finally, what if, more than forty years after the executions, the government released previously secret material that showed that my father had committed a series of armed robberies in which no one was killed, and the government said: "See, that proves they were guilty." I would have a hard time denying my father committed the robberies *if all this were true*, but government institutions and agents, not my parents, would be murderers.

The more I thought about it, the more confounding it became. I've discussed this with family members and friends. They all get my point, but I have never seen anyone raise it in print. Perhaps that is not surprising. Those who tout Venona as proof positive of my parents' guilt can hardly be expected to point out how devastating it is to the government's case. And those who dismiss Venona as disinformation can't accept the accuracy of any of it.

Michael and I concluded that the Venona material was probably neither completely true nor completely false. In 1996 my brother and I wrote an article that pointed out that the Venona transcriptions might contain both accurate *and* inaccurate information. We provided examples in this article of transcripts relating to our parents' case we suspected had been doctored. We submitted this article to the weekly magazine that had provided the key progressive forum for the post–Venona release debate, but they said our 2,500-word piece was too long and refused to publish it. They offered instead to publish the 900-word portion of our article in which we analyzed what the implications would be if all the transcriptions were true. We refused because this would distort our central claim that the material contained both true and false information.

Michael and I included two examples of suspect transcriptions in our proposed article. One was the transcription dated March 5, 1945 (final reissue date: June 17, 1976), reporting that Liberal was paid four thousand dollars, a substantial sum in 1945. Ronald Radosh, writing in the *New Republic*, suggested that this might have been the source of the four thousand dollars David Greenglass testified about at my parents' trial in March 1951. At trial Greenglass swore that he received four thousand dollars from my father in May 1950, not long before Greenglass was arrested. According to this theory my father got four thousand dollars in 1945, stashed it for five years, and then gave it to Greenglass.

It is unlikely that our father ever received such a generous sum, given our family's poverty during those years. Michael has a vivid memory from the late 1940s of our father returning home and telling our mother with a big smile, "I saw my first fifty-dollar bill today." Michael clamored to see it, but our father said he had already given it to a creditor. Would someone who had received or was hiding a lump sum of four thousand dollars get excited over a fifty-dollar bill? Given Greenglass's trial testimony, my brother and I believe at least one of Venona's custodians plugged the four-thousand-dollar figure into this transcript after the trial to bolster the government's case.

While the transcriptions seemed inconclusive, they forced me to accept the possibility that my father had participated in an illegal and covert effort to help the Soviet Union defeat the Nazis. Although I didn't think it was wrong to help the Soviets defeat the Nazis, I still found this possibility disquieting. Could I really approve of the father of two small children acting this way? That's not what I would have done after my kids had been born. But I didn't want to deal with these feelings, and decided I didn't have to because my father might not have done anything illegal. I suppressed these feelings and focused instead on trying to figure out what had happened.

The Venona transcriptions also cast new light on other information I received during this time.

Over a year before Venona's 1995 release a researcher told me that he had made contact with a man in Russia who claimed to have been the former KGB agent who worked directly with my father. Over the next several years this researcher and a Russian colleague wheedled a series of statements out of retired KGB agent Aleksandr Feklisov, whose story became the primary source of a 1997 hour-long television documentary. Feklisov's book was published in 2001.

The researcher importuned my brother and me to become involved in his project. Feklisov, he said, wanted very much to meet us. We refused. Feklisov appeared to us to be a disreputable character interested in self-aggrandizement and financial gain. But Feklisov's story dovetailed with Venona and might even represent independent corroboration of it. According to Feklisov my father knew nothing about atomic espionage, and my mother was just a housewife. But my father had supplied a steady stream of military-industrial information to Feklisov for several years during World War II.

We felt that meeting with Feklisov would place our stamp of approval on his assertions, and we suspected that his claims contained many untruths. Relatively early in the process the researcher provided me with a written summary of what Feklisov told the researcher's Russian colleague. The written summary contained several false notes. For instance, Feklisov related another agent's anguish over instructing the courier Harry Gold to use the phrase "I come from Julius," when he introduced himself to David Greenglass, because it was used against Julius at the trial. Michael and I knew better. Either the FBI agent interviewed in *The Unquiet Death of Julius and Ethel Rosenberg* originated the phrase that contained my father's name, or at a meeting arranged by government agents ten weeks before my parents' trial, Greenglass proposed to his fellow inmate, Gold, that possibly the code phrase contained Julius's name. Prior to December 28, 1950, Gold remembered the name "Ben" and Greenglass recalled the name "Dave," but neither mentioned Julius. It seemed extremely unlikely that a Soviet agent had made up a phrase that contained my father's first name, that Gold had used the name Julius in 1945, and that both Gold and Greenglass had forgotten it and substituted other names by 1950, but then hit on it again at the government-arranged meeting. Because the FBI file that reported the Greenglass-Gold meeting had received little publicity, only a few people knew of its contents. Feklisov was apparently making things up to fit the more generally known public record.

Many other details described by Feklisov are similarly flawed. There are instances in which the written summary the researcher gave to me tells one version of a story, while Feklisov tells another on camera in the television documentary and yet a third in his book. While it would be foolhardy to take much of what he said at face value, inconsistencies and embellishments do not prove that Feklisov never met my father or that my father never handed over classified information to him. But I would have to look elsewhere in my ongoing quest to pin down what actually happened.

Individuals still occasionally bring new information about my parents to my attention. In 1998 I attended a forum at Mount Holyoke College where Abraham Lincoln Brigade veteran Abe Osheroff discussed his experiences. I introduced myself afterward. He immediately told me that he regularly hung out with my mother and father and several other young communists after he had returned from the fighting in Spain. Abe said that around the time when the Soviet Union began to prepare for the inevitable German attack, my father said he had access to technical engineering information that could help the Soviet Union defend itself. We continued this discussion in greater detail at Abe's home in Seattle the following summer. Abe said my father told him he had specifications that would permit fighter planes to fire machine guns without damaging their propellers. My father asked him if he had access to Soviet officials in New York City to whom he could give this information. Abe responded that he didn't have such access, and told me that since the Soviets never developed a "variable-speed propeller," he assumed my father never contacted Soviet officials. After my father's arrest, Abe wondered if perhaps he had.

If I had been told this story in the late 1970s I would probably have dismissed it. But after Venona I considered it carefully. I do not question Abe Osheroff's integrity. He has lived a life of heroic antifascism from the battlefields of Spain to the villages of Nicaragua. True, memory can play funny tricks in the course of almost sixty years. Did Abe's memory detail the unrealized romantic dreams of a twenty-year-old engineering student, or an opening episode of espionage? I weighed the statements of other friends of my parents, which discounted the possibility that either one of them was involved in espionage, against others' statements that are more in line with what Abe told me. Though Abe's additional morsel tipped me more in the direction of thinking that my father might have helped the Soviet Union, it did not eliminate the possibility that my father was entirely innocent.

It is a humbling experience to have studied a discrete body of information for decades and yet realize the limitations of your knowledge. It never ceases to amaze me how many people who know relatively little about my parents' case think they have so many more answers. Although through legal action and personal contacts I have had access to more Rosenberg case–related material than almost anyone, I still can't untangle fact from disinformation. This is especially true for anyone dealing with governmental agencies staffed by professional deceivers. Many world-class historians, reporters, researchers, and experts grant blanket credibility to the information generated by these government bureaucracies or by those who worked for them. For instance, some of these professionals characterized the KGB as a cabal of sophisticated dissemblers while the Cold War raged, but now accept as gospel every word in the KGB's files or provided by retired

KGB agents. Researchers and interviewers have explained to me that they can tell when they are viewing false information or when they are being lied to. Such explanations fail to recognize the difference between being hard to fool and proving that you have not been suckered.

But the mere possibility that KGB, CIA, or FBI information *might* be false does not make it so. Many who refuse to accept information that might implicate my parents fail to understand the distinction between proving something false and proving that something *could* be false. Perhaps people have trouble with uncertainty. Career experts have a particularly difficult time admitting what they don't know, and media professionals want answers, not uncertainty. I've watched many interviewers squirm when I tell them I don't know if my father ever supplied information to the Soviet Union. The quick ones pounce: "So what do you think?" When I answer: "I think I don't know," their disappointment is palpable.

But one might still wonder, with the Venona transcripts, corroboration from retired KGB agents, information from politically sympathetic friends, and more, why I haven't become convinced that my father did something illegal? The agencies in charge of collecting, storing, and finally disseminating this information have a history of crafting disinformation. The American agencies helped orchestrate my parents' frame-up and wrongful execution. They have a huge stake in proving that at least one of my parents participated in illegal activities. In legal jargon, they have the means, motive, and opportunity to create false leads to show my parents' guilt. If anyone could create such effective but deceptive proof it is this group, and I was not, and still am not, going to spread their disinformation for them! Moreover, the stories of retired KGB agents and unverifiable reports of the contents of KGB files may only appear to be independent corroboration of our government's claims. They may be no more than the clever creation of mirror images based on the known record that professional manipulators have used to attract media attention and financial gain. Against this backdrop of continuing uncertainty I hung, twisting slowly in the breeze.

But strange as it may seem, I was not overly distraught. The RFC was flourishing, and I loved my work. I could not help being my parents' child. I was not responsible for Julius and Ethel's actions and was determined to make the best of whatever roll of the dice history left me. The RFC celebrated my parents' resistance; it did not proclaim their innocence. This focus was consistent with the RFC support for the children of targeted activists. We never claimed that the parents of our beneficiaries were either innocent or completely virtuous.

CHAPTER 9

Defeating Death

———◆◆◆◆◆———

PERHAPS THE UNCERTAINTY THAT SURROUNDED MY CONSIDERATION
of my parents' culpability caused me to seek firmer ground. I found
surer footing whenever I focused on their sentence, and in late 1995
for the first time in my life I plunged headlong into the anti–capital
punishment movement. But I got there by a somewhat circuitous
route.

Contacting potential beneficiaries for RFC grants is an ongoing
staff job. Targeted activists are often reluctant to ask for help, even if
they know of the fund's existence. Reaching out to prospective beneficiaries was one of my principal tasks during our first several years.

In 1992 I heard that an African American political prisoner,
Mumia Abu-Jamal, on death row had at least one child who might
qualify for RFC support. I had only a vague memory of his case. I
found out that in 1981 Mumia had been charged with killing a
Philadelphia policeman, and in 1982 he had been convicted and sentenced to death. I learned that Mumia had been a radio journalist
called the "Voice of the Voiceless," and that he had been the minister

of information for the Philadelphia Black Panther Party when he was a teenager. The title "Voice of the Voiceless" had a familiar ring to it.

I recalled one trip I had made to Philadelphia during the reopening effort. A very young black radio journalist had provided me a platform to discuss my parents' frame-up. Actually we agreed about so many things that the show became more of a discussion than an interview. At the end of the show he asked me a question that frequently came up at such times. He asked if I thought a judicially sanctioned, politically motivated killing—like my parents' execution—could happen again in this country. We discussed this briefly and agreed that given the racism, class bias, and the political orientation of the U.S. courts, it could.

Afterward I didn't give the program or its conclusion a second thought. The years passed, and I never met the journalist again. In fact I retained a much clearer image of the space in which the interview took place—a small windowless room whose walls were lined with metal shelving piled to the ceiling with old-fashioned canisters of radio tapes—than I did of him. I remember thinking it was a good thing they didn't have earthquakes in Philadelphia. Even a minor temblor could have buried us so deep in tapes that we wouldn't be found for weeks.

In 1992 I realized that the interviewer had been Mumia Abu-Jamal. The person who had asked me the question about the possibility of something like my parents' case happening again now sat on death row. I had met and been interviewed by the first political prisoner in this country to face execution since my parents, and I hadn't even realized it until a decade after he had been sentenced to death!

The many political parallels between Mumia's case and my parents' struck me as I learned more. There were striking similarities: the nature of the political targeting, the resistance of the defendants, and the wide range of viewpoints held by the participants in the movements that evolved to save their lives.

I had concluded long ago that my parents were killed not for any crime they may have committed, but because they were Communists who would not cooperate with the FBI. The FBI documents bear this out. For instance, the FBI report in 1953 to newly elected President Eisenhower did not describe my mother as an active participant in illegal activity but concluded that she was "cognizant and recalcitrant."

I learned that when Mumia began writing for the Black Panther Party newspaper as a teenager in Philadelphia in 1967, the FBI placed him under surveillance, and they continued to observe him until the day of his arrest in 1981, fourteen years later. The Philadelphia of Mumia's youth was notorious for police violence. Frank Rizzo, first the chief of police and then Philadelphia's mayor, was infamous for condoning police violence, particularly against citizens of color. As a radio journalist Mumia repeatedly exposed police brutality, earning him the enmity of Philadelphia's police. Like my parents before him, Mumia was not the typical death-row inmate, because regardless of what he had done, his most dangerous crime was his articulate resistance to the dominant forces of our society. It seemed to me that like my mother, Mumia's "capital" crime was being both "cognizant and recalcitrant."

Of course there are differences between the two cases. By 1992 Mumia had been languishing on Pennsylvania's death row for a decade. He hadn't come close to exhausting his appeals, and his execution did not appear imminent. In my parents' case the entire process from arrest to execution took less than three years. Also unlike my parents' case, his did not receive national attention at the time of his trial. To this day what actually transpired during his trial has not been adequately aired in the mainstream media.

In 1997 Amnesty International, which enjoys worldwide respect for its fair and independent investigations of trials with political overtones, released the following statement about his trial:

Amnesty International has serious doubts about the fairness of Mr. Abu-Jamal's trial, which may have been contaminated by the deep-rooted racism that appears to taint the application of the death penalty in Pennsylvania. Mr. Abu-Jamal's case serves to highlight some of the particularly egregious aspects of the application of the death penalty in the United States: racism in jury selection, questionable identification evidence, possible pressure on witnesses, the withholding of evidence from the defense, a questionable purported "confession," incompetent trial counsel, and inadequate funding for the defense.... The questioning of Mumia Abu-Jamal about his past political beliefs and affiliations at the sentencing proceeding alone presents grounds for commuting the death sentence.

But if this case was like so many others, why had a worldwide movement developed to save Mumia's life, while more than three thousand other death-row inmates remained virtually anonymous? I realized that my parents' letters, like Mumia's radio broadcasts and writing, sparked the movement by articulating their resistance. Both my parents and Mumia were conscious political actors, targeted for their resistance and glorified for their heroism.

I also felt an instant identification with Mumia's high-school-age son. I found myself comparing his situation with my own. Neither of his parents had been killed, but he'd grown up a young African American male in a city whose police force was clamoring for his father's execution. I thought that perhaps his experience was more like that of Morton Sobell's son, who was a couple of years younger than me. Mort's son had grown up while his father, my parents' codefendant, spent almost twenty years in prison. Neither of his parents was killed, but his father was branded a disreputable communist spy and sat in jail while his mother campaigned relentlessly for his father's release. I realized that my being able to confine my nightmare to a set time period enabled me to put it in a box—a key to my recovery. It would have been more difficult to endure this over a twenty-year period as both Mumia's and Mort's sons had. Maybe Mumia's son had the worst of both situations. He faced an endless nightmare that included a possible execution. He'd grown up with death's lurking presence. I wondered what I could possibly say to him?

And what could I possibly say to Mumia? I was leery of becoming too personally embroiled in the effort to save his life. I wasn't sure I could withstand reliving and possibly losing a struggle so much like the one that culminated in my parents' deaths. I thought maybe I should visit him, but I couldn't place myself in a scenario so much like my visits to Sing Sing forty years earlier.

But I was drawn to the effort to save Mumia's life. The material I read made it appear that the movement contained two camps—those who proclaimed Mumia's innocence, and those who argued that his trial had been so unfair that he deserved a new one to determine whether he was guilty. This also reminded me of my parents' case. Although the stalwart defenders of my parents whom I'd worked with during the reopening effort all believed passionately in my parents' innocence, the committee that fought to save their lives in the 1950s included many who did not believe my parents had received a fair trial.

It struck me that the core of both movements contained a disproportionate number of people who believed in the defendants' total innocence. Both, however, had to accommodate a much broader range of opinion if they wanted to forge the broad-based movement that was most likely to save the defendants' lives. By May 1995 I could see that the numbers working to save Mumia's had grown at least in part because they included individuals with a range of views. All those working to save Mumia might not be certain of his innocence, but most agreed he had been targeted for his activism, and all agreed that he never received a fair trial.

In May 1995 Pennsylvania governor Thomas Ridge issued a death warrant for Mumia, who suddenly faced death in August. Though I felt compelled to act, I pondered my role and my position. I knew that many of my parents' supporters and more traditional leftists were uneasy about championing the cause of someone convicted of killing a policeman. Many older progressive people have said to me in private that they had no way of knowing if Mumia was innocent. Unlike my parents' conspiracy case, where the evidence was oral and one couldn't even be sure a crime had been committed—let alone that my parents had done it—in this instance a policeman had been killed and Mumia was found moments later lying critically wounded near the slain officer. I wanted to play a role in presenting Mumia's case to a broader Left constituency, but I felt that, despite the urgency, I had to proceed very carefully.

I recalled how I'd embarrassed myself in the late 1970s by speaking out about a local case. Two union organizers had been charged with attempting to blow up trucks during a labor struggle. They and their lawyers claimed that the bosses were framing them. At their urging I wrote what became the cover story for the area's leading alternative newsweekly, the *Valley Advocate*, which proclaimed their innocence and compared their frame-up to my parents' case. Not long after its publication the defendants reached a plea-bargain agreement. They received probation in return for admitting criminal misconduct. It turned out they had been enticed by an undercover agent into planting very weak explosive devices that scorched the front-seat upholstery of two trucks. Antiunion forces wanted to make a mountain out of this molehill. It was a political prosecution, but it was not a frame-up. I had been used, gotten egg on my face, and determined never to make that mistake again.

I couldn't be sure of what happened the night Mumia was shot and the policeman was killed, although I'd read enough to be confident that Mumia did not receive a fair trial. My position was that while Mumia might be innocent, arguing over his innocence or guilt missed the point. I believed that only through the process of a fair trial could either be determined, and until he received a fair trial, discussion of his culpability would be inconclusive.

In 1995 news of Mumia's date with the executioner coursed through the Internet to all corners of the globe. Within weeks the movement to save his life became as massive as the one to save my parents had become in *a year*. I decided the most effective contribution I could make to this effort was to raise funds for it. We could not use RFC resources for this purpose, but I could write a personal appeal to our supporters, and use our own funds to produce and mail it. Elli and I and several other friends from the RFC board spent the weekend of July 15–16 stuffing and mailing five thousand letters to RFC supporters. The letter began:

> *I am often asked if something like what happened to my parents could happen again in this country. It is about to happen! Pennsylvania Governor Tom Ridge has set August 17 as Mumia Abu-Jamal's execution date. He is the first political prisoner in this country to face execution since my parents, Ethel and Julius Rosenberg.*

I am proud of the overwhelming response this letter generated. Tens of thousands of dollars poured into the coffers of the legal team just when they needed it most. Their efforts, coupled with agitation that reached global proportions, forced a stay of Mumia's execution just a few days before it was to take place.

I had relatively little involvement with the anti–capital punishment community prior to 1995, although by then I'd been opposed to capital punishment for at least a decade. I felt out of tune with the movement because many of its most ardent activists opposed the death penalty on religious grounds. While I also believed the death penalty to be morally wrong, my stance was based on humanist ethics. I was leery of any anti–capital punishment organizing strategy based on morality. Moral arguments are problematic because such core beliefs are not necessarily susceptible to rational persuasion. Some believe just as strongly in the eye-for-an-eye doctrine, and feel that it is not immoral for the state to execute people convicted of murder or even other crimes. No amount of moral argument is likely to change their minds. That's why I felt that it would be futile to raise my voice against capital punishment on this basis.

But, as is often the case with deeply divisive social controversies, there are also many people who remained undecided. Though I wanted the anti–capital punishment movement to concentrate on persuading these uncertain ones, I knew that doing so with arguments based on moral certitude would also be very difficult.

Fortunately there was at least one very powerful anti–capital punishment argument that had a logical rather than moral basis. I focused on this argument starting in late 1995, when I broadened my talks about my parents' case to include Mumia's case and capital punishment in general. I called it the "perfection argument."

Almost all of us accept that humans are imperfect beings. We make mistakes. Sooner or later all the safeguards in a human-built system will fail. It is unrealistic, therefore, to expect a mistake-proof justice system. A large majority of people will readily agree that capital punishment allows no room for error. It is, therefore, inevitable that mistakes will be made and innocent people will be executed. Once someone has been executed you can't say "Oops" and take it back.

And mistakes can be political as well as factual. People often look back at my parents' case and reflect that if they had not been tried at the height of the McCarthy period's anti-Communist hysteria their sentence would have been lighter. This acknowledges that people can get carried away by the political and cultural climate of the time. Sorry, but I get very little comfort from these more sober reflections.

I found it effective, especially on college campuses, to respond to someone who said that he or she favored capital punishment by stating that that meant accepting the execution of innocent people. My opponent would vehemently deny this, but ultimately, if she or he was honest, admit that the execution of innocents will happen. The stubborn may adamantly maintain their position, or rationalize that the chance of error is so small that it is worth the risk. I had to rein in my rising anger so that I could respond without snapping back: "Was it worth risking my parents?" Instead I asked the person if he or she would feel the same way about the risk of executing someone who was totally innocent or even not guilty of a crime warranting execution if a member of his or her family was facing the executioner?

Anyone who proclaims himself or herself willing to risk executing an innocent person in order to reap the benefits of capital punishment is not so subtly demonstrating his or her class and race biases. As studies have repeatedly shown, the poor and people of color inhabit death row in the United States. The white middle-class college student who is willing to "risk" the execution of innocents is not worried that his family or friends might be executed. White skin and class privilege protect those who are dear to such people.

As often happens in our mass society, a number of people began presenting variations on the perfection argument in the mid-1990s. One variation fueled the explosion of the moratorium movement in the final years of the decade. Mainstream organizations such as the American Bar Association, and pro–death penalty conservatives such as Republican governor George Ryan of Illinois, ultimately joined this group. They argued that executions should be suspended until there was greater assurance that we were not executing the wrong people.

The moratorium movement took on additional force after the remarkable Wrongful Convictions Conference at Northwestern University Law School in Chicago in November 1998. I joined hundreds of activists from all over the country to listen to the stories of eighty-one innocent people who had been convicted of capital crimes and ultimately cleared. Some had come within hours of execution. Others had been saved not by the judicial process but by the fortuitous intervention of crusading Northwestern University journalism students and their professor David Protess. The conference climaxed with a ceremony attended by several dozen exonerated former death-row inmates. Their names were called one by one; each walked onstage and said a few words about his or her case before concluding: "If the state had its way I would be dead today." Each then solemnly placed a single sunflower in a vase and took a seat at the back of the stage. As the vase and stage slowly filled, a tidal wave of emotional energy rolled through the audience.

There is an obvious difference between the moratorium position and the abolition movement. Some moratorium adherents believe that the capital punishment system can be fixed. However, the perfection argument demonstrates the impossibility of effectively reforming the death penalty to prevent the execution of innocents, and I believe that it will ultimately bring many moratorium supporters into the abolition movement.

In true Mush-Head style, when campaigning against the death penalty I did not confine myself to one argument. Whenever I spoke I also addressed the class bias and racism involved in the use of capital punishment in our nation. These arguments that the death penalty is unfairly applied had relatively little impact on many audiences. This sad fact probably reflects the class bias and racism still rampant in the United States. But perhaps these arguments are finally sinking in. The American Bar Association's 1999 call for a moratorium on all executions cited racial bias and the inability of poor defendants facing capital charges to receive effective legal assistance as reasons for suspending executions. In 2002 Maryland announced a moratorium so a commission could study the racial bias in its application of the death penalty.

•   •   •

By 1998 anti–capital punishment agitation was taking place within the context of a growing movement against more general issues related to imprisonment. At that time more than 1.5 million Americans were in prison, and young people of color made up a disproportionate percentage of this huge number. But by locking up that many people, "they" were unwittingly sowing the seeds of a mass response. This policy worked in tandem with the accelerating pace of executions to provoke a growing revulsion among a broader cross-section of citizens. As a result, in the later 1990s, many more young people joined the struggle against mass imprisonment and capital punishment.

A movement against what activists dubbed the prison-industrial complex began to coalesce. In September 1998 I spoke at the founding conference of the Critical Resistance Movement at the University of California at Berkeley. Critical Resistance was dedicated to creating a mass movement to battle the growing power of all those associated with building and maintaining prisons nationwide. The turnout of more than 3,600 activists from all over the country, mostly young people of color, overwhelmed the organizers of this event. I sat in the audience during the conference's culminating cultural performance, one of the few middle-aged white male graybeards amid a rainbow sea of youth, and let their energy and enthusiasm pulse through me. I'd been saying for years that fogeys like me would not lead the next mass progressive outburst, but I hoped to be astute enough to jump on the bandwagon. I grieved the absence of so many of my age mates, wondering why so few were in attendance, but felt lucky to witness this rebirth.

I sought to build bridges between the young radicals of color taking on the prison-industrial complex and the predominantly white middle-class movement more narrowly focused on abolishing capital punishment. Each group would increase its chances of success if they worked together, but each group would have to adjust its strategy in order to build such a coalition. I urged the activists at the Berkeley conference not to dismiss the anti–capital punishment movement as privileged liberal do-gooders. The broad spectrum of support for that movement could provide those taking on the prison-industrial complex with potential allies who might come to share more of our position and analysis over time. And we should not forget that this was a matter of life and death, not only for Mumia Abu-Jamal, but also for more than 3,500 others on death row in 1998.

Two months later, when I attended the emotionally powerful Wrongful Convictions Conference in Chicago, I argued for situating our anti–capital punishment efforts within the broader context of mass imprisonment. Isolating capital punishment from the less popular issue of mass imprisonment might at first glance appear to maximize the potential for producing a liberal, single-issue mass movement with a significant chance of achieving the elimination of capital punishment. But placing this effort in the context of these broader issues seemed essential in dealing with a problem that was rapidly assuming Holocaust proportions. It would be wrong to ignore preposterously long sentences, inhumane conditions in U.S. prisons and the disenfranchisement of millions of "felons" of color. Forever the Mush-Head, I argued that achieving successful compromise was critical to ending capital punishment and attacking the prison-industrial complex.

At both the Berkeley and Chicago conferences I also outlined the anti–capital punishment argument that resonates most deeply with me even though it is subtler than arguments about perfection and fairness. Capital punishment undermines and corrupts our democracy. It corrupts democracy by concentrating too much power in government officials' hands. A nineteenth-century British peer summed up the problem in nine words. Lord Acton said: "Power tends to corrupt, and absolute power corrupts absolutely."

It is possible that I feel this argument most keenly because of the relationship between it and the last week of my parents' lives. The Supreme Court's machinations during that time provide a potent example of just how corrupting the death penalty can be. As my brother and I demonstrated when we released *The Kaufman Papers* in 1976, previously secret FBI files and the widely publicized events that unfolded between June 15 and June 19, 1953, show that Attorney General Herbert Brownell and Supreme Court Chief Justice Fred Vinson conspired to obstruct justice in order to speed my parents' execution.

Of course, the argument that capital punishment undermines democracy applies to other cases besides my parents'. Some people follow a simple logical progression in determining that they favor capital punishment. They envision the most horrendous murderer, perhaps someone like Jeffrey Dahmer, who cannibalized his victims. They conclude that they support capital punishment because they would not object to his execution. But these same people quickly grasp that supporting the execution of one murderer is not equivalent to supporting the general practice of capital punishment. The logical sequence fails once the death penalty is seen as an institution.

Capital punishment is a national system set in motion by thousands of county prosecutors and district attorneys. The initial decision to charge someone with a capital offense is made by these elected officials. Although juries determine guilt or innocence, elected state judges control most of the trials and elected appellate justices often review the trial court's findings. And, of course, the final thumbs-up or -down is given by a governor or president.

I find it ironic that citizens who don't trust government officials to develop a fair tax code or even put up a traffic light are willing to grant these same officials the power of life and death. In the wake of a murder, the police must demonstrate their competence by quickly finding and arresting the killer. Once an arrest is made they are loath to admit a mistake. The prosecutor must show the electorate he or she is tough on crime by demanding the death penalty and by rapidly obtaining a conviction. If contrary evidence is uncovered it may be ignored or even buried. Trial judges won't make evidentiary rulings that might hinder a conviction. They fear the charge that they are coddling criminals. They guide juries with prosecution-oriented instructions to ensure this will not happen. Pro death-penalty governors and legislators stack the deck further by limiting funding for defense attorneys so that incompetent lawyers represent indigent capital defendants. The foursome of precipitous police action, suppressed evidence, prosecutorial misconduct, and judicial bias is a formula for injustice.

Since capital punishment allows no room for error, the stewards of this fatally flawed system must demonstrate that the institution they represent is perfect. I thought of George W. Bush as "Governor Death" when he was governor of Texas because he presided over the mass production of capital punishment in that state, and had ultimate responsibility for the execution of more people than any other person alive in our country today. Governor Death will still tell you, based on his faith in the system and his fifteen-minute review of each case just before the execution, that he is absolutely certain that each one of the 150 people killed during his tenure was guilty and deserved to die. Former Pennsylvania governor Thomas Ridge, who should have been known as "Governor Death Warrant," signed two hundred death warrants. He stated he was just as sure that every single one he signed before being appointed by Governor Death to run the office of Homeland Security was for someone who committed a capital offense. Two of those death warrants were for Mumia Abu-Jamal.

Capital punishment's demand for the appearance of absolute perfection also generates corruption. Appellate justices, Supreme Court justices, special boards of appeals, and gubernatorial review are ostensibly designed to prevent a miscarriage of justice. But these layers of bureaucracy often become mechanisms to demonstrate the system's perfection. Admission of error threatens the entire edifice of a system that requires flawlessness.

The need to prove infallibility leads groups of supposedly erudite individuals to nonsensical conclusions. For instance, a Texas appeals court ruled that a coerced confession constituted "harmless error" in a case where there was little other evidence. I was taught in my first-year criminal law course and reminded in my second-year evidence class that a defendant's confession is the most powerful evidence of guilt a prosecutor can have! But the Texas court found that the jury would have convicted the defendant even if they'd never heard the confession in a case in which the prosecution presented little other evidence of the defendant's guilt.

The Texas Court of Criminal Appeals also held, in the cases of Calvin Burdine, Carl Johnson, and George McFarland, that each defendant's attorney rendered a competent defense even though he slept through portions of each defendant's capital trial (Stephen B. Bright, "Indifference to Justice," in *The Death Penalty*, vol. 1, *Frontiers of Justice*, Claudia Whitman and Julie Zimmerman, eds. [Brunswick, Maine: Biddle Publishing Co., 1997], p. 58). The U.S. Supreme Court has found that proof of serious constitutional violations in a capital case are irrelevant if the paperwork is filed three days late, and that execution of an innocent does not, in itself, violate the constitution (*Coleman v. Thompson*, 501 U.S. 722, 1991; *Herrera v. Collins*, 506 U.S. 390, 1993). Through such manuevering, the Court charged with upholding our loftiest legal principles has turned its back on death row, proving that the corrupting influence of the death penalty has spread to the pinnacle of power.

Abolition itself is a valid goal, but ending capital punishment can have a broader salutary impact. Even if we could guarantee that the state would execute only those guilty of cold-blooded killing, and would do so without regard to politics, class, race, religion, gender, sexuality, or ethnicity, what purpose would such executions serve? Since, as numerous studies have shown, capital punishment does not deter people from committing murder, it can serve only to meet the needs of those who wish the state to act as a public instrument of their private desire for revenge. I believe Maureen Faulkner, the widow of police officer Daniel Faulkner, whom the State of Pennsylvania says was murdered by Mumia Abu-Jamal, and the Fraternal Order of Police (FOP) seek to use the death penalty for this purpose. The FOP has gone so far as to pay for a full-page ad in the *New York Times* urging Mumia's execution. They want their fallen comrade avenged.

Should the government act as a public outlet for private revenge? History provides horrific examples of what can happen when a society seeks to avenge perceived individual or communal wrongs. This road is lined with hatred, bigotry, homophobia, racism, lynching, ethnic cleansing, and those ultimate instruments of ethnic cleansing, the crematoria. Do we want our government pointed in that direction?

There is something deeply disquieting about the largest professional organization representing our nation's police forces lobbying for an execution. I gave a talk about capital punishment and Mumia's case at Kansas State University in the spring of 2000. During the question-and-answer period a young man attacked my position that Mumia did not receive a fair trial. He appeared to be using a prompting sheet of talking points, which I quickly determined was a printout from the FOP's Web site promoting Mumia's execution. His questioning and his demeanor reminded me of the method police officers use to question a suspect. Later, when confronted by an attorney who had helped organize the program, the questioner admitted he was an off-duty police officer from another county and that he was carrying a concealed weapon.

The specter of pistol-packing police officers attending public forums to give the third degree to those they disagree with is an intimidating one. The FOP's national agitation for an execution carries a whiff of vigilantism. This is especially so when it is placed within the context of the barely contained reflexive violence that appears endemic to police departments nationwide. Police have repeatedly demonstrated their barely contained rage, from the vicious attacks on Amadou Diallo and Abner Louima in New York to the pattern of violence committed against minority communities by police departments across the country.

Revenge is a base emotion. Wouldn't it be preferable for our social institutions and our government to reflect our highest aspirations? Leonard Weinglass, then Mumia Abu-Jamal's chief attorney, articulated this vision during a presentation he made at Hampshire College in Massachussetts in 1997. A student, whose family had been forced into exile from South Africa years earlier because they were African National Congress activists, said he understood Weinglass's opposition to capital punishment. But what, he asked, should we say to the families of those tortured and killed for working against apartheid?

Weinglass acknowledged this young man's anger, but pointed to the postapartheid South African government's Reconciliation Commission as an example of governmental power employed to reflect higher aspirations. Those who testified before the commission who committed crimes while either enforcing apartheid or struggling to overthrow it were granted immunity from prosecution if the commission found that they had fully and faithfully disclosed their actions. For all the commission's imperfections, and that nation's continuing troubles, the commission was a step in the right direction. In fact, institutions like the commission are essential for any strife-torn country to move beyond hatred and develop a functioning civil society.

I wish the United States would follow this example. I do not mean we should establish a similar commission, but that we must make it our priority to build institutions that foster reconciliation rather than inflict retribution. Capital punishment is an instrument of retribution that serves to deepen social divisions. I believe that we will reaffirm our common humanity if our government refuses to carry out socially sanctioned cold-blooded ritualized killings under any circumstances. This is how its abolition can help bridge the social fault lines that separate us. Alleviating those divisions will make us both freer and safer.

CHAPTER 10

Constructive Revenge

ELEVEN P.M., APRIL 26, 1997, JOHN M. GREENE HALL, ON THE SMITH College campus: The first public performance of *Celebrate the Children of Resistance* was over. Elli's brainchild of music, poetry, and dramatic reading that celebrated families who struggle for justice had been very successful. It was also the most ambitious production of my creation, the RFC. The program commenced with our MC, Ossie Davis, introducing Susan Sarandon and Mandy Patinkin, who read selections from the letters my parents wrote from the Death House forty-five years earlier. It climaxed with Kory and José, two young RFC beneficiaries, telling their stories onstage. Now after the finale I stood onstage and watched the audience of more than two thousand drain out of various exits, leaving clusters of stragglers engrossed in animated conversation. My day's work was almost done. Soon I would shepherd the performers to the postevent reception.

The reception was several blocks away at Bill Newman's house. Bill, who'd represented Pat at the Ohio Seven trial almost a decade before, was a founding and still committed member of our board of directors. Almost two hundred people were crammed into the spacious first-floor rooms by the time I arrived. I looked around for twenty-year-old José and eighteen-year-old Kory, our two beneficiaries who had spoken so beautifully during the performance, worried that they might feel uncomfortable so far from home amid the mob of middle-aged and elderly revelers. Even in this triumphant moment, I had found something to worry about, but my concern was unwarranted. José and Kory had found a third beneficiary, Robyn, who was also eighteen, and they seemed to be having a great time.

An RFC grant helped Robyn participate in a high-school-sponsored trip to France several years earlier. RFC grants had helped pay José's tuition at an arts-oriented high school. Now he was a drama major in college. The RFC had also funded Kory's attendance at a summer training program for environmental activists. Kory never applied for further support because, in the summer of 1997, several months after her participation in *Celebrate*, she became the youngest person to be awarded the one hundred thousand dollar Goldman Environmental Hero Award.

The evening's program had been dedicated in part to Robyn's mother, Mary Pitawanakwat. Mary was an indigenous activist who died of breast cancer in 1995, just one year after winning a ten-year legal struggle against sexual harassment and racial discrimination. Robyn and another family member drove two thousand miles to attend the event.

Seeing our three beneficiaries so happy and relaxed together rekindled a spark of an idea that had been smoldering since 1995. Several times the RFC board had discussed bringing our beneficiaries together for a conference. Each time we considered the expense, logistical complications, and our uncertainties about how to design an exciting but emotionally safe environment, we put it off. But now Elli and I were inspired to take this plan out of mothballs, and the board agreed. In 1998 at the board's request Kelly, the RFC's grantmaking coordinator, sent a questionnaire to more than sixty current and past beneficiary families to determine their interest in such a conference. Our beneficiaries loved the idea. But we remained daunted by the difficulties of organizing a program that would meet the needs of parents and children of all ages. We opted instead to focus on a more uniform group and began planning for what we ultimately called the RFC's first "Carry It Forward Gathering." *Carry It Forward* is the name of the RFC's newsletter and of our granting program for post–high school youth. We invited all past and present beneficiaries between the ages of fifteen and twenty-five to attend the gathering on a prep-school campus in western Massachusetts in late summer 1999.

It took more than two years to bring this idea to fruition not only because we wanted to make sure that we did it right, but also because the RFC's attention was diverted by a sudden increase in progressive activism. What I had termed the "third flowering" had finally arrived.

At receptions since the RFC's beginning I had argued to audiences of primarily middle-aged and older adults that despite differences, the progressive movements of the 1930s and 1960s shared a key similarity: Young people between the ages of fifteen and twenty-five were the mainstays of both periods. I stated my belief that a "third flowering" was coming, and those who were only eight, ten, or twelve years old at the time I spoke would lead it. As the first half of the 1990s passed I wondered if I had let my perpetual political optimism color my judgment.

While the explosion of youth activism did not attract widespread public attention until the mass demonstrations against the WTO in Seattle in 1999, the RFC seismograph sensed increasing rumblings of youth activism from 1995 onward. It wasn't just the upsurge of the Mumia movement, although I found it remarkable that the overwhelming majority of those who attended rallies on his behalf were younger than twenty-five. There was also increased attendance of young people at my talks about capital punishment on college campuses during this period. Finally, there was growing mass militancy among high school students of color in urban centers in California and the big cities of the Northeast.

My RFC work has brought to my attention how our society treats youth. After the collapse of the Soviet Union, some of the same law-enforcement agencies that sowed the fear of the foreign-sponsored Communist during the 1950s escalated their warnings about the growing menace of the youthful criminal in the street. Many adults apparently believed that swarms of young dark-skinned street criminals threatened our social fabric. Our society was increasingly frightened of its own children. And this fear had become the latest excuse to gut the Bill of Rights and to increase law enforcement authorities' budgets. The war on drugs and the battle against street crime had become code phrases for targeting young people of color throughout the nation, and America's prison population skyrocketed.

This increase in activism has long-term implications. I've lost track of how many times people in their sixties or seventies have told me that their involvement in the effort to save my parents' lives launched them on a lifetime of political involvement. Even after I started the RFC, a few very elderly people told me that in their youth, during the 1920s, they joined the struggle to save Sacco and Vanzetti and have remained active since. Young activists today are entering deep currents, and I remain hopeful that they will form the core of progressive movements for the next fifty years.

This increased progressive activity brought about dramatic changes at the RFC in 1997 and 1998. During the first half of the decade we'd been progressing steadily toward our goal of awarding $100,000 annually by the year 2000. In 1996 we awarded almost $62,000. But the new wave of activism and the RFC's heightened public presence produced a flood of new applications. In 1998 we awarded more than $100,000. This was very exciting, but by the time planning for our first Carry It Forward Gathering was in full swing, the RFC had become a much bigger and more time-consuming project. I worked with another full-time staff member at the RFC, and we'd hire a third person before the turn of the year. When I traveled on the fund's behalf people still occasionally asked me what I did for a living, assuming that the RFC was something I did in my spare time. I'd cover my annoyance with a joke that was becoming truer every day. "This started out as a full-time job and then it got worse."

As the Carry It Forward Gathering approached, I felt increasing excitement and anxiety. Thirty young people had signed up to attend, including twelve African Americans, ten Native peoples, three Latino, and five white participants. They would be arriving from every region of the country as well as Hawaii, Puerto Rico, and the Canadian prairie province of Saskatchewan. I had plenty to worry about as I arranged for thirty round-trip flights over a three- or four-day period and coordinated ground transportation.

I was more concerned, however, that these young people have a positive experience. Very few of the participants had met one another before, and I felt ultimately responsible for their happiness and welfare. Those from the RFC board and staff who worked on the program wanted to give all attendees an opportunity to share their experiences and express their emotions without feeling pressure to do so. We wanted the participants to understand and feel that they are not alone. We hoped that this sharing would help these young people to understand their parents' choices, that they would bond quickly and develop a mutual support network after leaving. We also wanted them to have fun—a lot to hope for in a weekend.

The Saturday morning workshops were designed to promote self-expression. Participants chose among poetry, art, theater, or a discussion group, and each group was asked to consider sharing some of their morning efforts with the whole assembly at the Saturday-night party. After the workshops and a two-hour hang-out time of sports or relaxation, we planned a three-hour "tell your story session."

As I greeted the first arrivals at the airport baggage claim, I realized how excited but conflicted I was to be meeting so many of the young people the RFC had been helping. I had always been reluctant to meet many of our beneficiaries. I told friends that I feared imposing myself on them, as adults had imposed on me when I was a child. That feeling was real, but it was also an excuse. I had not been entirely comfortable in the presence of the beneficiaries I'd met previously. Perhaps I feared the open expression of raw emotion that might result from our meeting. My childhood defense mechanism had been to pretend that I didn't understand the conflict and trauma I encountered, and to act as if nothing unusual was happening. All my life people I interacted with expressed wonder at how normal I appeared. I didn't think I was crazy, but I sometimes thought how could I not be. I feared losing emotional control. Would these young people see through my veneer and expose who knows what beneath it? Would I break down in front of them, or would these young people evoke feelings and memories in me that I had tried not to face?

I was relieved that the participants seemed so normal, so happy and healthy (except for the participant who'd fallen off his motor bike and arrived in cast and crutches). I knew about the terrible experiences they had survived and must have feared that the damage would be more obvious.

We started the Friday evening program with a group icebreaking exercise, and then it was my turn to speak. The board planning committee felt it would help participants feel more comfortable telling their stories the next day if they heard me tell mine first. The group of young people sprawled on couches, chairs, and the floor of the large common room and listened to what happened to me as a child when my parents were arrested, imprisoned, and killed, and how that ultimately led me to start the RFC. When I was finished talking, several of the participants asked with emotion-laden urgency why I didn't seem angry.

I told them that I *had* been angry. I recounted my teenage revenge fantasies. I described my desire to line the people responsible for murdering my parents up against a wall and mow them down. I said that although I also had broader political objectives during the 1970s reopening effort, I would have been satisfied with having the institutions responsible for my parents' death formally apologize and acknowledge the wrong they had done my parents. But as I got older, I came to realize that even such an apology would not be enough. Now I wanted to play a role in defeating the destructive social forces that killed my parents, and the RFC was my vehicle for doing this. That's all I told them. I did not wish to burden them by completing the thought. I didn't say that I viewed facilitating all the good work this incredibly diverse, talented, and energetic group of young people would accomplish as my sweetest revenge. I think they understood.

The tell-your-story session late Saturday afternoon provided the climax of the weekend. The session started slowly despite my ice-breaking the night before. But it wasn't long before the emotional dams burst as one young woman recalled the horror of having a mass of armed police invade her home and drag off her parents at gunpoint. Not everyone spoke, but several who passed at first added their stories later, after they saw how powerful it was to share experiences with others who really understood and were so supportive. I was amazed at how accepting they were of one another's different responses and how supportive they were of each other's painful memories. This support seemed to spring from a visceral understanding and identification with what they'd all been through.

I had never experienced such an outpouring of raw emotional power, and was rooted to my seat. A twenty-year-old young woman told how after her parents' arrest, when she was an infant, she became, in effect, a ward of the Puerto Rican Nationalist movement. She'd been spirited out of the country and raised by a foster family in Mexico to prevent our government from using her against her imprisoned parents. She said her foster parents did not tell her they were not her biological parents, and were emotionally abusive. She did not discover her true identity until she was a teenager and returned to the United States. The RFC had helped pay for years of therapy to enable her to cope with her inner turmoil. The three hours passed in a flash. By the time we broke for dinner, I'm sure I wasn't the only one who'd felt we'd just completed an emotional marathon.

The rest of the weekend was less charged, but retained an exceptional quality as many in the group explored the depths of their special bonds. The precious hours passed too quickly. Participants' main complaint when the weekend was over was that it was too short, and their chief demand was that we do it again as quickly as possible.

I felt great seeing how good the experience was for them. However, I wished I had been able to worry less and enjoy it more. I had worried about everything from their smooth arrival and departure to my own reactions to what they said. A number of the participants noticed my tension and even cajoled me to lighten up. I was supposed to help provide them with healing and here they were trying to comfort me. It was a positive experience, but it wasn't easy.

The participants treated their time together as a nonstop party, and left those of us who acted as chaperones with massive sleep deprivation. I yawned and smiled for several days afterward. But hearing the RFC's beneficiaries' stories and discussing my own with them stirred up a hornet's nest of thoughts that I did not resolve for more than a year. Their questions about why I wasn't angry haunted me, and I began to think about organizing my response into a talk or an essay. Several weeks later a friend provided me with a deadline.

On November 3, 1979, Marty Nathan's first husband, Michael Nathan, was killed by the Ku Klux Klan in Greensboro, North Carolina. Marty asked me to participate in a group discussion as part of the twentieth-anniversary commemoration of the Greensboro Massacre. During the last few years I had become good friends with this person so intimately connected to the event that had horrified me when I had worked at *SR*. I felt honored to be invited to join a panel that included Anne Braden, Lani Guinier, Reverend Nelson Johnson, who had been wounded in the massacre, and Columbia University professor Manning Marable, but that is not the real reason why I accepted this request.

I wouldn't say no to Marty. She had been a medical intern with a six-month-old child when her pediatrician husband and four members of the CWP were killed. She and a few others have fought back tirelessly to bring the responsible parties to justice and to educate the public about what really happened. She endured the humiliation of first a state and then a federal criminal trial, in which the shooters were found not guilty. This was despite copious evidence, including videotape taken by local television stations, showing the murderers' actions and identities. Along with family members of the other victims she mounted a third and ultimately successful civil suit against the Klan, the city of Greensboro, and its police department.

The Greensboro jurors evidently could not bring themselves to award monetary damages to the relatives of members of the CWP, and only found on Michael Nathan's behalf. Marty's murdered husband, Michael, was the only nonparty victim, and his widow was the only plaintiff awarded damages. Marty shared her award with the families of the other plaintiffs and used her portion to start the Greensboro Justice Fund. For the past dozen years the fund has built upon these reparations, has developed a national base of support, and has been providing grants to progressive grassroots organizing efforts throughout the South.

If I could answer the question of why I wasn't angry I could contribute something to the panel that would be particularly helpful to Marty and the other survivors of the Greensboro Massacre. There were more than a few survivors. Five were killed, but eleven more were wounded. Dozens of people, many of them children, had close relatives or friends killed or wounded. I decided to focus my talk on the children.

My childhood taught me some lessons about how children can

overcome repression and terror directed at their families. I am still in touch with what it feels like to be a small child and have a parent killed. Even though I'm almost twenty years older now than my parents were when they were executed, those of my parents' generation who fought to save my parents' lives still call me one of the Rosenberg boys. I found this annoying when, at twenty-five, I began to speak out about my parents' case. More recently I've found it flattering. At fifty-five I may finally understand it.

This apparent infantilization reflects one of the important ways children can be helped to overcome such experiences. After my parents were killed, my brother and I became, to some degree, children of the movement that fought to save them. At key times during my childhood I was surrounded and protected by this community of support. It is understandable that some of these many parents still think of me as one of the boys.

The specifics of my childhood, just like everyone else's, are unique. Many adults have survived terrible incidents as children. In fact most of us have negative experiences in our lives that can have a devastating impact. These events can defeat us, causing us to become passive and dead inside. We can strike back violently by attempting to retaliate by visiting the destruction we endured upon others. A third reaction turns the rage inward, allowing us to wallow in bitterness. I believe the most productive course is to harness that anger and use it to develop something positive. I call this fourth path "constructive revenge."

The desire for revenge is only natural, especially when family members have been killed. The destruction of our loved ones can render us powerless, and the craving for revenge is an effort to regain some control. I believe a passive response that reflects the abandonment of hope is even worse. But if we can't channel the destructive energy of that desire into something positive, we are condemned to lead destructive and destroyed lives.

In late 1991 the Marjorie Kovler Center for the Survivors of Torture applied for support. They requested funds to help run a group therapy session for Guatemalan refugee children whose parents had been tortured by that country's military because they struggled for democracy. This project fell within our guidelines. We funded it and have been helping many of these children (some now young adults who attended the Gathering) ever since. In 1992 I traveled to Chicago to meet with the psychologist in charge of the program, Dr. Antonio Martínez, to learn more about this group.

Dr. Martínez explained that he preferred the term torture survivor to torture victim. He said that torture was, in part, an effort to disempower those being tortured. Victims have been defeated, he continued, but survivors can regain their power. He told me about his work in Chicago's Guatemalan refugee community of thirty thousand. "We bring the children together to tell their stories," he said. This process, which he termed "naming their torturers," began the healing, but that healing remained incomplete until the children regained their power by becoming active community members who speak out in the public arena.

What Dr. Martínez said struck a responsive chord in me. The RFC was less than two years old, but I'd already received dozens of comments from people praising me for devoting my life to such a wonderfully altruistic project. I thanked these people for their supportive words, but did not share with them my feeling that the RFC was also my revenge. Dr. Martínez had just explained why I felt that way. Although this understanding did not fully crystallize until after our beneficiary gathering more than seven years later, I understood in 1992 that, like the Guatemalan children, I had found a way to connect with my community and make a positive public contribution despite my parents' execution.

Viewing the RFC as avenging my parents' execution may seem far-fetched. Almost all those responsible are now dead. But a system, not just individuals, killed them. I created the RFC not only to help children who suffered as I did as a child, but also to be part of the movement to change that system.

These thoughts about revenge kept churning while I prepared for the Greensboro panel discussion. The parallels between my experience and what happened to the Greensboro families in the wake of the killings more than twenty years ago were compelling. The authorities blamed the victims. Even some on the Left, like my colleague at *SR* in 1979, turned their backs on the survivors.

But others came to their aid, and the survivors formed a support network that helped the children just as my brother and I had been helped, and just as the RFC now helps the children of other targeted activists. The survivors kept in touch. Many of the children grew up in a sustaining environment of socially aware adults who understood that the children had special needs. As the children grew up they had one another and many "parents" who were leading healthy and productive lives. This helped them to develop a positive connection with their parents and an understanding of why their parents acted as they had. While this did not work well for everyone, it was helpful to many. Equally important, the community was not passive; it organized, resisted, and is resisting to this day.

I wanted to share with the children who survived the Greensboro Massacre a concept that would help them understand that they have the power to transform the violent attack upon their community into something that could help others while fulfilling themselves. Doubtless some already knew. And the hardest job, figuring out how each could accomplish this, I could not do for them. But after my talk in Greensboro that November, I saw the same recognition in the eyes of some of the Greensboro survivors that I had seen in the eyes of the RFC's beneficiaries that evening in August three months earlier. I believe some will find their constructive revenge and transform the fear and fury of the Greensboro Massacre into something powerfully positive that will improve their lives and the lives of many they touch.

But some participants who asked "Why aren't you angry?" at the Carry It Forward Gathering weren't asking why I wasn't angry at the people who killed my parents. The young people who the RFC brought together that August did not uniformly applaud their parents' actions. While some viewed their parents as heroes and wanted to follow in their activist footsteps, others respected their parents' decisions but planned different life courses, or, if they were activist-oriented, chose other activist work. Still others did not forgive their parents for making choices that had a negative impact on their families.

Some participants wanted nothing to do with activism and were not shy about proclaiming this to the group. One young woman I'll call Carol told how at age fourteen, upon her stepfather's arrest, she learned that several years earlier her mother had married an escaped political prisoner. Carol described the mortification she felt at school and her feeling that her mother had betrayed her. Her mother had written a letter to the RFC in which she told how Carol had screamed during an argument that the only good thing that had happened since Carol's stepfather's arrest was the flute lessons that RFC grants provided.

Carol wasn't asking why I wasn't angry about what the government had done to my parents. Apparently I so strongly wanted to avoid Carol's real question that I did not realize until many months after the gathering that I had misunderstood. She meant, Why wasn't I angry with my parents for the choices they had made?

All the years in which I'd been certain of Ethel and Julius's innocence it was easy to say that I wasn't angry because they had done nothing wrong. In fact I could proclaim that I wished I would have the courage to do what they did if I were confronted with the same situation. But wasn't this rather glib? Guilty or not, shouldn't I have had some resentment at what a three-year-old couldn't help perceiving as his parents' abandonment? I watched the RFC beneficiaries thrashing these issues out and wondered if I had ever really come to grips with my own feelings. Maybe that's part of what made me uneasy in our beneficiaries' presence. I began to wonder if I was hiding behind my current agnosticism about my parents' case in part to avoid confronting this issue. As long as I didn't know what happened, I didn't need to consider how I would have felt if my father, with my mother's blessing, really had engaged in illegal activity to help the Soviet Union defeat Hitler.

September 2000 would mark the tenth anniversary of the RFC. Except for a couple of weeks here and there, I'd spent a decade consumed with RFC work. Elli, now a pediatric nurse practitioner, had been working at Shriners Hospital for almost twice as long. We both needed a break, and with careful planning were able to arrange to take the months of August and September 2000 as a mini-sabbatical. The RFC could survive my absence, especially during August and the first half of September, the quietest period of our annual cycle.

We arranged to rent a small cottage on Vinalhaven, a rocky island thirteen miles off the coast of Maine at the mouth of Penobscot Bay. We wanted to get far enough away to lead different lives for a while in a place that was still relatively easy to reach. We both had writing projects to engage us. Elli wanted to write fiction, her newfound passion, and I would write essays. I also wanted to step back and think about where the RFC was heading, and finally get to the bottom of how I felt about my parents' actions.

Vinalhaven is an evergreen-covered island eight miles long and three miles wide, with more than two hundred miles of coastline. It is shaped like an amoeba with a multitude of irregular pseudopods. Its hills were once completely deforested and densely populated, with more than ten thousand residents employed by the massive granite quarries and bustling fishing industry. The quarries had been shut down for decades, but the island still boasted the largest lobster fleet on the Maine coast. Summer residents swelled its year-round population of one thousand to five thousand.

It is amazing how much difference thirteen miles can make. If you didn't own a boat or couldn't afford the tiny air taxi, access to the island was limited to six daily round-trips made by the Maine state ferry. Only a dozen vehicles and up to a hundred passengers could make each seventy-five-minute trip. The island had no traffic lights, and drivers waved to each other as they passed in opposite directions on the two-lane roads. While it was reasonably crowded in August, it quieted to dead calm by mid-September. We wrote in the morning, hiked in the afternoon, and returned to our waterside house for wine and a dinner of whatever fresh foods the ferry brought in. Then we watched what was often a spectacular sunset over the bay and distant mainland hills, read or played chess, turned in early, and did it all over again the next day.

It was an incongruous setting in which to consider how I felt about the possibility that my father had provided the Soviet Union with classified information even though doing so might jeopardize his family. I now felt that my father's involvement in the kind of thing described in the Venona transcriptions was a real possibility. The question was simple but profound: How would I feel if the information about my father contained in the Venona transcriptions was accurate? How would I feel if it could be proved to my satisfaction that Julius Rosenberg helped organize a group of young scientists and engineers during World War II to provide cutting-edge industrial and military information to the Soviet Union to help defeat the Nazis, and that my mother knew about and supported his actions although she did not actively participate in them? I forced myself to accept this premise.

In my father's final letter to his attorney, Emanuel Bloch, he wrote: "[N]ever let them change the truth of our innocence." In my parents' last letter to me and my brother they wrote: "Always remem-

ber that we were innocent and could not wrong our conscience."
Were these self-serving lies?

Perhaps I am rationalizing, but that is not the way I feel about my
parents' claims of innocence. The information in the Venona transcriptions indicates that neither Julius nor Ethel was guilty of the
crime for which they faced the executioner. This material shows that
Ethel was not a spy and that Julius was ignorant of the atom bomb
project. It supports their claim that they were innocent of stealing the
secret of the atom bomb. They were fighting for their lives. They
were not in a position to explain to their six-year-old son the subtle
distinction between not being guilty of stealing atomic secrets and
blanket innocence. They probably were aware of such subtleties and
chose their words to have the maximum galvanizing effect on those
working to save them, as well as to help their loyal codefendant, who
faced thirty years' imprisonment, and to strike back at their execu-
tioners. I will not for an instant begrudge them any of that.

How they could engage in such high-risk activities that could
potentially leave their children orphans was a critique that had a lot of
force in the relatively calm domestic political landscape of August
2000. But the world was a different place in the early 1940s. Titanic
forces representing the sharply divergent social formations and
worldviews of fascism, capitalism, and communism were engaged in a
violent globe-spanning conflict to determine the world's fate. Vast
numbers of people chose sides in this life-and-death battle. How
many tens of thousands of American men with young children will-
ingly went to fight during World War II knowing that they might not
survive the conflict? Was my father, whose poor eyesight disqualified
him for military service, taking a greater risk by choosing this role in
the battle? The Venona transcriptions indicate that my mother did
not actively participate. Was this a conscious effort to ensure that at
least one parent would be free to raise the children if my father was
caught?

In the transcript I discussed earlier, the spy code-named Liberal tells his superiors that since he is ignorant of the atom bomb project, others should handle information related to it. Was this desire to involve someone else a father's effort to avoid the riskiest activity? We will probably never know the answers to these questions.

I will not judge my parents' actions of more than fifty years ago outside the milieu in which they were made. I can't predict what decision I would have made at that time, if I had been a child of the 1930s instead of the 1960s. I became more careful about my political activities when I became a parent. This may be because I knew from painful experience the terrible toll activist parents' decisions can take on their children, and I did not wish my childhood nightmare visited on my children. Perhaps Ethel and Julius would be horrified to hear me make this statement. But just as I will not view their actions outside the context in which they were taken, they and their age-mates should not judge *my* actions today outside the framework of *my* experience.

Perhaps some readers will conclude that what I've written above proves that Judge Kaufman was right when he pronounced that my parents loved communism more than they loved their children. But I have always felt supremely loved by my parents. Working to build a better world for our children is a key component of my definition of parenting, which also includes instilling a sense of humanity and justice in our children. Merely talking about such principles but not acting upon them sends a lukewarm and ultimately ineffective message. This is part of the RFC's vision and purpose. The RFC helps families who engage the world and take courageous actions even though they have children. Social activism should not be left to full-time professionals or be limited to those without children. I believe that the best chance of building a more humane and just society rests on the activism of ordinary citizens with family concerns. Some may find that what I've written in this paragraph contradicts what I wrote in the one before it. I do not find them mutually exclusive, but I acknowledge that there is a fine line to walk and we won't all draw that line in the same place.

I used to hope that when we finally got to the bottom of what really happened in my parents' case, the facts would show their unequivocal innocence. I no longer feel that way. Now I'd rather my parents had been conscious political actors than innocent victims. Shortly after I founded the RFC I had a series of discussions with Tsekei Murati, one of the leaders of the African National Congress (ANC) Youth Council. The ANC was getting close to victory and hoped to start programs to help the children of fallen activists once they came to power. We discussed the possibility of doing a joint fund-raiser that would, among other things, help fund the establishment of a South African version of the RFC. I cautioned my ANC friend that the RFC might not be the best organization for him to work with in the United States. When he asked why, I answered that a lot of people in the United States thought my parents were guilty. He looked at me as if I had two heads and said: "Nobody ever asks us to say Nelson is not guilty."

An ideal expressed by the civil rights movement was to treat all those who were a part of the struggle, no matter how flawed, as members of the "beloved community." Activism in the real world sometimes presents people with gut-wrenching decisions. Progressive activists do not always make the right choices, but they do remain part of the RFC's beloved community.

I know my parents would be considered a part of the RFC's community, but I've often wondered what my parents would think of the RFC. At least a hundred times since I started the RFC, contemporaries of my parents have told me how proud they thought my parents would be of what I am doing. I always smile, nod, and thank them, but I'm not so sure. First, this assumes that both my parents would agree.

While my parents might enthusiastically have supported what I am doing if they hadn't been denied that opportunity, I have no way of knowing if one or the other would conclude that what I am doing is not political enough. My mother or father might contend that I was engaged in a feel-good project that did not directly further the struggle. This is not just idle speculation on my part. Several of my parents' contemporaries have made this assessment of my actions.

I've occasionally held imaginary conversations with my parents about this question. Sometimes they castigate me for not following a more traditional course of left-wing activism. We've even had heated arguments: I tell them that I have to do what I think is right, just as they did; I tell them that the RFC's work may have a greater positive long-term social impact than their narrower concept of what constitutes real political work. I tell them that I am twenty years older and perhaps wiser than they ever became. I tell them that I don't require their approval; that I am doing this for myself, and for all the children who endured repression in response to their parents' actions. At other times they love the project, the conversation quickly becomes less personal, and moves on to events like the collapse of the Soviet Union.

Regardless of how they might feel about my activities, I am proud of my parents even if they may not have been unequivocally innocent. They acted with integrity, courage, and in furtherance of righteous ideals. They were worthy of all the support they received and more. They remain at the heart of my beloved community.

I returned from our sabbatical refreshed and more at peace with myself. Though I still wasn't sure if my father had been involved in supplying the Soviet Union with classified material, I had come to terms with the possibility that he had. And as 2001 began, there were exciting developments, particularly in the effort to abolish capital punishment, that filled me with hope.

In June 2001 I attended two extraordinary conferences. Murder Victims' Families for Reconciliation (MVFR) held its first national conference at Boston College. MVFR is an increasingly powerful voice in the battle against capital punishment that has continued to grow despite the ascension of Governor Death to the Presidency. With unique moral authority MVFR proclaims: "From experience, we know that revenge is not the answer. The answer lies in reducing violence, not causing more death. To those who say that society must take a life for a life, we say: 'not in our name.'"

MVFR views capital punishment as state-sanctioned murder and so includes in its constituency family members of those executed. I felt honored to make a presentation at one of the workshops, and found it particularly affecting to tell the story of my childhood and bring the work of the RFC to this group. It was humbling to discuss constructive revenge with people who, despite bearing the murder of one or more immediate family members, value forgiveness over even constructive revenge.

Perhaps we were merely using different words to describe the same response. But I suspect there are differences in our approach that spring from most MVFR members' religious faith. Religious faith remains something I have trouble fathoming, but it was eye-opening to see these beliefs spur such powerfully positive activity.

Ten days later I boarded a plane to attend the First World Congress Against the Death Penalty, held in Strasbourg, France, at the headquarters of the Council of Europe and the summer home of the European Union's parliament. The congress gathered more than five hundred activists and officials from six continents. Twenty-five leaders of national legislative bodies signed a declaration urging a worldwide ban on capital punishment. For me the most poignant moment of the conference was a brief but moving statement read by the president of the Cambodian parliament, Prince Norodom Ranariddh, explaining his country's renunciation of the death penalty. Cambodia, still reeling from the slaughter of five million during the late 1970s and early 1980s, has learned from bitter experience that state-sanctioned killing is not a solution to criminal violence.

Addressing hundreds of the world's leading death-penalty opponents from the dais of the Assembly Chamber of the Council of Europe was an unforgettable experience. I was one of several participants from the U.S. given an opportunity to speak in plenary sessions because the congress put special emphasis on abolishing the death penalty in our country. Although this unprecedented global event received substantial media attention internationally, I was dismayed that the American press virtually ignored it. But I was buoyed by the strength of international support for our efforts and I left energized, even more determined to carry the struggle to the United States. Plans to hold the Second World Congress Against the Death Penalty in the United States in 2004 are already taking shape.

By the summer of 2001 I was increasingly confident that the death penalty would be abolished in our country during this decade. I had a new fantasy. I'm helping to lead a charge of national, even international proportions, that is going to eradicate the barbaric practice of capital punishment in the United States once and for all. This is not entirely fanciful even though America now appears to be preparing for a new round of capital cases that will take place against a political backdrop even more hostile to the defendants than the McCarthy period was for my parents. But this gathering storm has only fueled my determination to eliminate the death penalty in America. It is fifty years too late for my family, but with more than 3,500 on death row in America today it is not too late for thousands of other families. I can almost taste the day when I'll be able to say with confidence that there can be no more Rosenberg cases in the United States because there will be no more executions.

Epilogue

I USUALLY ARRIVE AT MY OFFICE AT 7:30 A.M., AND SEPTEMBER 11, 2001, was no exception. I had no inkling of what had happened until I received a phone call from my daughter Rachel sometime after 9:00 A.M. A third-year law student at New York University, she'd flown out of Kennedy Airport the afternoon before, and was calling from Alabama, where she would spend the semester as a legal intern working for inmates on that state's death row. Unable to reach friends in New York City, she called me for information.

It was impossible to work. I talked to Elli and to my elder daughter, Jenn, who works for a campus-based service learning organization and lives in Providence, Rhode Island. Getting in touch with loved ones helped, but it was not enough. I felt powerless, and I could not dispel my sense of foreboding.

I called my brother and said: "This is terrible, and it is going to get worse." We had lived the first years of our lives in lower Manhattan. Knickerbocker Village is only about a mile from ground zero. Now living 150 miles to the north I too felt assaulted. I was angry, sorrowful, and afraid, and I knew many of my fellow Americans would demand terrible revenge. And even in the midst of my feeling of loss and vulnerability, I was equally frightened that the Bush administration would manipulate those very emotions to take maximum political advantage and shove its authoritarian agenda down our throats in the name of national security. Was September 11 the first day of a new McCarthy era?

My immediate post–9/11 sense of dread was compounded by the release of Sam Roberts's book *The Brother*, which is based on interviews with David Greenglass. I received a copy of the book on September 18. Reading about my parents' case from my uncle's point of view was thoroughly unpleasant, but I was even more appalled to read on page 472 of this 543-page book that Greenglass "agreed to cooperate fully on a book in return for a share of the proceeds." This meant that any response my brother or I made to the book would potentially generate more publicity and put money in Greenglass's pocket.

This was particularly troubling because I had already agreed to be a member of a panel about *The Brother* in October at the 92nd Street Y in New York City. This panel included the author, Sam Roberts, as the moderator. I felt I had no choice but to attack the method of the project, rather than the content of the book, during my presentation, although doing this with the author sitting near me was excruciating. Early in my talk I said:

> *It is one matter if David Greenglass agrees to talk because his conscience is troubling him. It is another if he agrees to talk in return for a share of royalties generated by the book's sales. In this instance David Greenglass's primary incentive is to help sell as many copies of the book as possible.*

I concluded:

And if putting money in David Greenglass's pocket doesn't deter potential purchasers, perhaps this additional fact will: Greenglass's voice pervades the book. Reading this book and getting this close to David Greenglass is like taking a bath in sewage. I can't imagine why anyone would want to do it.

These final words to the audience of almost a thousand produced a shocked pause followed by a standing ovation, but I felt drained rather than elated. I had done a necessary task, but I gained no satisfaction from doing it. But the most unbelievable event of that weird evening was yet to come.

Arnold Kramish also joined the panel. In 1945 he had been an army corporal working on the atom bomb project with David Greenglass at Los Alamos. After Greenglass's arrest in 1950, Kramish interviewed him to determine the value of the information Greenglass claimed to have stolen. At that time Kramish was a member of the Atomic Energy Commission's Intelligence Division. No Rosenberg partisan, he believed in my father's guilt, and during his initial presentation appeared to support the book's thesis. But as the evening drew to a close he asked for and was granted a final opportunity to address the audience. This elderly man walked slowly to the podium, turned toward the author, and said:

My main problem with your book is that it is full of errors perpetuated by David Greenglass. You believed everything he said about life at Los Alamos. . . . By depending on David Greenglass . . . as the ultimate authority . . . you have done a misservice [sic] to history.

My mouth dropped open. I could not believe my ears. The man who I thought was included on the panel to support the author had just demolished *The Brother's* credibility much more effectively than I ever could.

I felt pummeled by the intensity of my existence in weeks following September 11. I was scheduled to give a plenary address at the annual meeting of the National Coalition to Abolish the Death Penalty in Raleigh, North Carolina, at the end of October. Over the summer the meeting's organizers had asked me to provide attendees with historical perspective and to introduce them to another kind of capital case. The abolition movement has been exclusively focused on murder cases, and many of its militants did not even realize that someone in this country could be executed for conspiracy, as my parents had been.

I realized that my parents' case was no longer of merely historical or educational interest. Since the mass murderers who flew the planes into the towers were all dead, the government was likely to develop conspiracy cases against their colleagues and ask for the death penalty. My parents' case had been the only capital conspiracy in our country's history since the Civil War. I realized that Americans might soon face an unprecedented wave of capital conspiracy cases, and that these cases would present anti–capital punishment forces with a major new challenge.

Reaching this conclusion did not take much insight given my personal history. It punched me in the face. I consulted with friends in the progressive legal community. They were alarmed by the mass detentions, talk of military tribunals, and the general attack on civil liberties, but perhaps it took my personal history to anticipate the likelihood of a new round of capital conspiracy cases.

Touring in October and November 2001 to sound the alarm about capital conspiracy had a different feel than my previous RFC travels. I felt a mix of urgency and concern that bordered on fear. Ashcroft and his cohorts appeared to be using George Orwell's *1984* as a manual for manipulating the public and quashing dissent. Perhaps I was a bit paranoid, but I couldn't help wondering if big brother was watching what *I* did. I felt exposed as the son of "Communist atomic spies" attacking the government's policies in wartime. The country was undergoing a paroxysm of patriotism, dissent was equated with treason, and for many citizens of the United States the names Ethel and Julius Rosenberg were synonymous with *traitor*. It didn't take long before I got a dose of just how true this was.

In early November the ACLU and the Fund for Santa Barbara invited me to talk about capital conspiracy at the main branch of Santa Barbara's public library. On my way into town from Los Angeles that morning I stopped to do a radio talk show. About halfway through the program a caller peremptorily demanded: "Your father was a traitor, yes or no?"

That depends on your definition of treason, I responded. We sparred back and forth, but soon the next caller turned the conversation in another direction. I felt that my answer had been inadequate and worked for the next several days at developing a more satisfactory response. I knew I could have responded in a narrow manner: My parents were not charged with or convicted of treason. Furthermore, treason requires helping an enemy, but my parents were charged with conspiring to help the Soviet Union during World War II when the USSR was our ally. But such responses missed the heart of the matter.

Treason and politics are inextricably entwined. A charge of treason may reveal more about the politics of the accuser than the actions of the accused. The Founding Fathers recognized this and defined the crime in our Constitution to minimize its potential abuse for political purposes. The Constitution defines treason as follows:

> *Treason against the United States, shall consist only in levying war against them, or in adhering to their enemies, giving them aid and comfort. No person shall be convicted of treason unless on the testimony of two witnesses to the same overt act, or on confession of it in open court. (Article III, section 3.)*

This definition showed me what I should have said to the caller. I should have read the definition to him and asked what he considered to be the greatest act of treason against the United States in our history.

I've told this story and posed this question to a number of audiences since November 2001, and with just one exception my question has been met with silence. I've prodded people by saying that the answer seemed slam-dunk obvious to me, but the silence lengthened. Ultimately I have given the answer away with a question. When in our history did a group seek to destroy our nation by conducting a war within its borders that led to the deaths of more than a million American soldiers? Finally someone would say, often with a bit of wonder in his or her voice: "The Civil War."

That's right! Despite its ultimate defeat, the Confederacy was by far the most massive and successful traitorous conspiracy in our history. And to this day the Stars and Bars flag, the symbol of that great treason, is displayed, in some cases with official sanction not only in the South but also nationwide. Perhaps some people who would be quick to call my parents traitors have a Confederate flag decal on their vehicle's back window! One person's treason is another's heritage. We've buried the Confederacy's treason so deep that the vast majority of us are shocked to hear the Confederacy described that way.

What constitutes patriotism is subject to the same political manipulation. Could my parents be considered patriots? Even if they never engaged in spying, they were members of the American Communist Party. The right wing in our country claims a monopoly on patriotism. They equate love of country with blind obedience to authority and with the belief that our country is better than all others and that Americans, or at least white Christian Americans, are superior to all other people.

I grew up believing that the most patriotic acts are those taken to improve the quality of life for all our nation's inhabitants. Abel Meeropol concluded his patriotic song "The House I Live In," "but especially the people, that's America to me." Ethel and Julius Rosenberg identified with poor and oppressed people in the United States and around the world rather than a government that they believed served the will of a privileged few. Ethel and Julius believed that defeating fascism would help Americans and the world. Whatever actions they took sprang from their love of humanity, not from a particular allegiance to the Soviet Union. Based on this understanding of patriotism, I believe that my parents acted patriotically even if Venona is accurate.

Since September 11 I've had emotional flashbacks to how I felt about "them" as a small boy. Today many U.S. citizens live with a pervasive fear of "them." Our government is fueling this with its perpetual warnings. As a small child I tried to keep beneath "their" radar, and nest in the heart of a supportive community. As a teenager I dreamed of revenge.

As an adult citizen living in post–9/11 America, I am opposed to the Bush administration's repressive domestic policies in the name of eradicating terrorism. There is little evidence that Tom Ridge's Homeland Security plans and John Ashcroft's Justice Department have increased domestic safety. Instead the Bush administration has mounted the most effective attack on our civil liberties since the McCarthy period. How ironic that our government and the citizens willing to follow it blindly, not those who attacked the World Trade Center, have exposed the fragility of our freedom.

It took me almost forty years to figure out how to overcome my fear, harness my anger, and transform the destruction that was visited upon my family into something constructive—something to benefit my community. America today is confronted with a similar challenge. I don't doubt for an instant that if we put our minds to it we could use this moment to create something powerfully positive on a global scale. We could channel our fear and anger and use our immense power to protect ourselves by spreading economic and social justice throughout the world and by fostering international and cross-cultural understanding. This is a positive way to respond to the murderous impulses that spawned the September 11 attacks. This is the way to find *our* constructive revenge.